Making a differe

Judith Bennett, John Holman,
Robin Millar and David Waddington (Eds.)

Making a difference
Evaluation as a tool for improving science education

Waxmann Münster / New York
München / Berlin

Bibliographic information published by Die Deutsche Bibliothek
Die Deutsche Bibliothek lists this publication in the
Deutsche Nationalbibliografie; detailed bibliographic data
are available in the internet at http://dnb.ddb.de.

ISBN 3-8309-1508-X

© Waxmann Verlag GmbH, 2005
Postfach 8603, 48046 Münster, Germany
Waxmann Publishing Co.
P. O. Box 1318, New York, NY 10028, U. S. A.

www.waxmann.com
E-mail: info@waxmann.com

Cover Design: Verena Hane, Kiel
Print: Druckerei Runge, Cloppenburg
Printed on age-resistant paper, DIN 6738
All rights reserved
Printed in Germany

Preface

The Leibniz-Institute for Science Education (IPN) at the University of Kiel in Germany and the University of York Science Education Group (UYSEG) in the UK are amongst the strongest centres of science education. The activities of both span many aspects of science education research and development. In recent years they have become synonymous with the drive for scientific literacy at all levels of school education, in particular with the development of courses based on ideas of context-based learning.

Two years ago, the two centres decided to inaugurate a series of symposia on specific themes. The intention was that the conferences would involve a maximum of 30 participants, drawn equally from the two centres and from internationally-renowned experts in the chosen topic. Papers would be written prior to the meeting and much of the time at the meeting would be taken with discussing the contributions.

The first two topics chosen for these meetings were evaluation and context-based learning in science education. It was thought that the papers discussed at these meetings could be of interest to a wider audience and thus it was decided to publish these as books. This first book contains papers presented at the inaugural meeting on evaluation.

Manfred Prenzel, IPN, Kiel
Bob Campbell, UYSEG, York

January 2005

Contents

	Preface	5
	Introduction	9
Part A	**Setting the scene**	11
	Introduction to Part A	13
Chapter 1	Evaluating educational programmes: Issues and perspectives *Robin Millar*	15
Chapter 2	Fit for purpose: Appropriate methods to provide evidence to inform potential users of research in education, with special references to randomised controlled trials and systematic research synthesis *Diana Elbourne, David Gough*	33
Part B	**Examples of curriculum development and evaluation**	49
	Introduction to Part B	51
Chapter 3	*Chemie im Kontext*: Curriculum development and evaluation strategies *Cornelia Gräsel, Peter Nentwig, Ilka Parchmann*	53
Chapter 4	An evaluation of a large-scale curriculum development project: *Salters Advanced Chemistry* *Judith Bennett, John Holman*	67
Chapter 5	Developmental research: Improving the learning and teaching of science topics *Kerst Boersma, Marie-Christine Knippels, Arend Jan Waarlo*	85
Chapter 6	Evaluating Educational Impact- the CASE experience *Philip Adey*	99

Chapter 7	Science education for citizenship: Introducing the discussion of socio-scientific issues into the curriculum *Stein Dankert Kolstø*	109
Chapter 8	Evaluation of the 'Children Challenging Industry': A primary school science industry links project *Joy Parvin*	125
Chapter 9	What can we learn from different forms of evaluation? Experiences from a quality-development program in science and mathematics instruction *Christian Ostermeier, Manfred Prenzel*	145
Chapter 10	Teachers' transformations of innovations: The case of visual language *Jaume Ametller, Roser Pintó*	159
Chapter 11	Critical reflections on the evaluation of small-scale innovations *Bob Campbell, Fred Lubben*	173
Chapter 12	A long-term and systemic approach to science curriculum development, implementation and evaluation *Bat-Sheva Eylon, Avi Hofstein*	187

Part C Conclusions 203

Chapter 13	Evaluating innovations in science education: Some reflections *Judith Bennett, Robin Millar*	205

Participants at the Conference 212

Biographies of the authors 213

Introduction

This book is divided in three sections. **Part A**, *Setting the Scene*, contains two papers which together provide an overview of some of the key issues that have engaged educational researchers and potential 'users' of educational research, as regards the evaluation of educational practices. They provide a framework of ideas and issues against which to locate the specific examples of science curriculum innovation, and the ways in which these have been evaluated, which are presented and discussed in **Part B** of the book.

In this second – and largest – section of the book, we draw on ten examples of science curriculum innovation to illustrate different approaches to evaluation. In each chapter, the authors describe the nature of the innovation, the problem it was intended to address and the data that have been collected to evaluate it. They describe what has been learned from these data, and what other workers in science education might learn from them.

In the final section, **Part C**, Bennett and Millar in a chapter entitled *Evaluating innovation in science education: Some reflections,* identify common features in the approaches used to evaluate the programmes in Part B. They comment on the contrast between the approaches adopted and those advocated 'by some parties' in what they term as 'the wider debate about educational research and its quality' and why this may have come about.

PART A:
Setting the scene

Part A: Introduction

The first section of the book consists of two chapters looking at general issues concerning the evaluation of educational practices, whether established or innovative. These chapters raise a number of general issues about evaluation methods and approaches in education, some of which have their roots in more wide ranging questions about the nature of social knowledge and the research methods which are most 'fit for purpose' in attempting to find answers to certain types of question. In the context of curriculum evaluation, the questions we are most commonly interested in are: 'What happens when this intervention is used?', 'How does it produce the outcomes that it does?' and 'Is it successful (or perhaps more successful than other approaches) in achieving its objectives?'

Millar presents a broad overview of issues concerning educational evaluation. Noting that evaluation studies can be quite different in emphasis and purpose, he highlights nine dimensions that might be used to characterise any given evaluation study. He then goes on to outline the approaches to evaluation that have dominated the educational literature over the past half century, beginning with Tyler's 'objectives based' view of evaluation, and discussing why and how 'illuminative' approaches grew in popularity in the 1970s. The chapter then briefly explores the recent debate about educational research, in particular the strong advocacy by some educationalists of evidence-based education – the evidence being provided by experimental studies using randomly selected samples, that can provide sound evidence that one approach 'works' better than another. Some of the issues raised by this approach are briefly discussed. The concluding section of the chapter then contrasts the perspective of educational researchers (giving priority to quality of generalisable evidence) and of teachers and other potential users of a curriculum programme or innovation (giving priority to professional judgment of its 'fit' to local situations and needs).

Elbourne and Gough also discuss very general issues concerning educational evaluation. The first half of their chapter makes the case for using randomised controlled trials in educational contexts, to gather evidence that one approach is, or is not, better than another. The analogy with medical research, frequently used in the recent debate about educational research methods, is used to illustrate what is judged to be possible and desirable in education. The second half of the chapter then goes on to argue the value of systematic reviews of research on specific topics, to make available to policy makers and practitioners practically useful syntheses of 'what research tells us' about these topics. Elbourne and Gough explain how the Evidence Informed Policy and Practice in Education Initiative (EPPI) has developed a method which different review groups can use in a consistent and transparent manner to conduct systematic reviews in different areas of educational interest. A recent review by OECD of educational research in England (OECD, 2002) highlighted and welcomed the development of systematic review methods, seeing it as a potentially significant means of improving the interface between educational research on the one hand, and policy and practice on the other.

Thus these chapters provide a framework of key ideas and issues which have been used in the writing of the next set of papers which form Part B of the book. These are concerned with examples of science curriculum innovation and the ways in which these have been evaluated.

Reference

OECD (Organisation of Economic Cooperation and Development) (2002). *Educational Research and Development In England. Examiners' Report.* Paris: OECD.

Chapter 1

Evaluating educational programmes: Issues and perspectives

Robin Millar

Department of Educational Studies, University of York, York YO10 5DD, UK

Evaluation in educational contexts

Evaluation – assessing how well things are going – is a central and essential part of the educational process. It provides the information on which we can take decisions of different kinds:

- Decisions about individuals: identifying the needs of the pupil in order to plan his/her instruction, selection and grouping, and providing feedback to the individual learner.
- Administrative regulation: judging how effective a school is, how good individual teachers are, whether resources are adequate, and so on.
- Course improvement: deciding whether instructional materials and approaches are satisfactory and where change is needed. (Cronbach, 1963)

The focus of this chapter (and of this book) is on the third of these – evaluation for the purposes of course improvement. Our central interest is in curriculum evaluation, or – to use the term commonly used in the American literature – programme evaluation. Indeed 'programme' may be the more useful term as it focuses attention on a specific teaching intervention and the instructional materials on which it is based. A programme, in this sense, could be a national initiative, or a course which students follow over several years, or – at the other end of the scale – a teaching episode lasting only a few lessons. So the literacy and numeracy strategies in primary schools in England, Salters' GCSE Science (a two-year science course for 15-16 year olds) and Salters' A-level Chemistry (a two-year course for 16-18 year olds) are programmes. So too are short courses which propose new ways to teach atomic theory, or genetics, or energy ideas, or to develop students' ability to analyse and discuss socio-scientific issues. A programme is a planned intervention, designed with some purpose in mind. It is, to use another analogy, a 'treatment', given or applied to a learner in order to effect a certain change, or to promote a certain outcome.

Defining 'evaluation'

In everyday usage, evaluating something means assessing its merit or worth. So evaluating an educational programme means asking: How good is it? Does it do what we want it to do? Does it work? This, of course, implies a criterion (or criteria) on which this judgment is based – which may be more or less explicitly declared.

Questions like these will be familiar to anyone who has been involved in curriculum development and innovation; they are very much the kinds of questions that inevitably form in the mind of anyone who is engaged in designing and producing new materials and approaches for teaching their subject. Most science educators who become involved in curriculum development do so because they want to improve some aspect of science education. From their teaching experience, or through their reading or research, they have come to see a problem that they believe can be solved, or a weakness that they think can be addressed, by doing something differently. They want not merely to alter practices, but to improve them. The aim is not merely change, but improvement. Curriculum development is a necessary means of articulating their vision of how they think this aspect of teaching their subject can be improved, for communicating it to others in the hope that they too will be persuaded to take it on, and for supporting those who are persuaded to put it into practice.

But this inevitably raises the question of how the products of such work can be assessed and judged. How might a curriculum developer know if his/her efforts have been successful? What claims can reasonably be made? And what would count as evidence? Questions such as these emphasise judgement. Some educational researchers, however, have resisted this judgmental emphasis, arguing that evaluation should be seen as:

> *systematic examination of events occurring in and consequent on a contemporary program – an examination conducted to assist in improving this program and other programs having the same general purpose. (Cronbach et al., 1980: 14)*

Here, the focus is not on judging something to be good or bad, but on learning from it. Most people, however, expect an 'evaluation' to do more than simply describe. A compromise viewpoint might be to see evaluation as providing the information on which judgments can be made by any of the people or groups involved in the situation. From this perspective:

> *Educational evaluation is the process of delineating, obtaining and providing useful information for judging decision alternatives. (Jenkins, 1976: 6)*

'Information' in this definition can be as wide a category as we wish it to be. It may include test scores of students who have gone through the programme in question, but is not limited to this. It can also include a wide range of other data, collected from documents, from observation, from interaction with students, teachers and others involved. It might include measures of practical competencies (or skills), and attitudes or feelings or responses, as well as measures of cognitive change.

Dimensions of evaluation

This attempt to define 'evaluation' has already highlighted one dimension on which evaluations may differ, the judgmental – descriptive dimension. Stake (1986) identifies a total of eight dimensions that can be used to characterise research designs for programme evaluation studies.

1 *Formative – summative*
   This distinction is between studies carried out during the development of a programme and those carried out after development has been completed. The former focus on improvement of the programme or decisions about its future direction, the latter on assessing its effects. An evaluation that is summative for one development can, of course, be formative for a subsequent one.

2 *Formal – informal*
   Informal evaluation is a normal and inescapable part of everyday life. Formal evaluation is more open to scrutiny and must therefore be more systematic, with an obligation to aspire to accuracy, reliability, validity, objectivity.

3 *Case-particular – generalisable*
   The issue here is whether the outcomes of a programme evaluation apply only to that programme, or to others with similar features or characteristics. If the latter, then the outcomes can inform future programmes. But it may be difficult to identify these general features or characteristics, or to obtain the kind of evidence that would safely permit such generalisation.

4 *Outcome – process*
   Some evaluations may focus entirely on the outcomes of the programme. Others are interested in the processes by which these outcomes are achieved. Treating a programme as a 'black box' may make it easier to gain evidence of effects, at the expense of understanding how these are achieved.

5 *Judgmental – descriptive*
   This has already been explored in the previous section.

6 *Preordinate – responsive*
   Studies differ as to the extent to which the issues of the evaluation are determined in advance. A more responsive evaluation will allow at least some

of the issues explored to emerge as the evaluation proceeds. This gives more scope for unanticipated outcomes to be observed.

7 *Holistic – analytic*
Some approaches consider the programme as a whole; others may focus on specific aspects of it.

8 *Internal – external*
A programme evaluation may be carried out by people involved in the development, or by people who have not been involved. An external evaluation may carry more weight with wider audiences. Conversely, the developers may have a clearer sense of some of the key features that need to be evaluated, and of the outcomes the programme is aiming for.

Rather than see each of these as dichotomous choices facing a researcher who is designing an evaluation study, it may be better to think of them as continuous variables. A given study might sit close to one end, or adopt a compromise (or hybrid) position somewhere in the middle. Taken together, they help to locate a given evaluation within the whole 'space' of possibilities. They may also highlight some of the tensions within a single evaluation study, for instance, between the views and priorities of the sponsors or funders of the curriculum development, and those of the developers. The audience for an evaluation report may significantly influence its location on these dimensions.

Judging effectiveness

As the preceding discussion has already highlighted, the feature which most clearly distinguishes evaluation from other kinds of educational research is its focus on questions of impact and effectiveness. It may therefore be useful to explore in a little more detail what we mean by the 'effectiveness' of a curriculum development or innovation. Figure 1 shows the main stages of the curriculum development process, and the factors which may influence each stage. It refers to science curriculum development, but the general principles would apply to curriculum development in any subject. It is adapted from a model (Figure 1) proposed by Millar, Tiberghien and Le Maréchal (1998) for analysing the effectiveness of practical laboratory tasks in science teaching and learning.

The starting point (box A) is the developers' objectives – the things that the students are intended to learn, or become able to do, as a result of the new approach. Three kinds of external influences may shape the developers' choices at this stage. One is their view of science – what they see as important to teach within the topic that the development deals with, and the 'image' of that content they wish to convey.

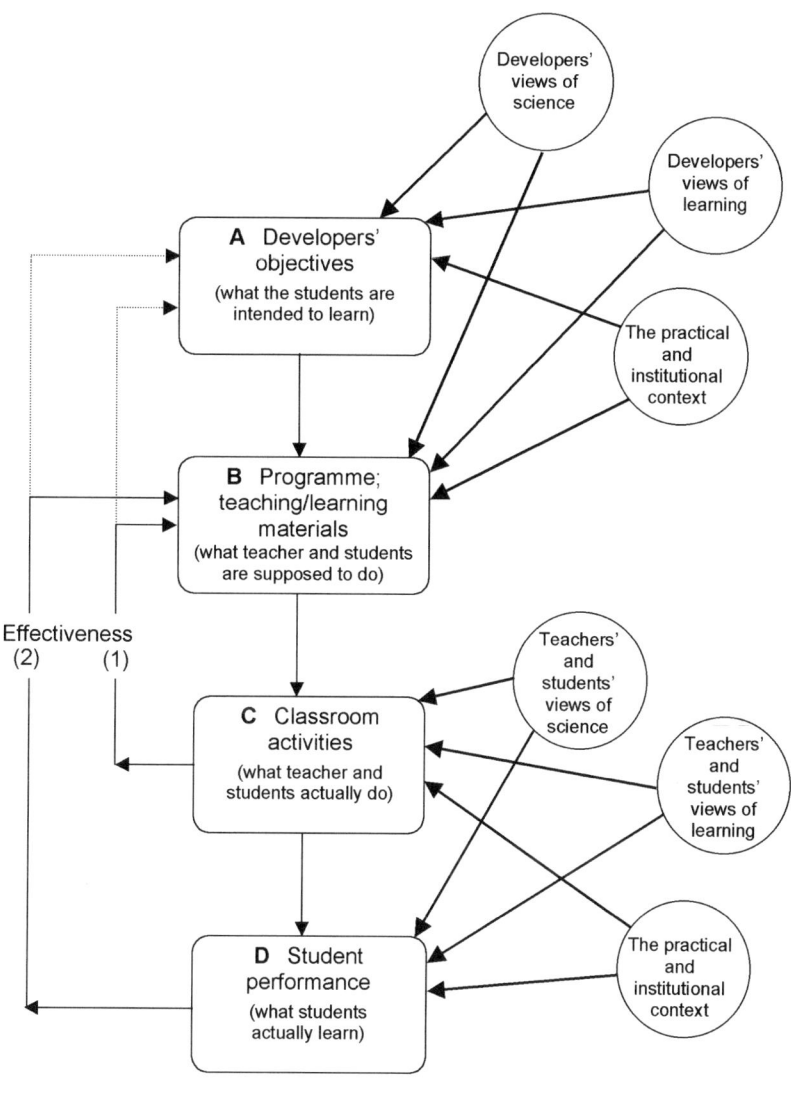

Figure 1: A model of the process of curriculum development and evaluation

Another is their view of learning, which is likely to have its greatest influence on box b but may also influence the choice of objectives. The third influence is the practical and institutional context; objectives must take account of what is practically feasible and what other influential stakeholders value.

Following on from the choice of objectives is the documentation (in whatever form) of the programme itself and the teaching and learning materials which comprise it (box B). The instructional materials indicate, to varying degrees of detail, what a teacher using the approach and his/her students are expected to do in the classroom or laboratory. Again, these will be shaped by the same three kinds of influence that apply to the objectives, though in different, and perhaps more detailed and specific, ways. For instance, the developers' view of learning will be reflected in the learning activities proposed – and may vary from topic to topic within the programme.

When the programme is implemented, it will result in certain activities – actions – in the classroom or laboratory. What the teacher and students actually do (box C) may be different from the developers' intentions. For example, a teacher may modify a given lesson plan so that it departs from that intended, in ways which the developers may regard as unimportant or as highly important. These differences may be due to misunderstanding of what was intended (a failure of communication), or deliberate choice. Similarly, the actions of the students in carrying out the planned activities may not be what the developers and/or the teacher intended. For instance, developers may design a science activity as 'guided discovery', expecting students to investigate a phenomenon carefully to collect the evidence to prompt a change in understanding – whereas students may do the task in a rather desultory fashion, as they know the teacher will tell them the expected outcome at the end anyhow. The students' (and the teacher's) actions are again likely to be influenced by their views of science and of learning, and by the context in which they are working. For example, they may be more strongly influenced by the implicit views of science and of learning that are embodied in the examination process than those of the developers and/or the teacher, if the two are at odds.

The end point of the process is box D, what the students actually learn from a lesson or from the programme as a whole. The same three types of external factor are also influential here.

We can then differentiate two senses of the term 'effectiveness'. The first, 'effectiveness (1)' in Figure 1, is the match between what the developers intend to happen in the teaching situation, and what actually does happen. The second, 'effectiveness (2)', is the match between what the developers want the students to learn and what they actually do learn. If either of these matches is not as good as we would wish, that may suggest a need to go back to review box B (and modify the instructional materials), or even to rethink box A and ask if the objectives are realistic, or correctly specified.

Another way to think about these two senses of 'effectiveness' is in relation to the curriculum framework used by the International Association for the Evaluation of Educational Achievement (IEA) for the Third International Mathematics and Science Study (TIMSS) and its predecessors (Robitaille et al., 1998). This distinguishes between the intended curriculum, the implemented curriculum and the attained curriculum. Effectiveness (1) is then concerned with the match between the intended and the implemented curriculum, and effectiveness (2) with the match between the intended and the attained curriculum. These may be useful distinctions to bear in mind in considering any specific example of curriculum development and evaluation.

Approaches to evaluation

There has been, and continues to be, much debate about approaches to evaluation in educational settings, about the appropriate methods to use, the assumptions underlying them, their implicit value commitments, and so on. Many commentators trace curriculum evaluation as a distinct field of educational research back to the work of Tyler in the 1930s and 1940s. Tyler (1949) saw curriculum planning as a four step sequence:

$$\text{objectives} \rightarrow \text{content} \rightarrow \text{organisation} \rightarrow \text{evaluation}$$

Programme evaluation then is:

> *essentially the process of determining to what extent the educational objectives are realised by the program of curriculum and instruction. (Tyler, 1949: 105-6)*

In the case of new or innovative programmes, this may involve comparing the extent to which the educational objectives in question are realised by the new approach and the established one. This, in turn, implies that evaluation studies use experimental research designs, in which two matched groups are compared on the same outcome measure(s).

This perspective on evaluation was very influential in the US at the time of the major wave of curriculum development projects (in many areas and subjects, including science) in the 1960s. Its attraction to politicians and policy-makers was that it appeared to offer a means of monitoring the benefits arising from (often very significant) expenditure, to ensure their 'value for money'. In practice, however, the evaluation studies carried out often departed from the ideal, and showed small or inconsistent effects which provided little clear guidance on policy (Norris, 1990). Nonetheless, the power of experimental designs, in principle at least, to provide sound evidence of causal links – and hence to demonstrate that a programme 'works' – has ensured their continuing influence on debates about educational evaluation methods.

Tyler's perspective on curriculum evaluation rests on a view of curriculum design that has been labelled the 'objectives model', or 'rational curriculum planning'. It assumes that it is desirable and possible (though acknowledging that it may, in some cases, be difficult) to specify educational objectives in advance. To be of value, these objectives must be precise and 'measurable'. In Tyler's view:

> *One can define an objective with sufficient clarity if he can describe or illustrate the kind of behaviour that the student is expected to acquire, so that one would recognise such behaviour if he saw it. (Tyler, 1949: 105)*

By the 1970s, however, other voices were beginning to be heard, challenging the objectives model. One key argument was that, in many areas of the curriculum, it is neither possible nor desirable to specify objectives – learning outcomes – in advance. Stenhouse (1977), for example, argued that the study of Hamlet can be defended simply on the grounds that Hamlet is worth studying. It is not necessary (or possible) to say in advance what individual learners will gain from studying it. Successful learning is not measured by observing the learner display some specific predetermined behaviour; its worth is reflected precisely in the fact that it may evoke a range of responses and consequent actions. This objection may, however, apply with greater force to the study of literature than to science education, where it may be both easier, and more justifiable, to consider that the key objectives can be specified in advance.

Tyler's model of evaluation in terms of predetermined objectives was also criticised on the grounds that it treats the classroom as a 'black box', focusing only on the inputs and outputs but telling us nothing about the processes in between. So even if we find that a programme does achieve the intended outcomes, we learn nothing about how it does so – and therefore cannot apply what we have learned to other situations. And if an evaluation produces a null result, showing no significant difference between two approaches, we learn almost nothing beyond the simple fact that we might equally well use either.

One contribution to the evaluation debate that proved particularly influential was Parlett and Hamilton's (1972) paper 'Evaluation as illumination: A new approach to the study of innovatory programmes'. In it, they criticised what they termed the 'agricultural-botany' approach to evaluation: comparing the performance of an experimental group with a matched control group on one or more pre-specified objectives. Parlett and Hamilton argued that matching groups is impossible in educational settings, because there are so many potentially important variables that would need to be controlled. Even worse, we do not know, for any situation, what all the relevant variables are. They also argued that a tight focus on pre-determined objectives means that we may not observe other unexpected side effects. In its place they proposed an approach which they termed 'illuminative evaluation', based on the methods of social anthropology, studying an innovation in context, without any parallel control group. This starts with a phase of relatively open-ended data collection to identify issues, followed by a more focused phase in which these are explored in greater depth. The outcome is a detailed case study of the programme in use.

Others have similarly argued for research designs that do not involve comparisons. Cronbach (1963), for example, concluded that:

> *Since group comparisons give equivocal results, I believe that a formal study should be designed primarily to determine the post-course performance of a well-described group with respect to many important objectives and side effects. (p. 405)*

In the UK, Stenhouse (1980) and others argued for study of cases rather than of samples, placing greater trust in sensitive and informed observers than in measurements (Hamilton et al., 1977). Through the late 1970s and early 1980s, the non-experimental, illuminative approach became the norm for the evaluation of major curriculum projects. As Hopkins (1989) observes, 'what had appeared dangerously radical 10 years earlier was now commonplace' (p. 8). It has remained influential since, and not only in the UK. In the specific case of science education, the majority of papers in the major journals and presented at conferences that might be classified as 'programme evaluations' use non-experimental research designs.

Illuminative evaluation, however, raises a number of fundamental methodological issues, many of which apply to any research that uses case study methods. A central issue is how to conduct and report a case study 'objectively', that is, in such a way that the findings can be seen to arise from the evidence, rather than from the views and preferences of the researcher. Procedures such as triangulation in data collection, and audit trails to show the stages in data analysis, are proposed to minimise researcher bias. In place of reliability and validity – key criteria for judging the quality of measurements – new terms like 'trustworthiness', 'credibility', 'transferability' and 'confirmability' are introduced (Denzin and Lincoln, 2000) with associated criteria that might be used to assess them. These may reduce the subjective element, though questions may still remain about the extent to which conclusions are entailed by the evidence collected.

Even if the findings of a case study are convincing, there remains the question of how far they apply to other cases. If they apply only to the case itself, then why should they be of any interest (and hence worth reporting) to anyone not directly involved in the case? A case is of wider interest only if it is a case of something. But by saying what we believe it to be a case of, we make implicit claims about the generalisability of the findings. Bassey (1981) argues that, rather than make or imply more general claims, the researcher should provide the details that would allow the reader to judge how far the outcomes might apply to his or her own situation. He proposes that:

> an important criterion for judging the merit of a case study is the extent to which the details are sufficient and appropriate for a teacher working in a similar situation to relate his decision making to that described in the case study. The relatability of a case study is more important than its generalisability. (p. 85)

Many reports of illuminative evaluations, however, in journal articles, book chapters and conference papers, fall somewhat short of these ideals. In the space available in these forms of publication, it is often not possible to provide enough rich description of the case setting to allow a reader to assess with confidence its 'relatability' to other situations. They are, as Roberts (1986) has remarked, often 'case stories' rather than 'case studies'.

Since the mid 1980s, the pendulum has swung back towards the judgmental (as opposed to the descriptive) end of the evaluation spectrum. In many countries this was associated with a growing climate of accountability and managerialism in education, and a concern with standards. In the UK, a significant event in shaping policy was a speech in 1976 by James Callaghan, the then Prime Minister, at Ruskin College, Oxford. In it, he emphasised the complexity of modern life and argued that standards in many areas, including education, needed to rise. This initiated a national debate on the curriculum, the relationship between school and working life, and educational standards. It also led directly to the setting up of the Assessment of Performance Unit (Hopkins, 1989). The shift of emphasis towards standards and effectiveness also reflected a common perception of educational researchers as talking mainly to each other, and not to wider audiences of potential users of the research – and that much of what they have to say to practitioners is unconvincing and provides little clear guidance on practice.

In the past decade, the value of educational research has been prominently debated in many countries. In the UK, a lecture by Hargreaves (1996), exploring the extent to which teaching can be said to be a research-based profession, encapsulated the concerns of policy-makers and triggered a vigorous debate, which is still continuing. Hargreaves dismisses the view that the problem is one of communication – that research findings are not disseminated effectively to teachers and other 'users'. Rather, he argues:

> There is no vast body of research which, if only it were acted upon by teachers, would yield huge benefits in the quality of teaching and learning. One must ask the essential question: just how much research is there which ... demonstrates conclusively that if teachers change their practice from x to y there will be a significant and enduring improvement in teaching and learning. (p. 5)

Teachers are not, of course, the only potential 'users' of educational research. A review of educational research in 1998 for the UK Department for Education and Employment concluded that 'the actions and decisions of policy-makers and practitioners are insufficiently informed by research' (Hillage et al., 1998, p. xi). The same point was expressed more bluntly by David Blunkett (2000), then Secretary of State for Education:

> *We need to be able to rely on ... social scientists to tell us what works and why and what types of policy initiatives are likely to be most effective. (p. 2)*

As an example of research that tells practitioners 'what works', Hargreaves (1996) identified clinical medicine and the growing emphasis on evidence-based medicine. The aim of evidence-based medicine is that doctors' decisions about the treatment of a particular patient should be based on evidence that the prescribed treatment leads to better outcomes (or is more likely to lead to better outcomes) than other alternatives – rather than on traditional or established ways of proceeding. The parallel term 'evidence-based education' entered the discussion, later softened by some to 'evidence-informed' or 'evidence-aware' education.

A move towards more evidence-based education would involve addressing research questions of the form: *Does approach (or programme) y have a better outcome than approach (or programme) x in terms of achieving outcome z?* This seems at first sight to be precisely the kind of question that curriculum development raises, either explicitly or implicitly. Some have argued, however, that such questions have no unique answer. Bassey (1999) makes the point that:

> *teaching situations are so varied that it is rarely, if ever, possible to say with certainty 'Do y instead of x and your pupils will learn more'. (p. 48)*

Similarly Roberts (1980) argues that 'the unique events of practice' make it impossible, in principle, to generalise about the relative effectiveness of teaching methods, approaches or materials. But unless we believe that it is impossible to compare two ways of doing something (and that any claim that one is 'better' than the other is meaningless), it seems reasonable to hope that research might be able to show that doing y instead of x is likely to result in better learning outcomes for more pupils, more of the time.

Questions of the type, *Does approach (or programme) y have a better outcome than approach (or programme) x in terms of achieving outcome z?*, seem to be very much the kind that curriculum or programme development raises. And thinking of curriculum innovation in this way has some clear benefits, in particular that it obliges developers to be clear about intended outcomes, and about how they will recognise when these have been achieved. This is likely to be rather easier for small-scale tightly focused programmes than for large-scale ones, with multiple aims. But even for the latter, the effort of specifying the intended outcomes, and thinking about how we can recognise if they have been achieved, is valuable.

Davies (1999) argues that, for such questions, 'evidence consists of the results of randomised controlled trials or other experimental and quasi-experimental studies'

(p. 114). Other advocates of evidence-based education have also argued for greater use of randomised controlled trials (RCTs) in education (Boruch, 1997; Fitz-Gibbon, 2000; Torgerson and Torgerson, 2001). The great advantage of random sampling is that it solves the problem of attempting to control multiple (and often unknown) independent variables, highlighted by Parlett and Hamilton (1972), provided that the sample is large enough. Other researchers have pointed to the difficulty of implementing RCTs in educational settings, where 'treatments' are usually applied to classes, rather than to individuals, teachers' implementations of the same 'treatment' may vary widely (and with outcomes that are often strongly dependent on the teacher's level of commitment to the treatment), and 'measures' (or indicators) of outcomes may be imprecise.

There is also a further, important reason for caution about the use of experimental research designs for curriculum evaluation. It is that many innovative programmes are not simply attempts to achieve more effectively the same objectives as the current programme. Rather they are attempts to change those objectives, to a greater or lesser extent – for example away from recall and towards understanding and application, or away from content and towards process, or whatever. Their implicit or explicit claim is not that approach (or programme) y is better than approach (or programme) x for achieving outcome z, but that outcome z is not the outcome we should be aiming for. A better goal is outcome w - and new programme y achieves this better than old programme x. So approaches x and y are not seen as two ways of achieving the same learning – which might therefore be compared – but as routes to two rather different targets – and therefore incommensurable (Figure 2).

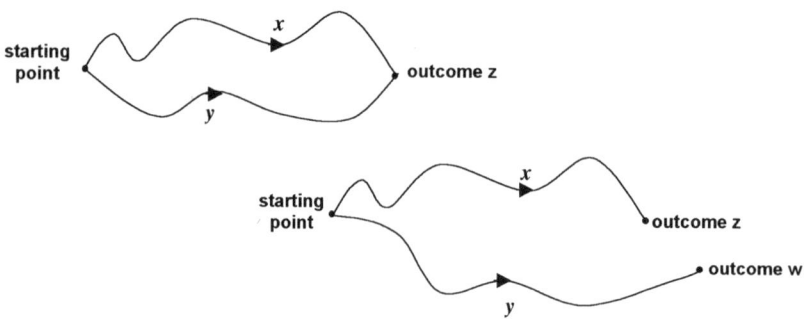

Figure 2:   Approaches x and y: comparable or incommensurable?

Recent debate about educational research in the US has some similarities to that in the UK. In 2000, the National Research Council (NRC) (a body which represents the National Academy of Sciences, the National Academy of Engineering, and the Institute of Medicine) set up an expert panel to advise on 'Scientific Enquiry in Education'. The choice of title is in itself an interesting comment on current issues and perspectives. The report begins by noting that:

> there is long-standing debate amongst scholars, policy makers and others about the nature and value of scientific research in education and the extent to which it has produced the kind of cumulative knowledge expected of scientific endeavors. Most recently, this scepticism led to proposed legislation that defines what constitutes rigorous scientific methods for conducting education research. (Shavelson and Towne, 2001: 1).

The legislation referred to is a proposal by some politicians that only research studies designed as RCTs should be supported from public funds. 'That proposal', the NRC report continues, 'coupled with rising enthusiasm for evidence-based education policy, led to this National Research Council study to examine and clarify the nature of scientific enquiry in education' (p. 1). The NRC committee argue that whilst there is no agreed account of 'the scientific process', it might be characterised by six 'principles of inquiry':

- Pose significant questions that can be investigated empirically
- Link methods to relevant theory
- Use methods that permit direct investigation of the question
- Provide a coherent and explicit chain of reasoning
- Replicate and generalise across studies
- Disclose research to encourage professional scrutiny and critique. (p. 36) As regards research methods, the committee's view is that 'the research question drives the design, not vice versa' (p. 70), and that:

> The design of a study ... does not make the study scientific. A wide variety of legitimate scientific designs are available for education research. ... To be scientific, the design must allow direct, empirical investigation of an important question, account for the context in which the study is carried out, align with a conceptual framework, reflect careful and thorough reasoning, and disclose results to encourage debate in the scientific community. (p. 4)

The NRC committee also offer a useful classification of educational research questions. They suggest that 'a great number of educational research questions fall into three (interrelated) types: description – What is happening? cause – Is there a systematic effect? and process or mechanism – Why or how is it happening?' (p. 70) Research studies of each of these three types may then follow the six principles of inquiry to varying degrees. This three-way classification may be useful for science curriculum developers as a means of clarifying the focus of an evaluation. That is, it may be important to decide, and to make clear, whether the main interest is in questions of impact (what happens when it is implemented?), cause (does the innovation 'work'?), or process (how or why does it 'work'?).

Engineering change

The approaches discussed above draw strongly on images of science and of what it means to approach a problem 'scientifically'. To round off this overview of perspectives on evaluation, it may be useful to look briefly at some ideas which draw on a different set of analogies and metaphors of the development and evaluation process. In evidence-based education, an educational intervention is seen as a 'treatment', which is given or applied to students to effect a desired change. To the teacher, however, the decision to adopt a new teaching programme or approach may feel more like choosing a new product or manufactured artefact than prescribing a new treatment. The basis of the decision is more like that of a consumer choosing a new car or washing machine than that of a doctor deciding what to prescribe for a particular patient. Campbell et al. (1994), for instance, writing about the development of Salters' GCSE Science, a two-year programme for 15–16 year olds, suggest that:

> *curriculum development is ... like a technological problem-solving activity. ... the developer is aiming to produce something which will appear, to potential users, to be a solution to some of their current problems, as they perceive them. The success of the development will depend on how many people see the product as a solution, and on the extent to which, in practice, it does provide a solution. (Campbell et al., 1994: 420-1)*

The decision to adopt a particular approach is a judgement *in a particular context*. It is chosen because the teacher thinks it would 'work' with *their* pupils, in their department. In many cases, the new approach appeals because it has some feature or emphasis that the teacher already favours, but has not yet been able to implement. It may be something they have always wanted to do – but perhaps not seen how to. So it is congruent with the teacher's values (Harland and Kinder, 1997). The decision is 'evidence-based' or 'evidence-informed', but the evidence is not of the sort that comes from RCTs or other tightly designed experimental studies. For early adopters of a new programme, the two kinds of evidence that seem to matter are:

(i) evidence of the failings of the current programme (likely to be local, personal and unsystematic);

(ii) evidence that certain characteristics of the new approach have, in other situations, led to 'successful' lessons (again likely to be personal and experiential, and focusing on classroom process rather than learning outcome).

At a later stage, there may additionally be evidence from the experience of others who have adopted the new approach. A case study discussing in detail how the approach worked in another school may have greater impact than the findings of a controlled experiment. Indeed the latter may be dismissed on the grounds that 'it may work in those schools, but I very much doubt it would work here'.

There is, however, a difference between what people find persuasive, and what actually provides sound evidence. In other words, we may be able to explain why people are persuaded to take an innovation on, but are they right to be so persuaded? There is clearly a risk that packaging and presentation become more important in ensuring uptake than evidence that the new approach is an improvement – that it 'works'. If use is intimately tied up with context, what we need is a method of evaluating educational programmes in their actual contexts of application and use that is capable of generating sound evidence of the effects of the programme, including its outcomes. One approach which has attracted attention in recent years is that of the 'design experiment' (Brown, 1992; Collins, 1993). Brown and Collins begin from Simon's (1971) distinction between the natural sciences and the sciences of the artificial (architecture, engineering, computer science, medicine and education). In the former, the aim is to understand how natural phenomena can be explained. In the latter, it is to determine how a designed artefact performs under different conditions, in order to understand the factors which affect its success. In the case of an educational programme, this would include the factors that influence the initial decision to implement it, the quality of the implementation, the decision to continue using it, and its eventual acceptance as an established feature. The design experiment approach recognises, for instance, that the implementation of any design involves many decisions that go beyond the design itself. So the implemented design is inevitably variable, from case to case. Evaluations can only be made of particular implementations. The challenge is to see what general messages, if any, can be drawn from these.

Brown (1992) argues that the evaluation of complex interventions – and a large-scale science curriculum programme would certainly count as such – should involve both studies in naturalistic settings (classrooms) and more focused studies of specific elements using experimental designs. Within the overall 'design experiment', each informs the other. The design experiment would aim not merely to generate hypotheses, but also to test them. In this way, she argues, it is possible both to advance understanding (theoretical knowledge about teaching and learning) and to improve practice. It will be necessary to have some more published examples of completed design experiments before a decision can safely be reached on the viability and usefulness of the approach. But it does appear to offer a framework which science curriculum developers may find useful, particularly for evaluating large-scale, more complex innovations, which would be difficult or impossible to evaluate using experimental methods.

Conclusion

This chapter has set out to provide an overview of key issues and approaches in curriculum evaluation, and to provide some frameworks for classifying and characterising specific examples of curriculum evaluation. Its aim has been to explore briefly the strengths and weaknesses of several major approaches, rather than to advocate any single approach. In fact, new programmes and the contexts in which they are implemented and used are so varied that it is unlikely that any one approach is best for all. But by considering these options, and the issues they raise, we may be able to analyse the evaluations that have been carried out and perhaps to learn more from them, so that we may design better evaluations of the programmes we are currently involved in developing, or hope to develop in the future.

References

Bassey, M. (1981). Pedagogic research: On the relative merits of search for generalisation and study of single events. *Oxford Review of Education*, 7 (1), 73-94.

Bassey, M. (1999). *Case Study Research in Educational Settings*. Buckingham: Open University Press.

Blunkett, D. (2000). Influence or irrelevance: Can social science improve government? London: Department for Education and Employment. (Reprinted in *Research Intelligence*, 71, 12-21.)

Boruch, R. (1997). *Randomised Experimentation for Planning and Evaluation: A Practical Guide*. London: Sage Publications.

Brown, A. (1992). Design experiments: Theoretical and methodological challenges in creating complex interventions in classroom settings. *Journal of the Learning Sciences*, 2 (2), 141-178.

Campbell, R., Lazonby, J., Millar, R., Nicolson, P., Ramsden, J. and Waddington, D. (1994). Science: The Salters' Approach – A case study of the process of large scale curriculum development. *Science Education*, 78 (5), 415-447.

Collins, A. (1993). Towards a design science of education. In E. Scanlon and T.O'Shea, (eds.), *New Directions in Educational Technology* (pp. 15-22). New York: Springer Verlag.

Cronbach, L., Ambron, S., Dornbusch, S., Hess, R., Hornik, R, Phillips, D., Walter, D. and Weiner, S. (1980). *Toward Reform of Program Evaluation*. San Francisco: Jossey Bass.

Cronbach, L. (1963). Course improvement through evaluation. *Teachers College Record*, 64, 672-683. Reprinted in M. Golby, J.Greenwald and R. West (eds.) (1975), *Curriculum Design* (pp. 399-413). London: Croom Helm.

Davies, P. (1999). What is evidence-based education? *British Journal of Educational Studies*, 47 (2), 108-121.

Denzin, N. and Lincoln, Y. (2000). The discipline and practice of qualitative research. In N.Denzin and Y.Lincoln (eds.), *Handbook of Qualitative Research*. 2nd edition (pp. 1-28). Thousand Oaks, CA: Sage Publications.

Fitz-Gibbon, C. (2000). Education: Realising the potential. In H.Davies, S.Nutley and P.Smith (eds.), *What Works? Evidence-based Policy and Practice in Public Services* (pp. 69-92). Bristol: Policy Press.

Hamilton, D., Jenkins, D., King, C., MacDonald, B. and Parlett, M. (eds.) (1977). *Beyond the Numbers Game*. London: Macmillan.

Hargreaves, D. (1996). Teaching as a research-based profession: Possibilities and prospects. Teacher Training Agency Annual Lecture 1996. London: Teacher Training Agency.

Harland, J. and Kinder, K. (1997). Teachers' continuing professional development: Framing a model of outcomes. *British Journal of In-Service Education*, 23 (1), 71-84.

Hillage, J., Pearson, R., Anderson, A. and Tamkin, P. (1998). *Excellence in Research on Schools*. Research Report RR74. London: Department for Education and Employment.

Hopkins, D. (1989). *Evaluation for School Development*. Milton Keynes: Open University Press.

Jenkins, D. (1976). *Open University Course E203, Curriculum Design and Development. Unit 19:Curriculum Evaluation*. Milton Keynes: The Open University.

Millar, R., Le Maréchal, J-F., and Tiberghien, A. (1999). 'Mapping' the domain - varieties of practical work. In J. Leach and A.C. Paulsen (Eds.), *Practical Work in Science Education: Recent Research Studies* (pp. 33-59). Roskilde, Denmark: University of Roskilde Press, in association with Kluwer: Dordrecht.

Norris, N. (1990). *Understanding Educational Evaluation*. London: Kogan Page.

Parlett, M. and Hamilton, D. (1972). *Evaluation as illumination: a new approach to the study of innovatory programmes*. Occasional Paper No. 9, Centre for Research in the Educational Sciences, University of Edinburgh. Reprinted in D.Tawney (ed.) (1976). *Curriculum Evaluation Today: Trends and Implications* (pp. 6-22). London: Macmillan; and in Hamilton, D., Jenkins, D., King, C., MacDonald, B. and Parlett, M. (eds.) *Beyond the Numbers Game* (pp. 6-20). London: Macmillan.

Roberts, D. (1980). Theory, curriculum development, and the unique events of practice. In H.Munby, G.Orpwood and T.Russell (eds.), *Seeing Curriculum in a New Light* (pp. 65-87). Lanham, MD: University Press of America.

Roberts, D. (1986). What counts as quality in qualitative research? *Science Education*, 80 (3), 243-248.

Robitaille, D., Schmidt, W., Raisen, S., McKnight, C., Britton, E. and Nicol, C. (1998). *Curriculum Frameworks for Mathematics and Science*. TIMSS Monograph 1. Vancouver: Pacific Educational Press.

Shavelson, R. and Towne, L. (eds.) (2001). *Scientific Inquiry in Education*. Washington, DC: National Academy Press.

Simon, H.A. (1971). *The Sciences of the Artificial*. Cambridge, MA: MIT Press.

Stake, R. (1986). Evaluating educational programmes. In D.Hopkins.(ed.), *Inservice Training and Educational Development*. London: Croom Helm. Reprinted in Hopkins, D. (1989). *Evaluation for School Development* (pp.16-18). Milton Keynes: Open University Press.

Stenhouse, L. (1977). Some limitations of the use of objectives. In D. Hamilton, D.Jenkins, C.King, B.MacDonald and M.Parlett (eds.) *Beyond the Numbers Game* (pp. 115-121). London: Macmillan.

Stenhouse, L. (1980). The study of samples and the study of cases. *British Educational Research Journal*, 6 (1), 1-6.

Torgerson, C. and Torgerson, D. (2001). The need for randomised controlled trials in educational research. *British Journal of Educational Studies*, 49 (3), 316-328.

Tyler, R. (1949). *The Basic Principles of Curriculum and Instruction*. Chicago: University of Chicago Press.

Chapter 2

Fit for purpose: Appropriate methods to provide evidence to inform potential users of research in education, with special references to randomised controlled trials and systematic research synthesis

Diana Elbourne* and David Gough

Evidence for Policy and Practice Information Co-ordinating Centre, Social Science Research Unit, Institute of Education, 18 Woburn Square, London WC1H 0NR, UK

There are many different methods for evaluating innovations in education. The challenge is to choose methods which are appropriate to the particular questions being addressed ('fit for purpose'). This challenge applies equally to research which is 'primary' or 'secondary' (i.e. to reviews of the research). Ideally, the review of already existing evidence should come before any new primary research is initiated. In both contexts, it is important that the process is transparent – including a clear protocol for the research, with the question, the background to justify addressing this question, the specific aims of the research within that broad question, the choice of methods for answering it, and plans for dissemination of the results. In this chapter we consider three broad research questions: what is happening? why or how might it be happening? is there evidence of a causal effect? We then examine the place of particular study designs for addressing these questions, either for the primary research or for inclusion into a review of research. We particularly consider the role of randomised experiments to provide evidence about 'what works'. Whatever the study design, we underline the importance of taking into account the quality of that research. We also stress the crucial importance of assessing the views of relevant people such as teachers, students, LEAs, potential employers, policy makers, particularly in determining which are the most relevant questions to ask. Finally, we show how these principles are applied in secondary research where the systematic synthesis of evidence from many primary research studies provides stronger evidence about the different educational interventions. The work of the EPPI Centre in this area is also described.

Introduction

Education for people at all different ages in a variety of settings is not a static process. Sometimes innovations, such as the use of new practical examples for

*corresponding author

teaching about magnetism, are introduced by individual teachers to their pupils. At other times, the innovations are introduced at national level, such as the science strategy in the National Curriculum in England (QCA, 2001). Ideally, whatever the innovation, it seems sensible that its problems and benefits should either already be known before being introduced to children, or the introduction should include an evaluative stage.

There are many reasons why some new approach should be introduced, including innovative ideas, policies, designs and developments as well as fashions and politics and competing interests for competing resources. That there are such a multitude of possible influences does not preclude the role of research to assess the nature and extent of expected and unexpected effects of any approach to teaching and learning. Research may be only one player at the table, but that is not a reason for it not to be systematic and reliable. Some argue (see for example Millar's discussion of Stenhouse in Chapter 1) that it is not possible to specify learning gains in advance and that they may evoke a range of responses and consequent actions. Not withstanding this creative and unpredictable nature of learning, it is possible to study whether certain gains have or have not been achieved and whether teaching approaches vary in the extent and nature of range of learning responses achieved.

In the US, recent federal legislation requires states and school districts to rely on scientifically-based research in choosing school improvement programmes. Although there is currently no such legal framework in the UK promoting this approach, there are numerous pointers to changes towards research informed decision making for both policy and practice (Davies, 2000; Hammersley, 2001). For instance, in 1999 the White Paper on Modernising Government was published (Cabinet Office, 1999), which led to the establishment of the Centre for Management and Policy Studies within the Cabinet Office, directly responsible to the Prime Minister, to ensure that policy makers have access to the best research, evidence and international experience, including piloting initiatives to assess their impact. In addition, the 2002 Spending Review considered the effectiveness of existing programmes, with a greater emphasis than previously on the evidence base for policy-making.

In the area of education, these changes may have been prompted, at least partly, by criticisms about the quality of the research evidence and its accessibility (Hillage et al., 1998; McIntyre and McIntyre, 1999; Tooley and Darby, 1998; Cullen et al., 2002). Hargreaves (1996) also argues that teachers over-rely on procedural craft knowledge rather than making a balanced use of craft and research based declarative research knowledge, and contrasts this to an evidence-based culture in medicine. This rather over-simplifies the position. Although there is, indeed, a strong legal framework requiring sound scientific evidence for new drug therapy, other interventions such as surgery, non-pharmaceutical treatments and health promotion, as well as broader health policy initiatives, are much less likely to have been subjected to rigorous evaluation. The extent to which unevaluated interventions are introduced into the science curriculum teaching or any other areas of education is largely unknown. The argument is not that teachers should have to use certain approaches on teaching and learning but that there is at least a responsibility to discover what is known from research about a particular approach before 'inflicting' it upon students. In this chapter we first briefly discuss conceptual ideas about scientific research in education, stressing the need to fit the type of primary research design to the purpose for which it is intended. This serves as an introduction to a discussion of the role of one particular method (randomised controlled trials) to address questions of the efficacy of teaching and learning interventions. Finally, we discuss the limitations of individual research studies and the need for systematic research synthesis to inform policy and practice. Throughout, we put particular weight on the role of the users of this research.

Scientific Research in Education

Shavelson and Towne (2001) discuss some of the key principles behind scientific enquiry:

- Pose significant questions that can be investigated empirically
- Link research to relevant theory
- Use methods that permit direct investigation of the question
- Provide a coherent and explicit chain of reasoning
- Replicate and generalise across studies
- Disclose research to encourage professional scrutiny and critique

These principles are not specific to educational enquiry, but may be appropriate to a wide range of disciplines and substantive topic areas. Education may, however, have some features which, while not individually unique to the field, may be unusual in their combination. It is a highly value-laden area, involving a variety of different players at many levels i.e. not just teachers and pupils, but also their families, schools and the wider societal context.

This diversity is also reflected in the many disciplines, both qualitative and quantitative, which are involved in education research. It means that many different research questions may need to be addressed in order to understand the complexity of a broad topic. In addition, each of these questions will be better answered by some types of research rather than others, in order to operationalise the principle of using 'methods that permit direct investigation of the question'. As Millar describes in Chapter 1, three key questions in assessing new innovations are: (1) what is happening? (2) why or how might it be happening? and (3) is there evidence of a causal effect?

Although conceptually separable, there are many circumstances in which the questions become inter-related, and individual studies may address more than one of these questions.

Types of research question

What is happening?
This first question is largely descriptive. For instance, we may want to know how many students are being taught science according to different programmes; or the differential results of students on these programmes or in different science disciplines. Alternatively, we may wish to conduct a survey to examine the age profile of science teachers in secondary schools for human resource purposes, or in terms of approaches to and understanding of science. Successive surveys can be used to consider trends over time. Using valid and reliable data collection instruments with a large random sample of teachers, and achieving high response rates, will allow credible and generalisable conclusions to be drawn. In addition, well-designed ethnographic studies describing the way science teachers are working in the classroom can provide rich examples of practice in particular contexts. Descriptive studies may also provide the basis for new theoretical models.

Why or how is it happening?
The second question attempts to explore processes and mechanisms. For instance, in order to establish theories about how children create and develop gender-stereotyped ideas about scientists, researchers could observe the behaviour of children in the playground and the interactions between teachers and children in science lessons in the classroom. Further studies correlating the gender, age and family background of the teachers could also help to explore possible mechanisms for the observed gender-stereotypical behaviour.

Is there an effect?
This third question investigates causal relationships in terms of outcomes, in particular to find out 'what works'. Research aimed at testing whether there are systematic effects is usually under-pinned by both descriptive and theoretical work, and establishing what works often loops back into exploring how and why? Sometimes all these questions are addressed in a single evaluative study.

Research to assess the value of an innovation in education needs to incorporate ideas about how various concerns are valued. In practice, this means the choice of measures used to assess outcome. For instance, the basis for considering an innovation to be valuable may be that is it acceptable to those involved, or that it proves feasible to carry out in practice, or that it does not further stretch resources which are already strained. The weight placed on these type of 'outcome measures' may need to be put alongside measures of whether the innovation 'works' in terms of that it is intended to achieve, and also whether it works better than current or alternative polices or practices.

Randomised Controlled Trials

Different research designs vary in the extent that they contribute evidence to questions of what is happening, how is it happening, and to what effect. In terms of assessing effectiveness, it may be valuable to consider different study designs within a hierarchy of the strength of evidence they supply. Many different study types can contribute. For instance, case studies of problem-based (PB) approaches to learning about electricity may be of help to describe in detail what is going on in a classroom, and may alert researchers, practitioners and policy-makers to the possibility of a potentially effective innovation. Without a comparison (control) group, however, it is possible that the effects in terms of, say, children's enjoyment of the lessons, or their results in tests, would have happened anyway, and cannot be reliably attributed to the approach.

A common type of control group is known as a historical control, when a comparison is made between these outcomes before and after (pre and post) instituting a PB approach. The difficulty with this design is that children change so much over time anyway, and any effects seen over the time period may be due to secular trends or children's normal stages of development.

To get over this, comparisons are sometimes made with contemporaneous controls. For instance, children are taught both as a whole class, and also in smaller groupings. Within a class, half the pupils in the class may be learning using a PB approach, and the other half may be being taught in whatever was the usual pedagogic style for teaching that area of the science curriculum. Although this addresses some of the problems of historical controls, we do not know why the children were being taught in these different ways. It is possible that they have made a choice themselves, and so the sort of children who might be attracted by learning through addressing problems will be more likely to succeed using these methods. Alternatively, the teacher may have selected the brighter children or more sociable children for the new (experimental) style. Clearly the concern here is that the children learning in the two different ways were themselves different at the start, and it is these differences, rather than the teaching which have resulted in their differing test scores or enjoyment.

Characterising the children in terms of their initial achievements or their sociability and then arranging that similar numbers with different levels of these attributes are represented in the two comparison groups, either by individually matching them, or matching the groups, can be a way of trying to control these potential confounding factors – especially if these factors are indeed the primary predictors of the later outcomes. The difficulty lies in the fact that this approach can only control the known confounders, but not those confounders which are not known to influence the way in which PB learning may affect the outcomes under consideration.

All the designs already discussed could be based either on existing innovations (with retrospectively collected information), or those manipulated prospectively. One method, that of randomised experiment, can only be prospective. This has a contemporaneous control group, but instead of children being selected to receive one teaching approach or another, the decision about which approach they will be allocated is based on chance – random assignment. As long as there is a large enough sample, this assignment allows not only the known factors, but also the unknown factors, to be evenly balanced between the two teaching styles – any imbalance is then due to chance and can be appropriately adjusted for in any statistical analyses.

An experimental study, if well designed and conducted, is the most rigorous for the evaluation of effectiveness questions (Boruch, 1997). An experiment which is poorly designed or conducted may be as misleading as any other study of low methodological quality. There are several steps in which an experiment can be problematic. For instance, studies are often reported as having random allocation, when, in fact, the assignment was haphazard, and/or known to the participants in advance, such as when allocation is based on date of birth. Sometimes the randomisation is well conducted, but then there is study attrition such as when only a small proportion of the children are assessed. This is even more of problem if the attrition is different between the two comparison groups. Such later selection biases may destroy the benefit of creating two comparable randomised groups initially. Biases can also arise in 'unblinded' trials if the tests are conducted in such a way that they favour one randomised group over another, especially if the assessor has some prejudices (conscious or unconscious demand characteristics) in favour of one or other teaching style. There may also be such demand effects from differential expectations of the services by the pupils in the two groups. Another problem can arise if the sample is too small to reliably detect differences. This may lead to a falsely negative conclusion about the benefits of an innovation. Although these concerns are not specific to experiments, they serve as a reminder that even the most methodological rigorous design can be methodologically weak in its application.

Regardless of their methodological quality, many objections have been raised to the principle of experimental research in education. For instance, the multi-layered characteristics of much educational practice may mean that the simplest design in which individual children are randomly allocated to be taught in different ways is not always appropriate. This does not mean the experimental design should be abandoned, but rather that it should be appropriately adapted. One concern might be that the children learning about electricity using a PB approach may influence their classmates, for example, by being seen to be having such fun that the other children in the class want to switch to it too. This so-called 'contamination' between the two types of polices for learning may necessitate a design in which groups of children such as classes or schools, rather than individuals pupils within a class, are randomised to one of the two approaches. This group or cluster randomisation (Murray, 1998) is very useful in social research as well as a number of health settings (Donner and Klar, 2000). The design can allow the two policies to remain separated, and may also have the extra benefits of preventing the teachers getting confused about which children they were teaching in which way, and may also allow a group effect to enhance the teaching and learning process. These benefits need to be counter-balanced against serious problems with this design if not correctly designed and analysed (Campbell et al., 2001). The potential problems arise from the fact that the effects on individual pupils in a class may be correlated with each other. This lack of independence between the children requires larger (sometimes very much larger) sample sizes to provide the same statistical power as an individually randomised trial, and the analysis must be adapted to take the clustering into account. If these issues are properly addressed, however, a cluster randomised trial can be a highly successful experimental design for the evaluation of diverse innovations in education. For example, a cluster randomised trial conducted in Texas, evaluated the effect of a specific multi-component violence prevention intervention (Students for Peace) on reducing aggressive behaviours in students. Eight schools were randomised to receive this programme, or the school's usual violence prevention curriculum (Orpinas, 2000). This design was also used in the RIPPLE trial to randomise 27 schools in the UK either to receive a peer-led sex education programme or to act as controls providing their usual sex education curriculum. Outcomes include the knowledge, attitudes and behaviour of the students, as well as sexually transmitted diseases and pregnancy rates (Strange et al., 2001).

Although there are problems with all research designs, these are often overstated or misunderstood in terms of experimental designs (Oakley and Fullerton, 1996). There are many myths about randomised controlled trials and in some cases it has become an ideological issue about whether one favours different methodologies rather than using whatever research tool is best suited to the purpose at hand (Oakley, 2000).

Some researchers have stated that randomised controlled designs are by their nature unethical. One of the reasons that randomisation may be considered unethical is that control groups may not receive some service that it is widely believed should be made available to all. An extreme example might be when, in order to assess the value of schooling, a control group does not receive any formal education. In general, however, withholding an educational intervention from some children is only unethical if the intervention was already known to be effective (Torgerson and Torgerson, 2001). Indeed, it could equally be argued that not rigorously evaluating educational interventions is the more unethical path. In the health field, it is considered necessary to test drugs in this way to ensure that drugs are safe and effective. Interventions in education, if they have the potential to be beneficial, also have the potential to be harmful, and randomisation can at least ensure that if the intervention does turn out to be problematic, only half rather than all the children will be disadvantaged.

Randomisation can be particularly relevant and acceptable if the intervention being assessed is a rare resource which cannot be offered to all. For example, in a randomised controlled trial of nursery provision where there are not enough places for everyone, random methods can be a fair way of allocating the scarce resource (Toroyan et al., 2000). The group not receiving the scare resource can then go on a waiting list. In many cases, however, it is not necessary to have a 'no treatment' control group. Instead, the design can compare different types or levels of intervention where it is not known which is the most successful (whatever outcome is of interest).

Another concern is that experimental designs may only be feasible in highly artificial conditions, and therefore their findings cannot be widely generalised. Although this is not invariably the case, this potential imbalance between internal validity in a small tightly controlled randomised experiment and external validity derived from large numbers in a more natural setting can be overcome if experiments become more common in education and do not necessarily disturb the normal pattern of provision. In the health setting, such trials are termed pragmatic (Schwartz and Lellouch, 1967).

Even if randomised experiments are undertaken in realistic settings, some argue that the specificity of professional decisions as judgements in particular contexts (Millar, Chapter 1) makes it unlikely that professionals will make decisions on the basis of experimental evidence. The experimental evidence is based on probabilistic data just as in health research, but this does not preclude doctors combining such evidence with their professional skills and judgements of the individual patient's particular situation and context. There is no reason to believe education is different in this regard.

Even more fundamental criticisms of randomised experiments are that they are atheoretical and that they are too simple to analyse the complexity of human social behaviour. In some ways, such an experiment is atheoretical, as it is simply a methodological tool. The theory is implicit in the research question and outcome measures applied. Any research method including case studies that are used without thought (mechanistically) is atheoretical. The criticism is not of the method but of its use. Experiments use a relatively simple methodology, but it is a misunderstanding to believe that they are too simple to cope with multivariate complex phenomena. Their whole rationale is to randomise the effects of such complexity rather than allowing it to be a source of confounding variables as in many other designs. Health research examines the effect of interventions on the human body which is also highly complex and individualistic in response. Doctors do not know for certain if any action or any well-known treatment will or will not have particular effect on a particular patient. Experiments may be thought as a crude methodological tool, but their ability to focus down upon the simple but bottom line question of whether any initiative or change in service provision has any effect is, in fact, their strength.

Finally, it is commonly considered that randomised experiments are too expensive, although they are no more expensive than any other well-conducted prospective study without randomisation. Indeed, it may be argued that the risk of providing an educational programme that has no effect or is even harmful may turn out to be more expensive in the long run. In medicine, there are many examples of clinically accepted and valued treatments which have been shown by research to not have the effects believed. Individual professionals may be highly skilled but may not see the breadth of cases or may not be able to differentiate the effects of different factors on their patients in the way possible in an experimental study. Similarly individual teachers, classes and schools can not be sure whether any changes, consequent in the use of any specific approach, are really the direct effect of that approach.

In the next section, we move from primary to secondary research. Just as individual teachers may not be able to have the breadth of experience or control to assess efficacy, individual research studies are also limited by their own contexts. One study cannot provide as much evidence as many studies combined.

Accumulation of knowledge –
systematic reviews and research synthesis

Scientific enquiry is a:

> '*continual process of rigorous reasoning supported by a dynamic interplay among methods theories and finding. The accumulation of scientific knowledge over time is circuitous and indirect ….Rarely does one study provide an unequivocal and durable result. Formal syntheses of findings across studies are often necessary*' (Shavelson and Towne, 2001, page 2).

In this section, such syntheses of research findings are considered, particularly in the context of systematic reviews of the research literature, and with special reference to the work of the Evidence for Policy and Practice Information and Co-ordinating Centre (EPPI Centre).

We have argued above that primary research in education needs to be of high scientific quality, using a research design, which is appropriate to the questions it seeks to address. The same principles should apply to reviews of research. In reviews, however, the primary studies have already been completed. Hence it is the selection of these primary studies into the review, which needs to be appropriate to the questions addressed in the review.

The aim of many such reviews of the research evidence is to summarise what is known which can inform policy, practice, democratic debate, and provide a basis for deciding what more needs to be known by further research. This involves a belief in the ability to develop general laws of prediction by the creation and testing of hypotheses using procedural methods to increase objectivity and minimise bias often using quantitative data. This positivist approach (Noblitt and Hare, 1988) can be contrasted to interpretative qualitative synthesis which is more focused on developing discourses on human action and understanding (Denzin and Lincoln, 2000). We have argued elsewhere, that both approaches are helpful (Gough and Elbourne, 2002).

Traditional literature reviews have been criticised for not being sufficiently rigorous in specifying or utilizing an explicit methodology (Oliver and Peersman, 2001). As early as 1981, Glass (one of the pioneers of quantitative synthesis in education research) commented on a conception of traditional reviews

> *"in which the activity is viewed as a matter of largely private judgement, individual creativity, and personal style. Indeed, it is and ought to be all of these to some degree; but if it is nothing but these, it is curiously inconsistent with the activity (viz., scientific research) it purports to illuminate" (Glass et al., 1981).*

Given that it is not practical to expect people to read many original papers, an explicit methodology allows the reader to understand how the results of the review were reached, to make an assessment of their reliability and validity, and to understand why different reviews came to different conclusions. This also allows for replication and updating of reviews.

The main stages of a review include setting the research question, establishing the methods for the review; searching for the literature (with explicit inclusion and exclusion criteria), quality assessment of the studies, the synthesis; conclusions, and dissemination. At all stages, the role of potential users of the research is invaluable, but no more so than when choosing and refining the research question(s). User-led research synthesis is essential if research evidence is to be transformed into practice research knowledge (Desforges, 2000).

The same three broad questions considered for primary research can also be used as a framework for systematic reviews, and similar issues about fitness for purpose and methodological quality also apply – but this time to the range of studies included within the review. For instance, if the review is asking about the existing research on the extent to which PB learning is used in science teaching, the reviewers will search for relevant surveys, assess the quality of the information they provide, and synthesise the findings. Alternatively, if the review is asking about the evidence that PB learning is more effective than traditional pedagogical approaches for teaching about electricity, the reviewers will search for evaluations which have compared the two approaches, and assess the quality of the information they provide, before synthesing the evidence in order to inform policy, practice, and further research.

In the same way as we have seen in the discussion of experimental primary research, many of the criticisms of the systematic approach to reviewing the research in education appear ideologically driven. For instance, the dominance of research questions (and thus research methods) concerned with effectiveness within systematic research synthesis in medicine, (particularly in the international Cochrane Collaboration) has led some researchers to be concerned that statistical meta-analysis of randomised controlled trials will become the primary model for reviews in education (Vulliamy and Webb, 20001). This is in spite of the fact that the principles of explicit synthesis methodology can be applied to research questions other than evidence of efficacy, and are also relevant to the accumulation of evidence from qualitative data. Other commentators, such as Slavin (1984) have criticised over-simplistic use of the systematic review methods, but have made suggestions for adapting, rather than discarding the approach (Slavin, 1995).

Below, we discuss one approach, that of the EPPI Centre, which addresses some of these criticisms.

The EPPI-Centre

The EPPI Centre is part of the Social Science Research Unit (SSRU) at the Institute of Education, University of London. The SSRU undertakes descriptive, analytic and experimental primary studies on social interventions, systematic research syntheses in the EPPI-Centre, and related methodological work. Since 2000, the EPPI-Centre has an additional focus in education funded by the English Department of Education and Skills, facilitating education reviews which are primarily conducted by subject-specific review groups (RGs) using specialised EPPI-Centre procedures and tools. A basic principle behind EPPI-Centre reviews is transparency of methods, which allows replication, updating and sustainability of reviews, which will be freely available on the web.

The EPPI-Centre shares this principle with other initiatives in the education field such as the newly formed Campbell Collaboration (although, like its older sibling the Cochrane Collaboration, this has to date largely focused on experimental research). In contrast, EPPI-Centre reviews may also address wider questions, include data from both quantitative experimental and qualitative studies, and summarise the information in the form of tables and words, rather than (or in addition to) numbers, although still using tools and methods that enable transparency and sustainability. For example, one EPPI-Centre review has investigated firstly, evaluations of interventions to reduce the barriers to mental health in young people, and secondly, the descriptive studies about what young people, themselves, consider to be important barriers to their achieving good mental health. These two bodies of evidence were separately assessed for their methodological quality, and their findings synthesised, also separately. Finally, the barriers identified by the young people were integrated with the evidence about their effectiveness within a matrix (Shepherd et al., 2001). In using findings in this way from different types of primary studies, the reviews can be characterised as systematic narrative reviews in contrast to non-systematic traditional narrative reviews.

All the research synthesis initiatives argue for the importance of involving users such as (in education), teachers, students, LEAs, potential employers, policy makers etc. For the EPPI-Centre, user involvement is seen as a central driver for setting significant and relevant research questions (Oliver, 1999) (including explicit theoretical and ideological assumptions) and allowing more open democratic participation in research. This process is facilitated by having users involved in suggesting and prioritising topics for RGs, as members of RGs, as advisors to the RGs, as peer-referees for the RG proposals, review protocols, and review reports. Users are also involved in producing summaries of the reviews for different user groups.

EPPI-Centre systematic review methods involve the following stages: a protocol for the research question, giving the background to justify addressing this question; the specific aims of the research within that broad question; the choice of methods for answering it, and plans for communication of the results. The methods specify systematic and exhaustive searching methods, specification of explicit inclusion and exclusion and quality assessment criteria. Double data coding helps to assure the quality of the reviews. Although there are set stages for undertaking a review, it is not simply a mechanical process. All included studies are subject to an explicit judgmental process so that only studies meeting basic criteria for quality and coherence are included.

Seventeen education RGs have been registered in the areas of art and design, assessment and learning research; citizenship, continuing professional development; early years; English teaching; gender and education; inclusive education; Mathematics education, modern languages; motivation, Personal, Social and Health Education (school-based), post-compulsory education; school leadership, science education, thinking skills, and transitions. The first 22 reviews are freely available on the Research Evidence in Education Library (REEL) on the EPPI-Centre website (http://eppi.ioe.ac.uk/EPPIWeb/home.aspx).

Concluding remarks

In considering methods for primary research and systematic reviews of research to provide evidence to inform potential users of research in education, we have shown that there are many ways to address the variety of important questions for policy makers, practitioners and other users of education research. We have stressed the need to use research methods which are appropriate to these questions, and emphasised the need to take into account their methodological quality in order to be able to assess how much reliance to place on their findings. The involvement of policy makers, practitioners, and users of services is crucial in determining the questions that need to be asked, systematic research synthesis is also required to find out how much research evidence there is to answer such questions and what further (fit for purpose) research is required. Furthermore, research is more likely to influence policy and practice if there is clarity about the nature and source of the evidence. Indeed, transparency is essential to allow "science [to] advance through professional criticism and self-correction" (Lakatos and Musgrave, 1970).

References

Boruch, R.F. (1997). *Randomized experiments for planning and evaluation: a practical guide.* Thousand Oaks: Sage.

Cabinet Office (1999). *Modernising Government.* Presented to Parliament by the Prime Minister and the Minister for the Cabinet Office by Command of Her Majesty. Cm 4310 London: The Stationery Office.

Campbell, M.J., Donner, A. and Elbourne, D. (eds). (2001). Design and Analysis of Cluster Randomized Trials: *Statistics in Medicine*, 20 (3), 329-496.

Cullen, J. Hadjivassiliou, K. Hamilton, E. Kelleher, J. Sommerlad, E. and Stern, E. (2002). *Review of Current Pedagogic Research and Practice in the Fields of Post-Compulsory Education and Lifelong Learning.* Report submitted to the Economic and Social Research Council. London: Tavistock Institute.

Davies, P. (2000). The relevance of systematic reviews to educational policy and practice. *Oxford Review of Education*, 26, (3 and 4), 365-378.

Denzin, N.K. and Lincoln, Y.S. (2000). Preface in N.K. Denzin and Y.S. Lincoln (eds.) *Handbook of Qualitative Research, 2nd Edition.* Thousand Oaks: Sage.

Desforges, C. (2000). *Familiar challenges and new approaches : necessary advances in theory and methods in research on teaching and learning.* The Desmond Nuttall/Carfax Memorial Lecture. Cardiff: BERA Annual Conference.

Donner, A. and Klar, N. (2000). *Design and Analysis of Cluster Randomization Trials in Health Research*. London: Arnold.

Glass, G.V. McGaw, B. and Smith, M.L. (1981). *Meta-Analysis in Social Research*. Beverley Hills: Sage (page 14).

Gough, D. and Elbourne, D. (2002). Systematic Research Synthesis to Inform Policy, Practice and Democratic Debate. *Social Policy and Society* 1 (3), 225-36.

Hammersley, M. (2001). On systematic reviews of research literatures: a 'narrative' response to Evans and Benefield. *British Educational Research Journal*, 27 (5), 543-554.

Hargreaves, D. (1996). *Teaching as a research-based profession: possibilities and prospects*. Teacher Training Agency Annual Lecture. London: TTA.

Hillage, J. Pearson, R. Anderson A. and Tamkin, P. (1998). *Excellence in Research in Schools*. London: Department for Education and Employment/Institute of Employment Studies.

Lakatos, I. and Musgrave, A. (eds.). (1970). *Criticism and the growth of knowledge*. Cambridge, England: Cambridge University Press.

McIntyre, D. and McIntyre, A. (1999). *Capacity for Research into Teaching and Learning*. Final report to ESRC Teaching and Learning Programme. Cambridge: School of Education, University of Cambridge.

Murray, D. (1998). *Design and analysis of Group-Randomized Trials*. Oxford: Oxford University Press.

Noblitt, G.W. and Hare, D.W. (1988). *Meta-Ethnography: Synthesizing Qualitative Studies*. Beverley Hills: Sage.

Oakley, A. and Fullerton, D. (1996). The lamp-post of research: support or illumination? In A. Oakley and H. Roberts (eds.). *Evaluating social interventions*. Ilford, Essex: Barnados.

Oakley, A. (2000). *Experiments in Knowing: gender and method in the social sciences*. Cambridge: Polity Press.

Oliver, S. (1999). Users of health services: following their agenda. In: S. Hood, B. Mayall and S. Oliver (eds.). *Critical issues in Social Research: Power and Prejudice*. Buckingham: Open University Press.

Oliver, S. Peersman, G. (2001). *Using Research for Effective Health Promotion*. Buckingham: Open University Press.

Orpinas, P., Kelder, S., Frankowski, R., Murray, N., Zhang, Q. and McAlister, A. (2000). Outcome evaluation of a multi-compoent violence-prevention program for middle schools: the Students for Peace project. Health Education Research 15 (1), 45-58.

QCA [Qualifications and Assessment Authority] (2001). National Curriculum tests 2001. Implications for teaching and Learning - Key Stage 3 Science. London: QCA.

Schwartz, D. and Lellouch, D. (1967). Explanatory and pragmatic attitudes in therapeutic trials. *Journal of Chronic Diseases* 20, 637-48.

Shavelson, R.J. and Towne, L. (eds.). (2001). *Scientific Research in Education*. Report of Committee on Scientific Principles for Education Research. Washington DC: National Academy Press.

Shepherd, J., Garcia, J., Oliver, S., Harden, A., Rees, R., Brunton. G. and Oakley, A. (2001). *Barriers to, and Facilitators of, the Health of Young People*. London: EPPI Centre.

Slavin, R.E. (1984). Meta-analysis in education How has it been used? *Educational Researcher*, 13, (8), 6-15.

Slavin, R.E. (1995). Best evidence synthesis: an intelligent alternative to meta-analysis. *Journal of Clinical Epidemiology*, 48, 9-18.

Strange,V., Forrest, S., Oakley, A. and the RIPPLE team. (2001). A listening trial: 'qualitative' methods within experimental research, in: S. Oliver and G. Peersman (eds). *Using Research for Effective Health Promotion*. (Buckingham, Open University Press).

Tooley, J. and Darby, D. (1998). *Educational research – a critique*. London: Office for Standards in Education.

Torgerson, C.J. and Torgerson, D.J. (2001). The need for randomised controlled trials in educational research. *British Journal of Educational Studies*, 49 (3), 316-28.

Toroyan, T. Roberts, I. and Oakley, A. (2000). Randomisation and resource allocation: a missed opportunity for evaluating health care and social interventions. *Journal of Medical Ethics*, 26, 319-322.

Vulliamy, G. and Webb, R. (2001). The social construction of school exclusion rates: implications for evaluation methodology. *Educational Studies*, 27, (3), 357-370.

Part B :
Examples of curriculum innovation and its evaluation

Part B: Introduction

The place of science in the school curriculum has changed in the past 30 years in many countries, from a specialist preparation for an elite but economically important minority to become an entitlement for all. Across the world, often spurred by the results of international comparisons such as the Third International Mathematics and Science Survey (TIMMS) and the Programme for International Student Assessment (PISA), national education systems are grappling with the implications of this change. It is therefore not surprising that much effort and resource is invested in both small and large scale science curriculum innovation, but perhaps more surprising is the undeveloped state of expertise in evaluation of the effects of curriculum intervention. These chapters are a contribution to the development of that expertise.

Curriculum innovation may be on a large scale, involving the implementation of a complete curriculum and assessment scheme such as *Chemie im Kontext*, described by Gräsel and others in Chapter 3, or may involve smaller scale interventions. Evaluation poses different problems according to scale. A large scale innovation is likely to have a variety of objectives, not all of which can be addressed in a single evaluation study. In such a case, the collection of overall performance data, together with smaller and specific studies, as described for *Salters Advanced Chemistry* by Bennett and Holman in Chapter 4, may be the chosen approach. Boersma and his co-workers (Chapter 5) show the importance of both formative and summative evaluation to the whole curriculum development process.

Adey's description of the evaluation of the *Cognitive Acceleration in Science Education (CASE)* intervention illustrates the more experimental approach, advocated in Chapter 2, though not based on randomly selected samples as advocated by Elbourne and Gough . While taking a different, more 'illuminative' approach, Kolsto describes the evaluation of short-term interventions to teach about science for citizenship, and explores some general issues relating to evaluation on this scale (Chapter 7) and Parvin shows how a well-defined and limited intervention (in a primary context) lends itself well to focused evaluation (Chapter 8).

In all events, the delivery of curriculum innovations is ultimately in the hands of classroom teachers, and each will implement differently. In Chapter 9, Ostermeier and Prenzel not only acknowledge this but advocate an approach which places teachers at the heart of the curriculum development process; they identify some of the evaluation challenges raised by this approach. Amettler and Pinto, in Chapter 10, further explore the importance of taking account of this source of variability, even when the change involved is very limited and is a clearly defined one – and the challenge it poses to evaluators.

Clearly, there is no single model for the evaluation of science curriculum innovation: much will depend on the objectives of the innovation and the priorities placed upon them. In Chapter 11, Campbell and Lubben consider the appropriateness of a number of measures of success, including student participation and long-term interest as well as attainment. Eylon and Hofstein (Chapter 12) show through two examples how curriculum developers build on the work of their predecessors: if this is the case, it becomes even more important that each piece of work is rigorously evaluated so that the lessons can be clearly identified and passed on.

Although these papers show that evaluation procedures can vary, they still illustrate the key principles outlined in Chapter 1 by Millar.

Chapter 3

Chemie im Kontext – Curriculum development and evaluation strategies

Cornelia Gräsel[a], *Peter Nentwig, Ilka Parchmann*[b]
Leibniz-Institute for Science Education at the University of Kiel, D-24098

Summary

What is the innovation? A context-based curricular framework for chemistry teaching on lower and upper secondary level, which is developed and improved by teachers and researchers.

What need does it address? Fostering motivation and interest and enhancing the understanding of basic chemical concepts by using contexts that are relevant for students.

What is its scope? The development of *Chemie im Kontext* began in 1997 and is currently being implemented in about 120 schools in Germany.

What evaluation data have been collected? The first empirical investigations are formative and qualitative. Their goal is to get information about the realization of the conceptual framework in classroom practice, about learning outcomes and perception of the curriculum to guide improvement. One case study, which is described in this chapter, deals with students' perception of teaching and learning with the new conceptual approach (pre-post-design).

What are the key findings? The pre-post-study showed a significant increase in students' perception of relevance of chemical contents and the quality of instruction. Additionally, data showed that students with normally lower achievement showed a higher increase in their perception of teaching and learning. Other case studies give information about students' learning outcomes, for example the change and application of conceptual explanations for daily-life phenomena.

---

[a] Present address: University of Wuppertal, Faculty of Educational Studies, Department of Research on Learning and Instruction, D-42097 Wuppertal, Germany

[b] Present address: Carl Ossietzky University of Oldenburg, Didaktik der Chemie, Postfach 2503, D-26111, Oldenburg, Germany

Introduction

Many studies have been carried out to test students' science knowledge and understanding, long before TIMSS and PISA delivered their results, which were disappointing for many countries. Other research has examined the interest and motivation of students, and these studies too gave unsatisfactory results. Throughout the past decades one consequence of such studies has been the development of innovative curricula and concepts to enhance science learning. In most cases the objective was to improve interest and motivation as well as to lead students to a better understanding of science concepts. One way is to emphasize their relevance for real life problems. The 'Salters Approach' in the UK (see Bennett and Holman in this book) and 'ChemCom' in the US are two recent examples of such courses that have been implemented successfully. Other projects such as the Dutch physics course 'PLON' (Eijkelhof and Lijnse, 1988) and the German integrated science course 'PING' (Riquarts and Hansen, 1997; Reinhold and Bünder, 2001) have not been developed further, although some of their resources are still used in schools.

Many curricular approaches have been tried and have disappeared without a trace. Were the successful ones 'better'? Was it circumstance? Was it financial stamina alone? The success of curriculum implementation depends on a large variety of factors beyond well-meaning course-design. This contribution claims that the evaluation of curriculum success needs a variety of strategies and methods. This paper will outline how our research group tries to assess the effect of a new curriculum for grades 8 to 13.

Chemie im Kontext [1]

Chemie im Kontext (ChiK) is a curricular framework for lower and upper secondary chemistry lessons. The development started in 1997, mainly at the Universities of Oldenburg and Dortmund. In 1999, the project got a third base at the Leibniz-Institute of Science Education (IPN) at the University of Kiel. In 2002, the framework became the foundation of an implementation project funded by the German Ministry of Education (BMBF) and the participating states ("Länder"), which is being carried out under the leadership of the IPN and the universities of the Saarland and Dortmund.

---

[1] We adhere to the German expression *"Chemie im Kontext"* (also ChiK) in order to not be mistaken for either the college course "Chemistry in Context" of the American Chemical Society (American Chemical Society, 2000) or the secondary level chemistry book of the same name in the UK (Hill and Holman, 2000)

One central feature of *Chemie im Kontext* is that knowledge is developed from problems and issues, contexts, that are relevant to the students, either personally or for the society in which they live (Parchmann et al., 2000; 2001)ADDIN. Based on learning within authentic contexts, learners are supported to develop a deeper understanding of basic concepts. Chemical knowledge is acquired and used to elaborate the issue in question. This knowledge is then decontextualized for application in new contexts, and from there, a limited number of **basic chemical concepts** are abstracted. A third key feature in the philosophy of ChiK is the use of a large variety of teaching and learning methods to support the students' self-directed and co-operative learning.

Development of the curricular approach and the learning environments

Early development and first classroom tests were done by science educators in Oldenburg and Dortmund (Huntemann et al., 2000a, 2000b; Paschmann, et al., 2000). This work was strongly influenced by curricular approaches in other countries, and it shares many of the features especially with the *Salters' Approach* (Bennett, 1999; Lazonby et al., 1992).

In addition, the development of *Chemie im Kontext* was influenced by general theories of teaching and learning, especially by theories of situated learning (Spiro et al., 1987; Gräsel, 1997; Mandl, et al., 1997). There are visible similarities between ChiK and learning environments which were designed under the paradigm of situated cognition, namely the Cognition and Technology Group at Vanderbilt (Vanderbilt, 1990; 1997). As in *Chemie in Kontext*, self-determined and co-operative learning play a crucial role and such theories and related empirical findings will influence the future development of ChiK more and more.

Implementation of *Chemie im Kontext* in school

Some comments on the school system in Germany may be helpful to understand better our implementation approach. The general goals and contents of instruction are fixed in syllabi, which are determined by the educational authorities in the different states ("Länder"). The realization of the syllabi in the classroom is the teachers' own responsibility. They specify the general goals and contents of the syllabi, construct a lesson plan, select or develop teaching materials and assessment procedures and decide which learning methods are used in their classrooms. This responsibility is an important part of teachers' professional self-conception.

In Germany it is neither common nor would it be suitable to present a closed curriculum to teachers with pre-arranged teaching material, methodology and assessment instruments. ChiK therefore provides a conceptual framework rather than a 'teacher-proof' curriculum, that will be advanced, revised and improved by the core team and the co-operating teachers jointly during the implementation in schools. Groups of teachers will meet with members of the core group for a continuous process of curriculum development, self-evaluation and implementation of new ideas. This process is seen as a contribution to the professionalization of the teachers. Also, a closed curriculum would contradict the philosophy of ChiK, which is based on the *active* involvement of teachers *and* learners of the planning and structuring of lessons. Not least have we learned that top-down models of implementation most often fail to show the desired success.

The evaluation strategy of *Chemie im Kontext*

The open nature of *Chemie im Kontext* as a conceptual framework must have consequences on the evaluation strategy. Millar (in this book) differentiates two forms of effectiveness of curricula:

(1) The match between what the developers intend to happen in the teaching situation, and what actually does happen.

(2) The match between what the developers want the students to learn and what they actually do learn.

These two criteria of effectiveness can also be applied to ChiK. Millar's first item aims at the implementation of a new curriculum. What happens to the good intentions on their way from the curriculum developer into the classroom? What role do teachers play in this process, and how can they be supported to minimize disappointment? The evaluation of *Chemie im Kontext* aims to obtain more detailed information about important factors that influence the transfer of educational approaches into practice (e.g. teachers' beliefs, attitudes, school and organization variables). Furthermore, our implementation strategy itself will be evaluated and refined. This is the focus of the project, funded by the German Ministry of Education (BMBF). This project allows us to establish working groups of teachers in schools in several Laender (Zech et al., 2002). These groups co-operate to realise the framework of *Chemie im Kontext* in their classes by developing and revising units for context-based learning in chemistry.

Because of its open nature, there is no identical standard one can use to compare the intentions of ChiK and the results from the actual classroom processes. Depending on many influencing factors – e.g. syllabi, grade, content, prior knowledge of students – *Chemie im Kontext* can be realized in different variations. Therefore, a first important criterion for the success of our implementation is the assessment of the approach by teachers. They, as professionals, can judge whether our conceptual framework, our materials and our support in the working-groups are helpful for their teaching and learning. Additionally, we get information about limiting and facilitating conditions for the implementation of *Chemie im Kontext* in classrooms (e.g. syllabi). These views of the teachers, however, are only part of the evaluation. To know whether the activities of teachers and learners are in accordance with the philosophy of ChiK (use of contexts, decontextualisation of basic concepts, variety of teaching methods), we use a documentation of the teaching and learning activities and material in the classrooms. Finally, we are conducting case studies and collecting data from classroom observation.

Millar's second item was, what students are supposed to learn and what they actually do learn. Two questions can be distinguished regarding that aspect:

Does the course influence the learners' perception of the quality of teaching and learning? The course design involves theories about learning and motivation - e.g. the support of students' perception of motivation (Deci et al., 1997) and the use of relevant contexts (Reinmann-Rothmeier and Mandl, 2001). Before we tackle the question whether or not the course enhances students' motivation and interest in chemistry objectively, we want to know whether students subjectively perceive an improvement of these factors through the course design (Wierstra, 1984). When teachers participate in our working-groups and in-service training, the perceived quality of teaching and learning should rise.

"What are the cognitive learning outcomes of the course?" The general principle of *Chemie im Kontext* is to build a bridge from situated learning to the systematic development and understanding of basic chemical concepts. Several questions can be derived from this objective:

- Does the approach really foster an understanding of basic chemical concepts?
- Does the approach support students' use of scientific concepts in addition to or instead of so-called daily-life concepts?
- Do students develop different dimensions of knowledge and competencies, such as conceptual knowledge, transferable basic chemical concepts, meta-cognitive skills to apply mental models? (OECD-PISA, 1998; Anderson and Krathwohl, 2001).

To answer these questions, we are conducting case studies in which we investigate the learning outcomes in detail and with respect to the respective content of the course (see below). These studies focus on the effects of our teaching conception on student learning as well as on the professionalisation and perception of teachers.

First results of pilot studies

As the development and evaluation of *Chemie im Kontext* is still in progress, only the first results of our pilot studies can be presented in this paper. For this overview, we will refer to the key questions, as they are outlined above.

Does the course influence the learners' perception of the instructional quality?

Case studies for single units of the curriculum

Doctoral students, who have been engaged in the development of these units, designed questionnaires to ask students about their perception of the teaching and learning in the course, of the relevance of the topic used in the unit, and about their understanding of conceptual relationships (Huntemann et al., 2000a; Paschmann et al., 2000). The outcomes of these case studies were used primarily for further developmental work as well as for the improvement of the questionnaires, which will be used during the first year of the course's implementation. We noticed, for example, that students often saw the personal relevance of a certain topic (e.g. 'A Rusting World', 'Fuels in Discussion'), but did not always realise the issue's relevance for the society in which they lived. Another finding shows problems of cooperative learning, where we found the same difficulties that have been described in other studies (Renkl et al., 1995), for example the 'ruck-sack' effect, which gives active students the impression that they have to carry others with them and doing their work as well. These findings are helping to create tools for supporting and scaffolding self-directed and co-operative learning also for the weaker students.

Pre-Post study about the changes of the learners' perception of the quality of teaching and learning

On the basis of motivational theories and empirical studies about motivation and interest (Prenzel et al., 1998), a questionnaire was designed to investigate the students' perception of a number of criteria of teaching and learning quality that are important in the philosophy of *Chemie im Kontext* (Parchmann et al., 2001; Nentwig et al., 2005). This questionnaire contains 54 items on a five-step-scale. Following a factorial analysis, five variables were defined:

- interest in the chemistry lesson (6 items, $\alpha = .86$)
- perception of relevance (7 items, $\alpha = .74$)
- perception of own competence (5 items, $\alpha = .82$)
- perception of instructional quality (6 items, $\alpha = .75$)
- perception of learning atmosphere (7 items, $\alpha = .76$)

Because of the design of *Chemie im Kontext*, our expectation was that students' scores on these factors should rise after exposure to the new approach. The questionnaire was given to students before and after a unit of *Chemie im Kontext*. Each unit lasted for four to six weeks (15 – 20 lessons). To avoid incidental effects of single units, the questionnaire was used with 110 students from 8 classes in 5 secondary schools of Lower Saxony.

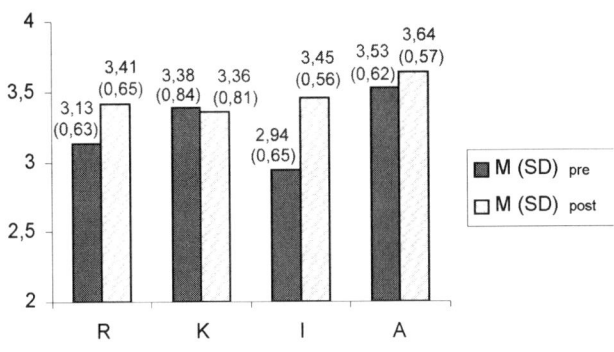

Figure 1: Results of a pilot study about the learners' perception of learning and teaching quality (variables: R – relevance of topic, K – perception of competence, I – quality of instruction, A – perception of learning atmosphere; columns: filled columns: pre-test, hatched columns: post-test)

We analyzed the pre-post differences of the five variables of teaching and learning quality for all students using T-tests for paired samples (Figure 1). We also looked for specific group effects, for example between boys and girls or successful and non-successful students (defined in terms of previous grades in chemistry).

We found significant positive effects for the perception of relevance of chemical contents and quality of instruction ($p<.001$; $\varepsilon = 0.4$ resp. 0.9).

Additionally, data revealed some interesting interaction effects. Students with lower chemistry grades in the previous school year showed a larger increase in all variables of teaching and learning quality than students with better grades (analysis of variance; repeated measures * previous marks). There were no significant differences between boys and girls concerning these variables. It may not be surprising that students with the lowest earlier grades, who are probably most dissatisfied with traditional chemistry lessons, show the highest increase. On the other hand, teachers had been worried that weaker students might not be able to follow context-based units and to cope with the demands of self-directed learning. At least according to the students' own perception, this was not the case.

The results of this pilot study are used in a formative way for the development of our implementation project, in which more than 100 classes are taking part. They are also being used for teacher-education workshops to indicate how the course was accepted by students, and why weaker students might have a better perception of their own competence in a course like *Chemie im Kontext*, compared to traditional classroom teaching.

What are the cognitive learning outcomes of the course?

Learning outcomes are difficult to measure, as they have many dimensions, and are highly dependent on changing factors beyond the control of curriculum developers. In recent years, various methods of assessing learning outcomes have been described, such as questionnaires with multiple choice and open questions (OECD-PISA, 1998; Baumert et al., 2000), mapping techniques (Rice et al., 1998; Fischer and Mandl, 2000), written texts (Sumfleth and Todtenhaupt, 1995), and – beyond paper-and-pencil tests – learning interviews (Gropengießer, 1997) or the analysis of students classroom work (portfolios) (Melograno, 1994).

Chemie im Kontext aims at the acquisition of knowledge within a context and the abstraction of basic concepts from there. To pursue this aim, we need deeper insight into this process from situated learning to decontextualization. Currently four doctoral studies are investigating this field. One is identifying the learning outcomes at the end of a unit; another is investigating the development and use of scientific concepts in real-life contexts; a third student is looking into the understanding and transfer of basic concepts and answers to contextualised questions, while the fourth student is investigating the use of scientific knowledge for decision making processes.

The understanding of contexts and concepts
As the course is aiming to develop different dimensions of knowledge and cognitive competencies, one test instrument has been developed in close relation to the process of learning in a *Chemie im Kontext* unit (Steinhoff, 2004). First, students are given problems related to the same contexts they have dealt with in the unit. They analyse the context and use the acquired scientific concepts to solve the problems. The second part of the questionnaire assesses the understanding of these chemical concepts, and in the third part of the test the same concepts have to be transferred for solving a problem in a new context. The example used for the questionnaire was a unit dealing with polymers (part one was concerned with polymers in cars, part two, the concept of structures and properties and part three was devoted to a new context, namely polymers in clothes and fabrics). The results show no significant differences

between the first and second part, while the students had more difficulties in applying the concept to a new context, as expected. We also found large differences between classes, which could not simply be correlated with content aspects that have been taught. To be able to identify criteria of successful and less successful teaching and learning in a 'ChiK-way', closer insight into the processes of learning are necessary (insight into the subsurface structure of learning, see Stigler et al., 2000).

The development and use of scientific concepts in Chemie im Kontext
A serious problem, described in several empirical studies, is the insufficient application of concepts that have been learned at school to real-life problems (BLK, 1997). Theories of situated learning and conceptual change therefore propose the integration of real-life problems and science concepts as part of the learning process (Driver et al., 1994; Schletter and Bayrhuber, 1998). *Chemie im Kontext* takes this into consideration by creating tasks that require the application of daily-life concepts as well as scientific ones. One study carried out in our group is looking into the understanding and the change of conceptual explanations during the course. Video documentation is also used to describe the development of conceptual understanding when students are asked to explain chemical processes on the sub-microscopic level of particles.

We also give students a daily-life question related to the unit taught at the time, which they are asked to answer before and several times throughout the unit. Each time, they are reminded of their own previous answers to comment, amend or correct. Thus, not only do we get information about the application of different concepts, but also the students gain insight into their own learning process. The first outcomes of this study confirm results of previous empirical studies, where typical pre-conceptions are described (Pfundt, 1982; Driver et al., 1994). During the course, the explanations of students change. They use scientific concepts more often, as was also found with other context-based approaches (Eijkelhof and Lijnse, 1988). The results also indicate that these explanations are strongly context-bound, because they are not used for all examples in the same way (Nieswandt 2001; Parchmann and Schmidt, 2003). Further results will have to give more information about how to design tasks or problems to support students' transfer.

In summary, the outcomes of these studies will mainly be used to improve the structure of the course, especially the design of context-based tasks, guidelines to support transfer, and the application of conceptual understanding. Follow-up studies, that compare the learning outcomes of *Chemie im Kontext* with those of other courses, might later be based on the developed instruments.

Discussion: Curriculum Development and Evaluation – what is it good for?

To discuss our approach to evaluation and to draw some consequences, we will follow five questions that Wottawa (2000) has posed for the planning and conduction of evaluation.

Where will the evaluation take place?
All investigations have been and will be carried out as field studies in the classroom using the same conditions under which learning normally takes place. Because of the difficulties with experimental designs and comparative studies at this early stage, we have developed qualitative and partly quantitative formative evaluation studies to get information about "How do students learn?" and "How can we support learning and teaching processes?". In a subsequent phase we will conduct comparative studies on the basis of the results of our present research.

What is to be evaluated?
Our current studies are dealing with processes and outcomes of the learning activities, concerning students' perceptions of the course as well as their knowledge. Until now we have used examples in which *Chemie im Kontext* was implemented in close obedience to the philosophy of the approach. Our ongoing projects shift the focus and ask about the success of the overall framework – the conception as well as the implementation in close co-operation between teachers and science educators. The goal of this evaluation is to gather information about limiting and facilitating conditions for implementation.

What is the relationship between costs, efforts and results?
Case studies are certainly time-consuming, but are also very useful as they deliver detailed information about learning processes and results. They can also be the basis for larger quantitative studies in future, once the design and methodologies are developed and piloted successfully. Another activity, costly in terms of time and both personal and material resources, is the transfer of research results to educational practice. Research has shown that publishing research findings rarely leads to change and innovation in the classroom (Krajcik et al., 2000). Other implementation strategies on the basis of working-groups and continuous activities have to be developed and evaluated therefore to avoid 'dead-end research' (Gräsel and Parchmann, 2004; Fey et al., 2004).

Which are the criteria for comparison with other programs?
Eventually, of course, we will have to show that *Chemie im Kontext* can, indeed, improve students' motivation and learning outcomes, compared to other courses on the basis of external standards. For the objectives of our formative studies, however, namely the improvement of the course design and a feedback and guidance for

teachers, criteria need to be defined by those users and their expectations. After all, a successful implementation will always be based on the personal satisfaction and 'innovation-need' of each individual teacher.

Chemie im Kontext is developing a conceptual framework, that should give teachers clear ideas, examples and guidelines to improve their teaching, but that also allows them the necessary flexibility to design their own units according to their particular situation. To achieve this, qualitative data are needed about the teaching and learning processes and about possibilities to support them as efficiently as possible. Later on, summative studies may follow, to answer the important question, **"Does it work?"**

References

American Chemical Society (2000). *Chemistry in Context*. Columbus: McGraw-Hill

Anderson, L. W. and Krathwohl, D. R. (Eds.). (2001). *A Taxonomy for Learning, Teaching, and Assessing*. New York: Addison Wesley Longman, Inc.

Baumert, J., Bos, W. and Lehmann, R. (Eds.). (2000). *TIMSS/III. Dritte internationale Mathematik- und Naturwissenschaftsstudie. Mathematische und naturwissenschaftliche Bildung am Ende der Schullaufbahn (2 Bände)*. Opladen: Leske + Budrich.

Bennett, J. (1999). *Teaching Scientific Principles Through Contexts, Does It Work?* Paper presented at the Proceedings 7th SAARMSE Conference (13. – 16.01.1999), Harare, Zimbabwe.

BLK. (1997). *Gutachten zur Vorbereitung des Programms »Steigerung der Effizienz des mathematisch-naturwissenschaftlichen Unterrichts« (Materialien zur Bildungsplanung und Forschungsförderung, Heft 60)*. Bonn: Bund-Länder-Kommission für Bildungsplanung und Forschungsförderung.

Deci, E. L., Kasser, T. and Ryan, R. M. (1997). Self-Determined Teaching: Opportunities and Obstacles. In J. L. Bess (Ed.), *Teaching Well and Liking It. Motivating Faculty to Teach Effectively* (pp. 57-71). Baltimore: The Johns' Hopkins University Press.

Driver, R., Asoko, H., Leach, J., Mortimer, E. and Scott, P. (1994). Constructing Scientific Knowledge in the Classroom. *Educational Researcher: A Publication of the American Educational Research Association*, 23(7), 5-12.

Eijkelhof, H. and Lijnse, P. (1988). The Role of Research and Development to Improve STS Education: Experiences from the PLON Project. *International Journal of Science Education,* 10(4), 464-474.

Fey, A., Gräsel, C., Puhl, T. and Parchmann, I..(2004). Implementation einer kontextorientierten Unterrichtskonzeption für den Chemieunterricht. *Unterrichtswissenschaft,* 33(3), 238-56.

Fischer, F. and Mandl, H. (2000). Mapping-Techniken und Begriffs-Netze in Lern- und Kooperationsprozessen. In H. Mandl and F. Fischer (eds.), *Wissen sichtbar machen. Wissensmanagement mit Mappingtechniken* . Göttingen: Hogrefe.

Gräsel, C. (1997). *Problemorientiertes Lernen.* Göttingen: Hogrefe.

Gräsel, C. and Parchmann, I. (2004). Implementationsforschung – oder: der steinige Weg, Unterricht zu verändern. *Unterrichtswissenschaft,* 33(3), 196-214.

Gropengießer, H. (1997). *Didaktische Rekonstruktion des »Sehens«.* Unpublished Dissertation, Carl von Ossietzky Universität, Oldenburg.

Hill, G. and Holman, J. (2000). *Chemistry in Context.* Cheltenham: Nelson

Huntemann, H., Haarmann, E.-M. and Parchmann, I. (2000a). Schüleraussagen zur Unterrichtsreihe »Treibstoffe in der Diskussion. *ChemKon,* 7(3), 131-136.

Huntemann, H., Vennemann, H. and Parchmann, I. (2000b). Ein Auto ohne Kunststoffe? – Eine Unterrichtseinheit aus der Konzeption *Chemie im Kontext.* *Praxis der Naturwissenschaften - Chemie,* 49(4), 19-24.

Krajcik, J., Marx, R. W., Blumenfeld, P., Soloway, E., Fishman, B. J. and Middleton, M. (2000). *Inquiry based science supported by technology: Achievement and motivation among urban middle school students.* Paper presented at the Symposium presented at the annual meeting of the American Educational Research Association, New Orleans, LA.

Lazonby, J. N., Nicolson, P. E. and Waddington, D. J. (1992). Teaching and Learning the Salters' Way. *Journal of Chemical Education,* 69(11), 899-902.

Mandl, H., Gruber, H. and Renkl, A. (1997). Situiertes Lernen in multimedialen Lernumgebungen (2., überarbeitete Auflage). In L. J. Issing and P. Klimsa (Eds.), *Information und Lernen mit Multimedia* (pp. 166-178). Weinheim: Psychologie Verlags Union.

Melograno, V. J. (1994). Portfolio Assessment: Documenting Authentic Student Learning. *JOPERD*(October), 50-61.

Nentwig, P., Parchmann, I., Demuth, R. and Ralle, B. (2005). Chemie im Kontext – A new approach to teaching chemistry in Germany. *Second International IPN- University of York Conference on Science Education, Kiel. In press.*

Nieswandt, M. (2001). Von Alltagsvorstellungen zu wissenschaftlichen Konzepten: Lernwege von Schülerinnen und Schülern im einführenden Chemieunterricht. *Zeitschrift für die Didaktik der Naturwissenschaften* 7, 53-68.

OECD-PISA. (1998). *Framework for Assessing Scientific Literacy. Science Functional Expert Group*: unpublished paper.

Parchmann, I., Demuth, R., Ralle, B., Paschmann, A. and Huntemann, H. (2001). Chemie im Kontext – Begründung und Realisierung eines Lernens in sinnstiftenden Kontexten. *Praxis der Naturwissenschaften – Chemie, 50*, 2-7.

Parchmann, I., Ralle, B. and Demuth, R. (2000). *Chemie im Kontext* – eine Konzeption zum Aufbau und zur Aktivierung fachsystematischer Strukturen in lebensweltlichen Kontexten. *MNU, 53*(3), 132-136.

Parchmann, A., deVries, T., Lüchtenborg, K., Arshadi, N. and Parchmann, I. (2000). Die Bedeutung der Ozeane im Kohlenstoffkreislauf – Eine Hinführung zum Begriff des Chemischen Gleichgewichts im Rahmen von *Chemie im Kontext*. *MNU, 53*(3), 170ff.

Parchmann, I. and Schmidt, S. (2003). Students´ pre-conceptions as a tool to reflect and to design teaching and learning processes – a study from the project *Chemie im Kontext. Paper presented at the ESERA conference, 2003*.

Pfundt, H. (1982). Vorunterrichtliche Vorstellungen von stofflicher Veränderung. *Chimica Didactica* 8, 161-180.

Prenzel, M., Drechsel, B., Kliewe, A., Kramer, K. and Röber, N. (1998). *Lehrermaterialien: Informationen zu Lernmotivation, Autonomieunterstützung und Kompetenzunterstützung* . Kiel: Institut für die Pädagogik der Naturwissenschaften.

Reinhold, P. and Bünder, W. (2001). Fächerübergreifender Unterricht. *Zeitschrift für Erziehungswissenschraft*, 4, 333-37.

Riquarts, K. and Hansen, K-H. (1997) Collaboration among teachers, researchers and in-service trainers to develop an integrated science curriculum. *Journal of Curriculum Studies*, 29, 661-676.

Reinmann-Rothmeier, G. and Mandl, H. (2001). Unterrichten und Lernumgebungen gestalten. In B. Weidenmann, A. Krapp, G. L. Huber, M. Hofer and H. Mandl (Eds.), *Pädagogische Psychologie* (pp. 603-648). Weinheim: Psychologie Verlags Union.

Renkl, A., Gruber, H. and Mandl, H. (1995). *Kooperatives problemorientiertes Lernen in der Hochschule* (Forschungsbericht Nr. 46). München: Institut für Pädagogische Psychologie und Empirische Pädagogik; LMU München.

Rice, D. C., Ryan, J. M. and Samson, S. M. (1998). Using Concept Maps to Assess Student Learning in the Science Classroom: Must Different Methods Compete? *Journal of Research in Science Teaching, 35*(10), 1103-1127.

Schletter, J. C. and Bayrhuber, H. (1998). Lernen und Gedächtnis – Kompartmentalisierung von Schülervorstellungen und wissenschaftlichen Konzepten. *Zeitschrift für Didaktik der Naturwissenschaften, 4*(3), 19-34.

Spiro, R. J., Vispoel, W., Schmitz, J., Samarapungavan, A. and Boerger, A. (1987). Knowledge acquisition for application: Cognitive flexibility and transfer in complex content domains. In B. C. Britton (Ed.), *Executive and control processes* (pp. 177-199). Hillsdale: Erlbaum.

Steinhoff, B. *Wissens- und Komptenzerwerb in einem Unterricht nach Chemie im Kontext.* IPN, University of Kiel, Unpublished PhD thesis.

Stigler, J.W., Gallimore, R. and Hiebert, J. (2000). Using Video Surveys to Compare Classrooms and Teaching across Cultures: Examples and Lessons From the TIMSS Video Studies. *Educational Psychologist* 35(2), 87-100.

Sumfleth, E. and Todtenhaupt, S. (1995). Redoxreaktionen aus Sicht der Schüler. *Chimica Didactica, 21*, 20-41.

Vanderbilt, Cognition and Technology Group at (1990). Anchored instruction and its relationship to situated cognition. *Educational Researcher, 19*(6), 2-10.

Vanderbilt, Cognition and Technology Group at (1997). *The Jasper Project: Lessons in curriculum, instruction, assessment, and professional development.* Mahwah: Erlbaum.

Wierstra, R. (1984). A Study on Classroom Environment and on Cognitive and Affective Outcomes of the PLON-Curriculum. *Studies in Educational Evaluation, 10*, 273-282.

Wottawa, H. (2000). Evaluation. In A. Krapp and B. Weidenmann (Eds.), *Pädagogische Psychologie* (4 ed., pp. 647-699). Weinheim: Beltz PVU.

Zech, L. K., Gause-Vega, C. L., Bray, M. H.,.Secules, T. and Goldman, S.R. (2002). Content-based collaborative enquiry: A professional development model for sustaining educational reform. *Educational Psychologist, 35*, 207-217.

Chapter 4

An evaluation of a large-scale curriculum development project: *Salters Advanced Chemistry*

Judith Bennett* and John Holman
Science Education Group, University of York, York YO10 5DD, UK

Summary

What is the innovation? A two-year pre-university programme in chemistry in which chemical ideas are developed from familiar contexts.

What need does it address? The perception that pre-university chemistry needs to be made attractive to a wider range of students.

What is its scope? The programme has been in existence for 10 years and is currently by 8,000 students each year in the UK. It has been adapted and translated in a number of other countries.

What evaluation data has been collected? Extensive data are available on uptake and national examinations results. Smaller scale studies have been carried out to produce data on a number of aspects of Salters Advanced Chemistry, including students' understanding of chemical ideas and views of chemistry. In some cases, these have involved comparisons with students following more traditional chemistry courses.

What are the key findings? The course is at least as successful as more conventional courses in developing understanding of chemical ideas, and there is evidence that students following the course are more likely to continue with their study of chemistry. The paper draws some general conclusions about the complexities of designing and undertaking evaluation of a multi-faceted, large-scale innovation.

Introduction

Art restoration, alternative fuels and the development of medicines may not be things which first come to mind when thinking about a pre-university chemistry course. However, they are exactly what students who have been following one particular course, *Salters Advanced Chemistry*[1], encounter in their lessons. They also provide a good illustration of the approach taken in the course which, in essence, involves using contexts as the starting point for the introduction and development of chemical ideas. From the national and international interest which *Salters Advanced Chemistry* has attracted since its inception in 1988, it would appear that such an approach is seen by many as a means of improving the experience of chemistry offered to students. What might these improvements be, and what research evidence is there to suggest that the course does result in such improvements?

This chapter has five main aims:

- to provide a brief outline of the materials and the approach used in *Salters Advanced Chemistry*;
- to give some details of the national background against which the course was developed;
- to identify some of the issues associated with evaluation of *Salters Advanced Chemistry*;
- to review the evaluation data which have been gathered on aspects of *Salters Advanced Chemistry*, and what those developing the materials have learned from such data;
- to consider some of the more general messages about the nature and purpose of evaluation of large-scale curriculum initiatives in science education which emerge from the various evaluations of *Salters Advanced Chemistry*.

The *Salters Advanced Chemistry* course and the 'Salters approach'

Salters Advanced Chemistry is a large-scale curriculum innovation in pre-university chemistry, comprising teaching and learning resources, assessment materials and in-service training of teachers. The original project was set up at the University of York in 1988 in order to develop a new pre-university chemistry course that would appeal to a broader spectrum of young people. The initial materials developed were used in a two-year trial before being revised into the final publication form. *Salters Advanced Chemistry* was a logical development of earlier context-based courses developed at the University of York for use with younger students: *Chemistry: the Salters Approach* (University of York Science Education Group [UYSEG], 1989) and *Science: the Salters Approach* (University of York Science Education Group

[UYSEG], 1990-1992). A fuller discussion of the development of the Salters courses and issues associated with large-scale curriculum development may be found in Campbell et al. (1994).

Salters Advanced Chemistry is studied over a two-year period and normally followed by students aged 17 and 18. It is one of a limited number of Advanced Level (A Level) chemistry courses available to students at the post-compulsory, pre-university level of education in England and Wales[2], where the formal school leaving-age is 16 and those who go on to university would normally do so at age 18+. At 16+, students also make decisions about the subjects they want to study at A Level. At the time when the course was first developed, students typically studied about ten subjects up to the age of 16, and then chose three for A Level study.

The original *Salters Advanced Chemistry* materials (Burton et al., 1994) were developed in the period 1988-1992, and have since been revised and published as a second edition (Burton et al., 2000). The development was a collaborative exercise between teachers, educators, professional chemists and industrialists: over 40 authors and nearly 100 expert advisers were involved. The three main course publications are a *Storylines* book, a *Chemical Ideas* book, and an *Activities* folder. These are supported by teachers' guides and technicians' guides. Additionally, an examination syllabus is available from the awarding body who sets the nationally validated external examinations (A Level examinations) taken by students at the end of the course. The *Storylines* provide the 'backbone' of the course, introducing the contexts within which chemical ideas and skills are developed, and indicating where students need to make excursions to the *Activities* folder and the *Chemical Ideas* book. Examples of storylines in the course are: *The Elements of Life, Developing Fuels, The Atmosphere, What's in a Medicine?, The Polymer Revolution* and *Colour by Design*. The *Chemical Ideas* book systematically draws together the chemical principles from the individual units and the different parts of the course.

The course has a number of aims. These are:

- to show the ways chemistry is used in the world and in the work that chemists do;
- to emphasise the frontier areas where new and exciting developments in chemistry are taking place;
- to broaden the appeal of chemistry by showing how it relates to people's lives;
- to broaden the range of teaching and learning activities to include computer modelling, debate, independent learning, fieldwork and a range of activities in addition
- to practical work;

- to provide a rigorous treatment of chemistry that will stimulate and challenge a wider range of students, laying the foundations for future studies yet providing a satisfying course for those who will take the study of chemistry no further;
- to follow on from balanced science courses, taken by most students between the ages of 11 and 16.

In addition to the use of contexts as starting points and the incorporation of a wide range of teaching and learning activities, the course was innovative in a number of other ways. Firstly, the *Storylines* book is unique in content and structure. Secondly, the course incorporates two particularly novel aspects within the teaching: a structured visit to a chemical industry and an extended practical activity, the *Individual Investigation*. Thirdly, the assessment model differs from that of more conventional courses in that it contains an open paper, and the teacher assessment of students' practical abilities is based wholly on the *Individual Investigation*. Fourthly, the style of questions used in end-of-course examinations differs from those in more conventional examinations, as the questions on Salters papers, in keeping with the 'Salters approach', use contexts as starting points for the questions.

The description above serves to illustrate that *Salters Advanced Chemistry* differs from more conventional A Level chemistry courses in several ways and could therefore be described as a multi-faceted innovation. This, coupled with the very broad aims of the course, points to one of the questions which needs to be addressed in any overall evaluation of the course: to what extent is it possible to attribute any effects to particular features of the course?

The formative evaluation of *Salters Advanced Chemistry*

This paper is principally concerned with summative evaluation: to what extent has this new curriculum succeeded in meeting its aims? However, formative evaluation played an important part in shaping the course and we will briefly summarise the process here.

Practising teachers were involved in every stage of the development of *Salters Advanced Chemistry*: planning, writing and trialling and the development of assessment procedures and examination papers. This extensive involvement of teachers followed the model established for earlier Salters curricula and is considered essential if the eventual implementation of the curriculum is to be as intended. The experience of past curriculum developments is that teachers rarely use curriculum materials as intended by their developers (Yager,1992; Elliott 1994; Fullan 1999). By involving teachers at every stage, the project team sought to ensure that the design of the curriculum reflected the realities of life in the school classroom, thus increasing the likelihood that the curriculum would be implemented as intended. This development process itself contributed significantly to the formative evaluation of the course. The matters discussed and debated at writing and training workshops, whilst not formally documented and reported, provided much very useful evaluation data for the developers.

The major formative evaluation of *Salters Advanced Chemistry* was carried out through its school trials, which were designed to evaluate the pilot (or 'beta') version of the teaching resources and the accompanying assessment framework. Prior to the trials of the full course, some of the individual units were tested. These 'unit trials' were of limited use because schools had to teach the unit within the framework of the curriculum they were already following, and in most cases the fit was not good. However, unit trials were influential in determining the format in which the teaching resources were produced for the full course trials.

The full course trials took place in 24 schools across England and Wales and involved 358 students. Although the schools were self-selecting in that they all volunteered to take part, they were a reasonably representative cross-section of types (comprehensive, selective, independent, mixed, single sex, 11–18 schools and 16-18 colleges). Volunteering for the trials was a significant act of faith on the part of these schools: only a small proportion of the course materials was available for inspection when the decision was made. Furthermore, schools were committing their students not only to a new two-year course, but also to the new assessment that accompanies it. Upon the results of this assessment depend the students' future prospects for university entrance.

The full course trials provided the evidence for on which the revision of the course materials was based. Evidence was collected from the schools using a number of different pro-forma reports.

- *A group profile report* provided basic data on the numbers, prior achievements and subject combinations of students in the teaching group.
- *Unit reports* provided feedback on each individual unit (of which there were 13 in the full *Salters Advanced Chemistry* course). These reports were completed by the teacher and gave information about the time taken to teach the unit, the reaction of students to its different components, the quality of students' learning of chemical concepts and how well these concepts followed on from those introduced earlier in the course. Teachers also annotated a copy of each unit and returned this with the unit report.
- *Student reports* in which students were asked to give their views on individual units: how interesting they found them, how well the activities helped them to learn and how they believed their understanding of chemistry had developed.

• *An end of trials review report* in which teachers were asked to give their evaluation of the course and assessment framework as a whole, including the drop-out rate, numbers of students wanting to continue to study chemistry, and the reactions of students, parents, teachers and school management to the course.

In addition to these pro-forma reports, feedback was collected from teachers who attended mid-course training workshops, and by making visits to trial schools to observe classes. Every unit was sent to expert chemists in universities and industry for checking: altogether, just under 100 experts were consulted.

These abundant data informed the project development team on both the macro and the micro scale. It painted a broad overall picture which confirmed that, taken overall, the new curriculum was working as intended. In addition, it gave detailed information about every component of the course to inform the editors, who made the final revisions.

The background against which *Salters Advanced Chemistry* was developed

In common with a number of other countries, there is concern in the UK over the uptake of science courses in the post-compulsory period of education. In the UK, a number of measures were taken at the national level to try and increase the numbers of young people choosing to continue with their study of science subjects, particularly the physical sciences, in the post compulsory period. The most significant of these changes was the introduction in 1989 of the National Curriculum in England and Wales which made it compulsory for all students to study some form of science course which included biology, chemistry and physics up to the age of 16+ (Department of Education and Science/Welsh Office [DES/WO], 1989). Prior to this, students had been able to opt out of one or more of the sciences at the age of 14+, and fewer than 30% of boys and 15% of girls had studied chemistry and physics beyond this point.

The introduction of the National Curriculum for 5-16 year olds coincided with the development of the *Salters Advanced Chemistry* course, and this points to a second question which needed to be addressed in any overall evaluation: to what extent is it possible to separate any effects of the course itself from the effects of more widespread changes in the nature and structure of educational provision which took place at the same time?

Some issues associated with the evaluation of *Salters Advanced Chemistry*

Those involved in the development of *Salters Advanced Chemistry* had a number of questions whose answers would provide important evidence against which to judge the success – or otherwise – of the course. What do teachers and students think of the course? How do they use the materials? How do students engage with the materials? What effects do they have on the understanding of chemical ideas? What effects do they have on the views students hold about links between the chemistry they are studying and the ways in which chemistry effects everyday life? More generally, what effects do the materials have on students' attitudes to chemistry? What are the effects on numbers choosing to continue with their study of chemistry at the tertiary (university) level? To what extent do these effects constitute improvements when compared with previous provision or with more conventional A Level chemistry courses? However, asking these questions is far easier than gathering the evidence to help answer them!

Two factors, both of which concern different aspects of relating effect to cause, have already been identified as issues in the evaluation of *Salters Advanced Chemistry*. Firstly, the very broad aims and multi-faceted nature of the course are likely to mean that it is difficult to attribute any effects to particular features of the course. Secondly, the scale of the innovation was such that it took place over a period of a number of years and against a background of other changes in educational provision aimed at increasing levels of participation in science subjects.

A third issue concerns the way in which *Salters Advanced Chemistry* was funded. The funding was provided to support the development and implementation of the materials, and did not include any resource linked directly to research-based evaluation. Such a situation is common in curriculum development, and there may be a number of reasons for this. Certainly those providing the funding very often see curriculum materials as a more tangible and useful return for their investment than the findings of research studies.

In practice, though no funding was provided for evaluation, a number of features of both the course and the development process have provided rich sources of evaluation data, as described in the next section.

Evaluation data on *Salters Advanced Chemistry*

Sources of evaluation data

One aspect of the course which has helped provide evaluation data has been its attractiveness to many teachers. This is demonstrated by its uptake over the last decade, with the number of schools and colleges now using *Salters Advanced Chemistry* rising from 24 when the course was first examined in 1992 to 330 in 2001 (Pilling et al., 2001). In a later section of this chapter uptake data are explored in more detail.

For a number of teachers using the course, their interest has extended beyond gathering informal evidence on its effects to exploring these effects on a more systematic basis. Thus a number of research studies, both at masters and doctoral level, have been undertaken on aspects of the use of *Salters Advanced Chemistry*. Masters level studies have typically been undertaken by teachers who are combining their teaching with part-time study, whilst the doctoral level studies have been undertaken by teachers taking time away from teaching to study full-time. Thus the masters level studies have generally taken the form of illuminative evaluation: case studies of aspects of the use of *Salters Advanced Chemistry* in the teacher's own institution. The doctoral studies, however, have drawn on data gathered from a number of institutions. Within this, there are some limited examples of experimental studies which have compared aspects of the experiences of students taking *Salters Advanced Chemistry* with those of students taking more conventional A Level chemistry courses.

The next section of this chapter reviews the research evidence which has been gathered on *Salters Advanced Chemistry* to contribute to the evaluation of the course. The evidence is presented under three main headings:

1. students' responses to the course,
2. teachers' responses to the course,
3. uptake and examination data.

Students' responses to the course

Information has been gathered on three aspects of students' responses to the course: understanding of chemical ideas, affective responses, and views on the course as a preparation for study at university.

Understanding of chemical ideas

The exploration of aspects of students' understanding of chemical ideas as a result of following the *Salters Advanced Chemistry* course forms the most extensive area of research, partly because of the implications of the approach for the learning of chemical ideas, and partly because there are well-established techniques for gathering information on students' understanding.

One implication of a context-based approach is that science ideas are introduced on a 'need-to-know' basis as they are needed to help explain and enrich understanding of features of the particular context being studied. This, in turn, means that it is unlikely that any one concept area, such as, for example, chemical equilibrium, will be introduced and developed in full in one particular context, as might be the case in more conventional courses. Rather, the concept will be revisited at different points throughout the course, with different aspect of the concept emerging from different contexts. This 'drip feed' approach clearly has implications for the development of students' understanding of chemical ideas. On the one hand, it could be argued that such an approach means that ideas will be revisited at different points in a course and thus provide more opportunities for students to develop their understanding. On the other, it is possible that such an approach fragments the curriculum, making it difficult for students to see the integrity of each conceptual area and hindering the development of a systematic picture of ideas and concepts.

Three studies offer evidence to support the claim that the 'drip feed' approach has no adverse effects on the development of students' understanding and may, in certain areas, enhance understanding. Barker undertook a large-scale, comparative, longitudinal study of 400 upper secondary level students at thirty-six schools in England following A Level chemistry courses (Barker and Millar, 1999; 2000). Within this group was a mix of students following conventional courses and *Salters Advanced Chemistry*. The study employed a series of diagnostic questions on key areas of chemical understanding, administered at three points over an 18-month period. Understanding of the following chemical ideas was probed: elements, mixtures and compounds, conservation of mass and reacting masses, characteristics of chemical reactions, chemical bonding, energy changes in chemical reactions, rates of reaction, and equilibrium reactions. The study indicated that the 'drip feed' approach does not impair learning of concepts and, indeed, may have benefits: for example, the gradual introduction and revisiting of some ideas (such as chemical bonding and thermodynamics) in different contexts at several points during the course appeared to improve understanding.

Two smaller-scale studies comparing students following *Salters Advanced Chemistry* with those following conventional courses provide additional evidence to support the claim that students' learning is not adversely affected by context-based approaches. Banks (1997) found that the 'drip feed' approach of the context-based course to teaching ideas about chemical equilibrium appeared more effective than the conventional approach. Barber (2000) used a range of added value performance indicators to compare predicted and actual grades in A-level Chemistry examinations for the two groups of students. Her study indicated that there was no particular disadvantage or advantage to students in either course in terms of the final examination grade they achieved. Although students' took different examination papers, all examinations have to meet both had to meet externally imposed standards, so the study provides some additional evidence to indicate that the learning of students on context-based courses is comparable with that of students on more conventional courses.

Students' affective responses to chemistry

Arguably, the most significant aspirations of developers of *Salters Advanced Chemistry* lay in the area of students' affective responses to chemistry. The hope was that the contexts used to develop the chemical ideas would motivate students by helping them to see the relevance of the chemistry they are studying, and, for some at least, motivate them to continue with their study of chemistry.

As yet, no studies gathering data on students' affective responses to chemistry as a result following *Salters Advanced Chemistry* have been undertaken. In part this may be due to the well-documented difficulties associated with gathering reliable and valid data on attitudes to science. However, one large-scale study involving 1200 students (Key, 1998) has compared perceptions of the chemical industry held by students following *Salters Advanced Chemistry* with those of students following three more conventional courses. Key found that those students who had gained first-hand experience of the chemical industry through a structured site visit – a compulsory requirement of *Salters Advanced Chemistry* and one of the other more conventional courses - demonstrated greater insight into the role of the chemical industry and an increased appreciation of its importance. This effect was most noticeable in the students who had followed *Salters Advanced Chemistry*.

Students' views on Salters Advanced Chemistry as a preparation for further study

It is interesting to compare *Salters Advanced Chemistry* with conventional courses as a preparation for the study of chemistry at university. Do students understand chemical principles any better or worse? How well prepared are they for the more independent study expected of them at university? In an informal survey of approximately 40 first year chemistry undergraduates, in three universities, the Salters students interviewed did not see themselves as different from their peers in terms of preparation for their university course (Pilling and Waddington, 1996).

> *When asked whether there were any areas in which they felt they were better prepared, almost all said they were able to adapt more easily to university life because they could organise their learning and were used to working on their own. Many said they were more confident in the laboratory because of the experience of working independently in the Individual Investigation. When asked if there were any areas where they believed they were less well prepared than their peers, Salters students often quoted particular topics, such as kinetics or organic reaction mechanisms, but the conflicting nature of the replies suggests that these may reflect local circumstances in the school rather than the content of the course (Pilling and Waddington, 2001, 2002).*

Teachers' responses to the course

Two studies have explored aspects of teachers' responses to *Salters Advanced Chemistry*. The first of these focused on views of one of the particularly innovative aspects of the course, the *Individual Investigation* and the second on the way in which teachers used the materials.

The *Individual Investigation* is undertaken over a two week period, and requires students to devise, execute, modify and evaluate an extended piece of practical work. The teacher's role is two-fold: initially to act as a facilitator during the investigation, and ultimately to assess the students' work, an assessment which contributes 20% to the final course assessment. Lubben and Bennett (1998) conducted in-depth interviews with nine teachers to explore their views on the *Individual Investigation*. Teachers reported finding the *Individual Investigation* challenging in terms of management and assessment skills, but felt it was a very worthwhile undertaking for their students. Unsurprisingly, teachers' main concerns centred on the tension between their twin roles as teacher and assessor. It is worth noting that this study also involved interviews with the national examiners, who did not share the anxieties over assessment expressed by the teachers.

A survey of just over sixty teachers using *Salters Advanced Chemistry* (Smith, 1995) looked at ways in which the materials were used in lessons. The study indicated that the materials were used by teachers in a wide variety of ways. At one end of the spectrum, some teachers adapted the materials such that teacher exposition still formed a significant component of lessons. At the other, the materials were being used by students in a supported self-study format, with teachers acting largely as learning managers (Lloyd, 1992).

Uptake and examination data

Fullan (1999) emphasises that teachers are only likely to make changes to their practice when they have become dissatisfied, for some reason, with their previous practice. Campbell et al. (1994) have described how teachers, dissatisfied with their current practice, may take up a new curriculum if they consider it will meet their needs better than the one they currently use, and thus allay their dissatisfaction. Thus, data about uptake of a new curriculum provides a significant source of evidence for evaluation: by taking up the new curriculum, teachers are indicating a positive evaluation. For a radical new curriculum, such a decision is not made lightly, especially in schools with a well-established curriculum that has been in place for several years.

In England and Wales, accurate data about uptake are available from the awarding bodies which administer the examination. All students who complete the course will take the examination, so examination statistics are a rich source of data. Table 1 compares the numbers of students completing the *Salters Advanced Chemistry* course with the total numbers taking other A level chemistry courses.

Year	A level Salters chemistry	A level chemistry other than Salters	Total A level chemistry nationally
1992	358	42 339	42 697
1993	868	40 107	40 975
1994	1639	39 592	41 231
1995	2177	40 116	42 293
1996	3550	36 868	40 418
1997	4125	38 137	42 262
1998	4470	38 355	42 825
1999	4654	37 073	41 727
2000	5018	35 838	40 856
2001*	5043	33 559	38 602
2002*	5292	31 356	36 648
2003*	5405	30 705	36 110
2004	5612	31 642	37 254

*Note: From 2001 onwards, students have taken a two-stage examination, made up of AS (first year) and A2 (second year). For comparability, the numbers given here are for the second stage, but in 2004 the numbers completing the first, AS stage were 7994.

Table 1: Numbers of students taking the A level Salters Chemistry examination and national numbers for chemistry

(Source: OCR awarding body and the Qualifications and Curriculum Authority)

These data show a sustained increase in the uptake of *Salters Advanced Chemistry* since its inception in 1992, in contrast to the national situation where the numbers are only just holding steady. Evidence from schools suggests that that the rising numbers taking *Salters Advanced Chemistry* come from three sources (Pilling et al., 2001).

• Schools changing to *Salters Advanced Chemistry* from other syllabuses;
• Schools, that previously offered the Salters course alongside another chemistry syllabus, moving totally to the Salters course;
• Increased numbers of students choosing to take chemistry in a particular school.

The data on uptake also provide evidence concerning gender balance. Table 2 compares the numbers of male and female students completing *Salters Advanced Chemistry* with the national numbers and shows that the proportion of female students has increased over the years and in 2000 actually exceeded that of males.

Year	Male/Female (Salters)	Male/Female (National)
1997	1.27	1.24
1998	1.12	1.19
1999	1.03	1.11
2000	0.96	1.07
2001	0.95	1.01
2002	0.85	0.98
2003	0.87	0.95

Table 2: Comparing numbers of male and female students for A level Salters chemistry with the total numbers for A level chemistry nationally (other than Salters)

(Source: OCR awarding body and the Qualifications and Curriculum Authority)

What those involved in the development have learned from its evaluation

Judging from data about the uptake of SAC, it is successful, at least according to the judgement of teachers. Furthermore, those studies which have been undertaken provide reassurance that *Salters Advanced Chemistry* is at least as successful as more conventional courses in developing understanding of chemical ideas, and students who do go on to study chemistry further feel at least as well-prepared as students who have followed more conventional courses, and better prepared in some ways, such at in their ability to work independently in the laboratory.

There is evidence to suggest that *Salters Advanced Chemistry* provides a worthwhile course in itself, but also does have a positive effect on numbers choosing to continue with their study of chemistry, although, as always the effects of individual teachers need to be taken into consideration (Pilling and Waddington, 2001). There is also evidence that *Salters Advanced Chemistry* has been successful in persuading students to continue with their study where other national initiatives (such as the introduction of a National Curriculum) have not, suggesting that the content and approach is a key determinant of success (Barber 2000).

It is clear from this paper that, with the exception of the gathering of data on student uptake and performance, and the formative evaluation undertaken during the course trials, all of the studies undertaken have emerged from interested parties in response to the publication of the course, rather than having been planned as an intrinsic part of the development itself. An evaluation agenda or 'wish list' to complement what already exists might include gathering comparative data on views of chemistry held by students following *Salters Advanced Chemistry* and more conventional courses; observation of *Salters Advanced Chemistry* lessons to explore how materials are used in practice; gathering data on novel features of assessment in *Salters Advanced Chemistry* such as the open book paper and assessing chemical knowledge and understanding through the use of context-based questions in examinations (a study is currently being developed in this area); gathering data on the practical skills and abilities of students who have undertaken the *Individual Investigation*; exploring gender effects

More general messages about the nature and purpose of evaluation of large-scale curriculum initiatives in science education

Although no structured programme of evaluation was formally designed for *Salters Advanced Chemistry*, and the picture of the development is therefore not as complete as we would like, a number of useful general messages have emerged from the studies which have been undertaken.

A key message concerns the central role that teachers have in contributing to the formative evaluation of a programme through their involvement in the planning, design and trial stages of development. This teacher involvement also ultimately determines the success of an innovation, as the discussion and negotiation with teachers as 'end users' of the programme results in a better match between the intended and the implemented curriculum.

The complexities of designing and undertaking evaluation of a multi-faceted, large-scale innovation have also become increasingly apparent. The most useful insights appear to be gained when one particular aspect which can be clearly defined (such as the learning of selected science ideas) is explored in detail. It is much harder to gather reliable and valid data on aspects of a programme which relate to broader aims. For example, *Salters Advanced Chemistry* aims to enhance students' views of science. However, with so many variables involved, it is difficult to gather data on affective responses which provide sound evidence to support claims that particular effects are linked to specific features of the innovation.

The more we have engaged in the process of curriculum development, the more convinced we have become of the desirability and value of the process involving a trial phase which is carefully and rigorously evaluated by an external agency who are involved from the earliest stages. This lesson has been learned by funders as well as developers; the latest Salters development, *21st Century Science* (Millar et al., 2002) includes, at the insistence of funders, a sum of £90,000 for an external evaluation to be implemented from the beginning of the pilot phase. The new *Salters Nuffield Advanced Biology* course (UYSEG/The Nuffield Foundation, 2002), currently under development, will also be formally evaluated by an external agency throughout the full course trial. We see this as a very positive move in curriculum development.

Notes

1. The course takes its name from one of the sponsoring groups, the Salters Institute of Industrial Chemistry, a charitable foundation dedicated to the improvement of science education.

2. Within the United Kingdom, England and Wales have a similar education system. Northern Ireland's system is slightly different, and Scotland's system is completely different from the other three countries. The Salters curricula were primary developed for England and Wales, and it is to those countries that this paper refers.

3. In the UK, education is compulsory to the age of 16. Up to this age, all students are educated in institutions known simply as 'schools'. Beyond the age of 16, students may remain in the school they are already attending, or they may move to an institution that caters for post-16 education only. Such institutions are known as 'colleges'. However, for the sake of simplicity, in this paper we refer to schools and colleges collectively as 'schools'

References

Banks, P. (1997). *Students' understanding of chemical equilibrium*. University of York, unpublished MA thesis.

Barber, M. (2000) *A comparison of NEAB and Salters A-level Chemistry: student views and achievements*. University of York, unpublished MA thesis.

Barker, V. and Millar, R. (1999) Students' reasoning about chemical reactions: what changes occur during a context-based post-16 chemistry course? *International Journal of Science Education*, 21 (6), 645-665.

Barker, V. and Millar, R. (2000) Students' reasoning about basic chemical thermodynamics and chemical bonding: what changes occur during a context-based post-16 chemistry course? *International Journal of Science Education*, 22 (11), 1171-1200.

Burton, W., Holman, J., Pilling, G. and Waddington, D.(1994). *Salters Advanced Chemistry*. Oxford: Heinemann.

Burton, W., Holman, J., Lazonby, J., Pilling, G. and Waddington, D. (2000) *Salters Advanced Chemistry*. 2nd edition. Oxford: Heinemann.

Campbell, B., Lazonby, J., Millar, R., Nicolson, P., Ramsden, J. and Waddington, D. (1994) Science: the Salters approach - a case study of the process of large scale curriculum development. *Science Education*, 78, 5, 415-447.

Department of Education and Science/Welsh Office (DES/WO) (1989). *Science in the National Curriculum*. London: HMSO.

Elliott, J. (1994). The Teacher's Role in Curriculum Development: an unresolved issue in English attempts at curriculum reform. *Curriculum Studies*, 2 (1), 43-69.

Fullan, M (1999). *Change forces: The Sequel*. London: Fulmer Press 13-30

Key, M. (1998) *Student perceptions of chemical industry: influences of course syllabi, teachers, firsthand experience*. University of York, unpublished DPhil thesis.

Lloyd, G. (1992) Experiencing Salters Advanced Chemistry. *Education in Science* 147, 27.

Lubben, F. and Bennett, J. (1998) Assessing pre-university students through extended individual investigations: teachers' and examiners' views. *International Journal of Science Education*, 20 (7), 833-848.

Millar, R., Holman, J., Hunt, A., Lazonby, J. and Milner, B. (2002). *21st Century Science GCSE Pilot Development. Report to the Qualifications and Curriculum Authority*. York: University of York Science Education Group.

Pilling, G., Holman, J. and Waddington, D. (2001) The Salters experience. *Education in Chemistry*, 38 (5), 131-136.

Pilling, G. and Waddington, D. (1996) *Unpublished survey of 30 first year students who had studied Salters Advanced Chemistry at the Universities of Leeds, Manchester and York.*

Pilling, G. and Waddington, D. (2001) 2001, *A Chemical Odyssey*. Proceedings of the 6th European Conference on Research in Chemical Education, Aveiro, Portugal. Cachupuz, A.F. (ed). Sociedade Portuguese de Quimica.

Pilling, G. and Waddington, D. (2002) Fifteen years of Salters Chemistry. *Chemistry in Action* 66, 6-13.

Smith, P. (1995) *How do schools and colleges use Salters Advanced Chemistry?* University of York, unpublished MA thesis.

University of York Science Education Group [UYSEG] (1990-1992) *Science: the Salters Approach: 22 Unit Guides for Key Stage 4.* York/Oxford: UYSEG/Heinemann Educational.

University of York Science Education Group [UYSEG] (1989) *Chemistry: the Salters Approach. 16 Unit Guides.* York/Oxford: UYSEG/Heinemann Educational.

University of York Science Education Group [UYSEG] (1990-1992) *Science: the Salters Approach. 22 Unit Guides.* York/Oxford: UYSEG/Heinemann Educational.

University of York Science Education Group [UYSEG]/The Nuffield Foundation (2002) *Salters Nuffield Advanced Biology (SNAB) trial materials.* York: University of York Science Education Group [UYSEG]/London: The Nuffield Foundation.

Yager, R. (1992). What we did not learn from the 60s about science curriculum reform. *Journal of Research in Science Teaching,* 19, 905 – 910.

Chapter 5

Developmental research: Improving the learning and teaching of science topics

Kerst Boersma*, Marie-Christine Knippels and Arend Jan Waarlo
Centre for Science and Mathematics Education, Universiteit Utrecht, 3544 CC Utrecht, The Netherlands.

Summary

What is the innovation? Domain-specific learning and teaching strategies for difficult or new science topics in secondary biology education. The strategies are based on the problem-posing approach.

What need does it address? The perception that domain-specific learning and teaching strategies are necessary to improve the quality of learning and teaching on specific science topics in secondary education.

What is its scope? Innovative learning and teaching strategies have been developed and tested in a limited number of case studies.

What evaluation data have been collected? Extensive qualitative formative data are collected on the feasibility and effectiveness of the learning and teaching strategies.

What are the key findings? The formative evaluation data show which learning and/or teaching activities of a preliminary learning and teaching strategy have to be adapted to improve the intended learning processes and to attain the desired learning outcomes. The desired learning outcomes are generally attained by the majority of the students participating in a case study, and learning difficulties reported in literature are generally avoided.

The 'developmental research' approach

Characteristics of developmental research

The 'developmental research' approach has been developed over the last two decades by curriculum developers and researchers of the Centre for Science and Mathematics Education of the Universiteit Utrecht, and is based on experiences with curriculum development (e.g. in the PLON-project). It is a research approach characterised by the following characteristics (Lijnse, 1995; Boersma, 1999):

- The aim is the development of didactical theory, which offers teachers a strategy for the learning and teaching of specific science and mathematics topics.
- The domain-specific didactical theory is based on a domain-specific philosophy of learning and teaching, rooted in social constructivism or cultural-historical theory, and in literature on learning and teaching difficulties and strategies (Gravemeijer, 1994).
- A developmental research study consists of a cyclic alternation of development and evaluation in a number of case-studies.
- Researchers employ an interactive working style with a limited number of teachers.

In this chapter the characteristics of developmental research are discussed, with an emphasis on the role of evaluation. A recent PhD-study on genetics (Knippels, 2002) is used as an example.

Developmental research is a time consuming approach, since PhD-students need approximately four years to complete their study. That means that, from the perspective of cost effectiveness, the question is when the developmental research method is appropriate and when it is an unnecessary investment of time and effort. Revisiting the studies recently completed, two conditions seem to justify the choice for developmental research.

The domain is (relatively) new, and uncertainty exists on the question which learning outcomes are desirable and attainable, and on the question which learning and teaching strategy should be employed. This condition was fulfilled in studies on biodiversity and the cell as a system.

- The domain is (relatively) well studied, but literature and experiences of teachers show that an effective learning and teaching strategy is not available. This condition was fulfilled in the study on genetics.

- *The study on genetics*

- Genetics is in many countries, including the Netherlands, considered to be one of the most difficult topics in biology courses for both students and teachers. The study revealed that a separation of inheritance from reproduction and meiosis (resulting in abstract subject matter) and the occurrence of heredity at different levels of biological organisation (its complexity) account in a considerable degree for learning problems. The 'yo-yo' learning and teaching strategy, developed to cope with these difficulties, was shown to be an adequate approach, and to promote the acquisition of a meaningful and coherent understanding of hereditary phenomena. In the 'yo-yo' strategy, students zoom in from the organism level to the cellular and molecular level and zoom out vice versa by means of content-related and well-sequenced questions. Emphasis is on thinking backwards-and-forwards ('yo-yo') between the levels of biological organisation, and on interrelating the genetic concepts on these levels.

Didactical theory

The aim of developmental research is not the development of curriculum materials, but the development of domain-specific didactical theory. Curriculum materials developed in developmental research are used as research instruments, necessary to develop a didactical theory.

A domain-specific theory consists of a domain-specific philosophy of learning and teaching, including the definition and validation of the desired learning outcomes, and learning and teaching strategy (or didactical structure). The learning and teaching strategy (LT-strategy) consists of a sequence of learning and teaching activities (LT-activities), which allows students to attain the desired domain-specific learning outcomes. A domain-specific theory prescribes teachers and curriculum developers which learning and teaching activities should be offered to the students and how they should be sequenced to attain the desired learning outcomes. However, a domain-specific theory is not only prescriptive. Since the relation between leaning activities and learning outcomes is studied in detail, it also explains why the intended learning outcomes are attained.

Most recent studies were following the so-called problem-posing approach, a LT-strategy derived from a domain-specific strategy for radioactivity (Klaassen, 1995). This approach has been applied since to a large number of topics: the particle model (Vollebregt, 1998), immunology (Janssen, 1999), decision-making on waste (Kortland, 2001), biodiversity (Van Weelie, 2001), the cell as a system (Verhoeff et al., 2001) and genetics (Knippels, 2002). That means that the problem-posing approach has a wide applicability in science education and can be considered as a general strategy for the reinvention of scientific concepts and complex skills. It means also that the domain-specific didactical theories developed in the PhD-studies are actually domain-specific elaborations of the problem-posing approach.

The problem-posing approach is based on the following two assumptions: (1) students should develop content-specific motives that guide them through a sequence of learning activities, and (2) the performance of the learning activities results in the reinvention of the desired learning outcomes. A domain-specific learning and teaching strategy consists of one or more problem-posing cycles. Each cycle consists of four steps (Figure 1).

I Development of a central steering question
↓
1 Development of a partial question, and motives to explore and answer the partial question
2 Selection of information and/or performance of one or more investigations
3 Application of extended knowledge in a new situation
4 Reflection: answering the partial question, verifying to what extent the central question is answered, and developing a new partial question

Figure 1:   The problem-posing cycle (after Knippels, 2002)

In the study on genetics (Knippels, 2002), the central steering question is *What makes you look like your parents without being identical to them?* In the yo-yo strategy, in which this question is answered, students are descending from the organism level to the cellular and molecular level, are ascending to the organism level again. On each organisational level one or two partial questions are answered. The yo-yo strategy seems applicable to all biological topics in secondary education in which structures and processes on both the organism level and the cellular and molecular levels are involved (e.g. evolution, metabolism, behaviour).

Domain-specific philosophies of education

A domain-specific philosophy of education is one of the components of a domain-specific learning and teaching theory. A preliminary version of such a theory is developed in the explorative phase of a study, and is based on (socio-constructivist or cultural-historical) learning theory, a domain-specific theory or philosophy of science, research literature and empirical data from science classroom practices. The domain-specific philosophy of education is also elaborated in aims and objectives. In the study on genetics, the philosophy was based on an extensive research literature, on focus group interviews with biology teachers and on an explorative case study.

The design of developmental research

Each study consists of a sequence of a limited number of case studies. In each case study the preliminary LT-strategy, based on the domain-specific philosophy of education, is elaborated in a scenario, and is put in practice in one or more cases (Figure 2).

In the design a number of curriculum levels are distinguished, ranging from very general to very specific.

The most general level is the domain-specific philosophy of learning and teaching, which includes the desired learning outcomes. The domain-specific philosophy is, if the problem-posing approach is applied, firstly elaborated into a sequence of questions or problems and secondly in a sequence of LT-activities. The learning activities provide the students the answers on the partial questions and evoke a next partial question. The sequence of questions and the sequence of learning and teaching activities constitute the LT-strategy. The predicted learning outcomes of each learning activity are included in the strategy. A preliminary LT-strategy is put into operation with one or more teachers by developing a so-called scenario.

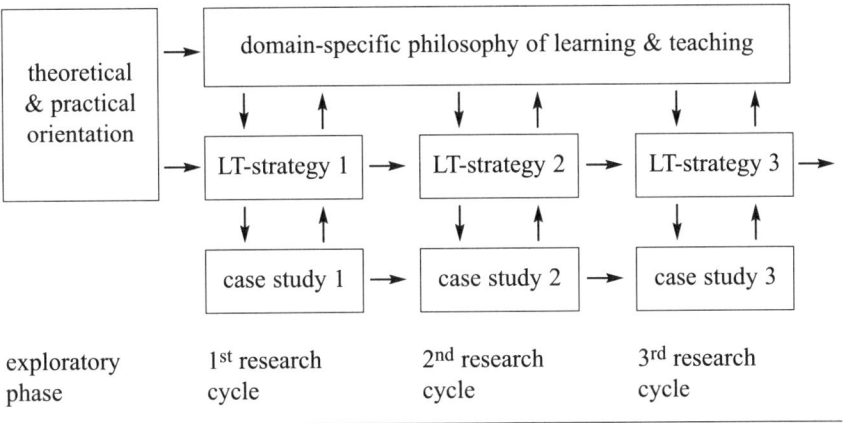

Figure 2:   Design of developmental research

A scenario describes in detail the expected behaviour and lines of reasoning of the students and the behaviour of the teacher that evokes it. Since a scenario takes the specific situation into account, wishes and abilities of a teacher, it is a context-specific document. Collaboration with another teacher would result in a different scenario. In order to estimate the context-specificity of a scenario, it is recommended that two different scenarios, with teachers from different schools, are developed simultaneously. This design was selected in the second research cycle of the study on genetics, when data collected in the first cycle showed that the learning and teaching strategy contained only a limited number of design errors.

The accessory LT-materials correspon with the scenarios. That means that the LT-materials are context-specific as well, although experience suggests that only minor adaptations to another context are required.

Finally, the scenario and its accessory LT-materials are tested in one or more biology classes. Extensive data collection through observation, audio or video recording of group and whole class discussions, interviews and written tasks, makes evaluation of the scenario possible.

Analysis of the data reveals where and frequently also which adaptations of the scenario and LT-materials are required. Data collection, in particular by written tests, also allows a summative evaluation of the students' learning outcomes.

More severe discrepancies between the scenario and the observed behaviour and/or learning outcomes do not only require adaptations of the scenario, but also adaptations of the LT-strategy. That means that, after a research cycle with one or more case studies, the sequence of LT-activities is reconsidered, to determine whether the LT-strategy should be adapted.

Experience suggests that the LT-strategy is saturated after two of three research cycles, which means that no further adaptations are required, or that it is possible to design a final, 'well enough' version. In the study on genetics it was possible after two research cycles to design a final version of the strategy.

Cooperation with teachers

A productive cooperation with teachers is considered as a prerequisite for the development of efficient and effective LT-strategies. In developmental research their role is indispensable, not because teachers are the major change agents in formal education, but because their practice knowledge and expertise is an indispensable addition to the theoretical knowledge of researchers. Many didactical problems in science education cannot be solved without the theoretical knowledge of researchers, since they can take an independent position. On the other hand, didactical problems cannot be solved either without the practical knowledge of good practitioners. They are familiar with the habits in science classes, have insight into the difficulties and capabilities of their students, and know how the requirements of the examination syllabuses have to be met.

The difference in expertise between researchers and teachers implies that a division of tasks is desirable. The preliminary LT-strategy developed by the researcher would, first of all, be discussed with the teacher(s), and, then, if necessary adapted by the researcher until agreement is reached about its expected efficacy and practicability. The scenario is generally developed in a process of co-construction. The accessory learning and teaching materials are generally developed by researchers, since they have more time available than teachers. When the scenario is put into practice, the teacher teaches according to the scenario and the researcher is collects data.

This division of tasks reflects that the responsibility for the study belongs to the researcher, and that the teacher remains responsible for his or her teaching practice. This difference in responsibilities also implies that the cooperation continues as long as both have a common interest. If the researcher is faced with a shortage of time, or with the necessity of testing the LT-strategy in other conditions, it is decided to select one or more other teachers. In the study on genetics, other teachers were invited after the first research cycle.

Differences with other research approaches

Developmental research is a research approach in the interpretative tradition. Since a study consists of a number of case studies, it is research according to the case study approach (Miles and Huberman, 1994; Yin, 1994).

Although the framework of developmental research as practiced by the Centre for Science and Mathematics Education of the Universiteit Utrecht was autonomously developed in the eighties and nineties from school-based curriculum development in curriculum projects like the PLON, it is not an unique approach. Similar or almost identical approaches were developed elsewhere, using different labels. In the Netherlands, researchers from Twente University developed an almost identical approach labelled as 'development research' (Van den Akker, 1999). In the US, these approaches were labelled as 'developmental research' (Richey and Nelson, 1996), 'formative research' (Walker, 1992) and design research or design-based research (e.g. Cobb et al., 2003; Kelly, 2004). Educational research practices using 'action research', a comparable approach, originated at several places, in particular in the UK (e.g. Elliott, 1991), and in the US (e.g. Greenwood et al., 1993).

Developmental research, action research and interactive curriculum development are approaches that are employed in the innovation of science education. The approaches have their interactive working methods in common but differ on some important characteristics (Boersma, 1999) (Table 1). It should be emphasised that intermediate forms are possible.

	Developmental research	Action research	Interactive curriculum development
Aim	Development of learning and teaching strategies	Solution of a problem in an existing practice	Development of learning and teaching materials
Research	The primary objective	Subordinate to the solution of the problem	Not aimed
Research questions	Defined by the researchers	Defined by the practitioners	Not defined
Learning and teaching materials	Developed as research instruments	Developed in some cases	The aim of the development
Evaluation	Systematic data collection and analysis	Systematic data collection and analysis if necessary	Limited data collection and analysis

Table 1: Differences between developmental research, action research and interactive curriculum development.

Evaluation in developmental research

Formative and summative evaluation

The role of evaluation in developmental research should be clarified at the level of the entire design (Figure 1), and the level of the specific case study in which a preliminary version of the LT-strategy elaborated in a scenario is tested.

In a case study, data are collected about the behaviour of the students and the teacher, the learning outcomes, of each learning activity, and learning outcomes of the students performed in a final test. Data about the behaviour of the students and the teacher, and the intermediate learning outcomes are formative on the level of the case study, since they are used to adapt the scenario when it is put in practice. At the level of the case study, the results of the final test are considered as summative data, since they reflect the final learning outcomes of the students participating in the case study. However, all data, including the results of the final test, are considered as formative data by the researcher and are used to adapt the preliminary LT-strategy. That means that at the level of the design all evaluation data have a formative meaning and may be used to construct a final LT-strategy. Walker' label 'formative research' (Walker, 1992) expresses this idea.

Evaluation of the feasibility and effectiveness

In all case studies, data are collected on the feasibility and effectiveness of the preliminary LT-strategy, elaborated in a context-specific scenario. Criteria for measuring the effectiveness of the preliminary LT-strategy are based on the learning objectives, expressed in the domain-specific philosophy of education. In the scenario, an indication is given about the LT-activities described in the LT-strategy that have to be performed and what learning outcomes of each discrete learning activity are to be expected if the learning and teaching activities are performed as planned. That means that by evaluating the feasibility and effectiveness of the preliminary LT-strategy the following questions are answered:

Feasibility

- Are the learning and teaching activities executed as planned? If not, what are the causes? Is revision required? If yes, what revision is required?

Effectiveness

- Are the learning outcomes of each learning activity as predicted? If not, what are the causes? Is revision required? If yes, what revision is required?
- Are the learning outcomes of the entire LT-strategy as predicted? If not, what are the causes? Is revision required? If yes, what revision is required?

Evaluation in the study on genetics

The study on genetics (Knippels, 2002) will be taken as an example to show how formative evaluation data on the effectiveness are used in the adaptation of a preliminary LT-strategy. This study on genetics consisted of three case studies; the second and third case studies were both based on the second version of the learning and teaching strategy. In all three case studies, data were collected through observations of the students' and teachers' behaviour, audio recordings of group discussions, class discussions, and the teachers verbal behaviour, worksheets, and written tests. The main line in the analysis of data were the transcripts of the audio-taped group and class discussions, because they contained the most complete and authentic information. In interpreting the transcripts the other data sources were used complementarily, which made triangulation possible.

In the first preliminary LT-strategy, among others, the following assumptions were tested:
- to reduce the complex nature of genetics it is necessary to distinguish the levels of biological organisation, and to interrelate the different levels and genetics concepts on these levels

- to reduce the abstract nature of genetics, it is necessary to relate the cellular and molecular level with the organism level.
- since students are familiar with the organism level, it is necessary to descend from the organism level to the cellular level.

The first LT-strategy was put in practice in the first case study. The next transcript of Iris' answer in the written final test, which tested if the students were able to perform these lines of reasoning, shows that Iris was able to descend the levels of biological organisation and to relate the genetics concepts on these levels, but that she did not explain how, from the molecular level, the pigment for the eye colour is formed.

Iris: A man and a woman would like to have children. In their bodies gemmates are formed by the process of meiosis. The sperm of the man fertilises the egg of the woman after sexual intercourse. In the gametes 23 chromosomes are present with one gene for eye colour. Imagine that the man has blue eyes (bb) and the woman brown eyes (Bb). The allele for brown is dominant, so she has brown eyes. The possibilities after fertilisation are: BB, Bb, bb. The child has a 25% chance to get blue eyes (the alleles are divided in the process of meiosis). The combination of Bb is passed on to the child after fertilisation, and now the zygote contains this information. The zygote will divide and after nine months a child with blue eyes will be born.

From this transcript and others, it was concluded that students did not ascend from the cellular level to the organism level by themselves, and that the LT-strategy should be extended with one or more reflection activities in which this relation is elaborated. The revised, second LT-strategy, which emphasised more the relations between the levels of organisation and included some LT-activities, which invited the students to ascend to the organism level again, was tested in the second and third case study. The next transcript illustrates how the questions of the researcher (co-assisting in a chromosome practical) guided students from the cellular to the organism level.

[R is researcher]
R: What do you think is a pair of chromosomes?
Josien: This is a pair of chromosomes.
Maud: Well, we think this is pair of chromosomes, after normal duplication, they are pulled apart.
R: Okay, we are now looking at a normal somatic cell, yes? Which indeed can divide. But what is a pair of chromosomes? How did you receive those pairs?
Loes: You have 23 pairs of chromosomes. And 46 ...

Josien:	... 23 of your father and 23 of your mother.
Loes:	Now we have three pairs.
Josien:	Father and mother [pointing at the chromosomes of a pair].
R:	Yes, that is a possibility. So you have so to speak a chromosome number 3 of father and one of mother. [...]
R:	So, now try to solve this problem.
Femke:	For if you have two of those pairs, ...
Josien:	One of mother and one of father ... So they are not the same!
R:	So, indeed they are not exactly the same.
Femke:	Oh yes, okay!

The researcher helps the students to ascend to the organism level by asking the question: *'How did you receive those pairs of chromosomes?'*. This question made students think about the origin of the homologue chromosomes and they indicated that one originated from mother and the other from father. So, they ascended to the organism level, and reflected on the reproduction process on that level, the formation of gametes and rediscovered the cause that resulted in a non-identical homologue pair.

Analysis of the data of the second and third case studies, including the data of the final written test, showed that most students attained the desired objectives. That means that they were not only in able to descend from the organism level to the cellular level and from the cellular level to the molecular level; but also to ascend to the organism level and to interrelate the different genetics concepts on these levels. Furthermore, the results of the written test showed that, although it did not have any focus in the strategy, most students were also able to solve genetic cross problems. This is a remarkable result, taking into account that the most frequently reported learning difficulties in genetics are dealing with genetic cross problems.

Discussion

In the study on genetics, the LT-strategies was developed by testing and improving preliminary strategies in three case studies. Evaluation of the preliminary LT-strategies showed what adaptations were necessary to improve its feasibility and effectiveness, and, therefore, made it possible to design a final LT-strategy.

Since the evaluations were mainly based on intersubjective interpretations of qualitative data, it cannot be excluded that other interpretations are possible and that a different design of the evaluation might have led to other adaptations of the LT-strategy. However, the validity of the analyses was improved by triangulation: analyses of transcripts of plenary and group discussions, were systematically compared with analyses of other additional data sources (interviews, observations, worksheets and written tests).

The domain-specific LT-strategy developed in the study is probably not the only possible learning strategy, since it is grounded in a domain-specific philosophy of education of which the problem-posing approach is a major component. It seems probable that, based on other philosophies, other strategies are possible. However, it should be kept in mind that genetics is a topic for which, considering the learning difficulties reported in literature, an effective LT-strategy was not available.

An important question is, of course, what other science researchers and teachers not involved in the studies may learn from it. The answers to this question depend on the perspective we choose, whether it is from the perspective of the teacher, or from the perspective of the researcher.

From the perspective of the researcher, it could be argued that the external validity of the LT-strategies was not empirically tested. However, Yin (1994) rejects statistical generalization for case study research, and advocates a replication logic. By selecting a number of case studies, it is possible to test and adapt the expectations or hypotheses, and to develop a theory, which is generalized to other comparable cases (case-to-case transfer). This procedure, which is followed in our studies, is called 'analytical generalization' (Yin, 1994) or 'theoretical generalization' (Smaling, 2000). To improve the theoretical generalisability cases were selected that differed with respect to important variables. In the study on genetics, cases were selected that differed with respect to the ability of the students (higher ability classes and pre-university classes), and the effective learning time (4th and 5th forms in higher ability classes, and 4th, 5th , and 6th forms in pre-university classes). Both from the perspective of the teacher and the researcher, it is necessary that other teachers and researchers, not involved in the study, are enabled to compare the results of the case study research with other cases (or their own case) by using analogical arguments (Smaling, 2000). The transferability of the results can be improved by the nature of the research report. Our research reports (e.g. Knippels, 2002) largely conform the criteria developed by Smaling.

Although the general ideas behind the LT-strategies are sometimes grasped by curriculum developers, we are not yet very successful in implementing our strategies among teachers. Of course, it is possible to give external explanations for that, like the fact that our research is insufficiently embedded in national innovations, but the question is whether these external explanations are satisfactory. There seem to be two related reasons why implementation of our strategies by teachers is not self-evident.

The first reason has to do with the concept of implementation. A mistake commonly made in implementation strategies is that they are implicitly based on a transmission paradigm. However, every implementation process should be considered as a learning process. And if, as in our developmental research, guided reinvention is chosen as foundation for a LT-strategy, it would be obvious that an implementation strategy should be based on the same strategy. The question is not 'what research says to the science teacher' but how teachers can get involved in learning processes aiming at the reinvention of specific LT-strategies like the yo-yo strategy.

The second reason has to do with the nature of our LT-strategies, since the transferability depends of course not only on the nature of the research reports. It can be questioned if our strategies do not prescribe too many details to teachers operating as professionals. And even if teachers do adopt our strategies, how reasonable is it to expect that they do adopt topic-specific strategies? Is it not preferable that teachers learn to adapt more general strategies like the problem-posing approach and the yo-yo strategy?

References

Boersma, K.Th. (1999). The Janus face of developmental research. Review of some designs of biology-didactical research. In O. de Jong, K. Kortland, A.J. Waarlo and J. Buddingh, (eds.). *Bridging the gap between theory and practice: What research says to the science teacher. Proceedings of the 1998 International Summer Symposium.* Hong Kong: International Council of Associations for Science Education.

Cobb, P., Confrey, J., DiSessa, A., Lehrer, R. and Schauble, L. (2003). Design experiments in educational research. *Educational researcher*, 32(1), 9-13.

Elliott, J. (1991). *Action research for educational change.* Milton Keynes: Open University Press.

Gravemeijer, K.P.E. (1994). *Developing realistic mathematics education.* Utrecht: CDß-Press.

Greenwood, D.J., Whyte, W.F. and Harkavy, I. (1993). Participatory action research as a process and as a goal. *Human Relations*, 46 (2), 175-192.

Janssen, F.J.J.M. (1999). *Ontwerpend leren in het biologieonderwijs.* (Learning biology by designing). Utrecht: CDß-Press.

Kelly, A.E. (2004). Design research in education: Yes, but is it methodological? *The Journal of the Learning Sciences*, 13(1), 115-128.

Klaassen, C.W.J.M. (1995). *A problem-posing approach to teaching the topic of radioactivity.* Utrecht: CDß-Press.

Knippels, M.C.P.J. (2002). *Coping with the abstract and complex nature of genetics in biology education. The yo-yo learning and teaching strategy.* Utrecht: CDß-Press.

Kortland, J. (2001). *A problem-posing approach to teaching decision-making about the waste issue*. Utrecht: CDß-Press.

Lijnse, P.L. (1995). 'Developmental research' as a way to an empirically based 'didactical structure' of science. *Science Education*, 79, 189-199.

Miles, M.B. and Huberman, A.M. (1994). *Qualitative data analysis: An expanded sourcebook*. London: Sage.

Richey, R.C. and Nelson, W.A. (1996). Developmental research. In D. Jonassen (ed.). *Handbook of research for educational communications and technology* (pp.1213-1245). London: Macmillan.

Smaling, A. (2000). Inductieve, analoge en communicatieve generalisatie. In F. Wester, A. Smaling and L.Mulder (eds.). *Praktijkgericht kwalitatief onderzoek* (pp.156-171). Bussum: Uitgeverij Coutinho.

Van den Akker, J. (1999). Principles and Methods of Development Research. In J. van den Akker, R.B. Branch, K. Gustafson, N. Nieveen and T. Plomp (eds.). *Design Approaches and Tools in Education and Training* (pp.1-14). Dordrecht: Kluwer Academic Publishers.

Van Weelie, D. (2001). Contextualizing Biodiversity. In: O. de Jong, E.R. Savelsbergh and A. Alblas (eds.). *Teaching for scientific literacy. Context, competency, and curriculum*. Proceedings of the 2nd International Utrecht/ICASE Symposium 11-13 October 2000 (pp. 99-116). Utrecht: CDß-Press.

Verhoeff, R.P., Waarlo, A.J. and K.Th. Boersma (2001). Systems Theory based Approach to Learning and Teaching Cell Biology in Upper Secondary Biology Education. In R.H. Evans, A.M. Andersen and H. Sørensen (eds.). *Proceedings of the 5th European Science Education Summerschool: Bridging Research Methodology and Research Aims. Gilleleje (Denmark), September 6-13*, 2000 (pp. 332-339). Copenhagen: The Danish University of Education.

Vollebregt, M. J. (1998). *A problem-posing approach to teaching an initial particle model*. Utrecht: CDß-Press.

Walker, D.F. (1992). Methodological issues in curriculum research. In Jackson, P. (ed.). *Handbook of research on curriculum* (pp. 98-118). New York: Macmillan.

Yin, R.K. (1994). *Case study research: Design and methods* (2nd edition). Beverley Hills/CA: Sage.

Chapter 6

Evaluating Educational Impact – the CASE experience.

Philip Adey

School of Education and Professional Studies, King's College London, Stamford Street, London SE1 9NN

Summary

What is the innovation? A two-year intervention programme for 12 – 14 years olds designed to develop their higher level thinking through science.

What need does it address? Inadequate general levels of thinking in the secondary school population.

What is its scope? The programme has been in existence for 20 years and is currently used, at some level, by around one-third to one half of all secondary schools in the United Kingdom, and by many overseas.

What evaluation data has been collected? Extensive data are available on the long-term effects of the intervention on national examinations results, using both quasi experimental methods with matched control groups and a 'value added' approach comparing CAE with non-CASE schools over many years.

What are the key findings? The programme has been shown consistently to (a) raise students' levels of cognitive development; (b) subsequently raise their levels achieved in National tests of science at ages 14 and 16 years; (c) also raise their test levels in remote subject areas such as English.

Introduction

"Cognitive Acceleration" means promoting the development of children's general cognitive processing capability (also known as 'general intelligence'). The original Cognitive Acceleration work was set in a science context, at the junior secondary level, that is with 11 – 14 year olds, and the project was called Cognitive Acceleration through Science Education (CASE) (Adey and Shayer, 1994). Subsequently, Cognitive Acceleration programmes have been developed in mathematics, technology, and arts subjects, and also with primary-aged children. This chapter describes some of the methods we have used to evaluate the effects of the original CASE project at the junior secondary level, and of the work we have done at Kindergarten level with 5 and 6 year olds. We will look at the effects of Cognitive Acceleration on students' cognitive growth and on academic achievement. In the Cognitive Acceleration programmes, we have taken a predominantly (but not exclusively) quantitative approach to evaluation. Our philosophy has been "if you can't attribute measurable gains in pupils to the programme, then what's the point?" Now, this stance begs all sorts of questions, and I will try to address those which are commonly put by audiences and reviewers. Firstly, however, the quantitative methods need to be outlined. In this chapter I will focus only on the quantitative measures, as these are becoming relatively unusual in educational research.

Pupil-level data and long term far transfer

In the original Cognitive Acceleration through Science Education (CASE) research project, funded by the British Economic and Social Science Research Council from 1984 to 1987, we used a classical quasi-experimental method with experimental and matched control groups in whole class units given pre-tests of cognitive level, post-tests after the two year intervention of cognitive level and science achievement, similar delayed post-tests one year later. We then collected grades students obtained in the General Certificate of Secondary Education (GCSE) Science examinations, which are nationally set and marked, and which were taken one or two years after the delayed post-tests. The design is represented in table 1:

Group	9/1985	2 years	6/1987	6/1988	6/1990
CASE	Pre test of levels of cognitive development	CASE intervention	Post tests of levels of cognitive development	Delayed post tests: cognitive development and science understanding	GCSE grades in science, maths, English
Control		Normal science			

Table 1: Experimental design for original CASE research

(Incidentally, although true randomised experiments are rare in education, there is one example from Finland (Hautamäki et al., 2002), where children from every primary school in one town were randomly assigned to one of three conditions: CASE only, CASE+CAME (the mathematics CA programme), or neither, and then children were bussed around once a week to experience the intervention programme assigned to them. A fascinating result is that although the CASE and CAME groups did significantly better than the control group, all three groups did better than expected from national norms. The most plausible hypothesis for this effect is that the CA groups generated more discussion and 'social construction' back in their regular classes, so that the cognitive acceleration effect was experienced also by the 'controls'.)

In the original experiment, CASE classes were chosen (1) from schools recommended by local government science education advisers as either being in need of help, or as likely to follow the programme as offered; and (2) within the chosen schools by the head of the science department as representing students with middle of the range ability. Control classes were also identified by the head of science in the same schools as being as similar as possible in mean ability to the selected CASE classes. In some cases, CASE and control groups were taught by the same teacher, in others by different teachers.

The pre-cognitive tests were moderately good predictors of success in the achievement delayed tests (science and GCSE) so the regression equation for those tests on pre-cognitive measures were found for the control group, and used to predict expected grades for the experimental groups if they had been no different. Comparing expected with actual grades gives the measure of gain – the residualised gain score of each pupil. Results have been extensively reported, (e.g. Adey and Shayer, 1993; 1994), but in brief summary it was shown that the CASE programme at the junior secondary level caused (a) significantly accelerated cognitive growth by the end of the two-year intervention; (b) significant gains by the experimental group compared with the control group on (i) science tests taken one year after the intervention and science GCSE grades taken two or three years after the intervention; and (c) significant gains in GCSE grades in mathematics and English as well as in science. On the GCSE grades, the experimental groups showed and effect size from .03 to 1.0 standard deviations over the control groups. These results demonstrate the long term, and far-transfer effects of cognitive acceleration.

The school-level value-added approach

After 1990 when results indicated long-term effects of CASE on academic achievement, which transferred from the science context into English, it became ethically improper to run similar experiments which would explicitly deny control groups the opportunity to participate in a beneficial experience. So we turned to an added value system, looking at whole school units rather than individual children or classes (although class-level analysis was used on occasion). The relationship between the mean cognitive level of a school's intake of 12-year olds expressed as a percentile and the mean GCSE grade in various subjects achieved five years later is more or less linear. We can see how much higher is the mean GCSE grade of CASE schools, compared with what would be expected from their Year 7 intake levels. Examples of this form of processing are given by Shayer (1996; 1999a; 1999b)

Recent work – experiments again

From 1999, the Cognitive Acceleration principles were used to develop stimulating activities for children in primary schools (Year 1; ages 5 and 6). We again used the quasi-experimental method to evaluate the effect. In this case, the experimental, CA, classes were pre-ordained by the source of funding, a special government budget targeted at a specific disadvantaged area of an inner city borough. We had to use all of the Year 1 classes in schools in that area, a total of 14 classes in 10 schools. For controls we identified 5 schools (8 classes) in an immediately adjoining area which was not quite as economically disadvantaged, but had a similar profile of ethnic mixture, numbers eligible for free school meals, and numbers and levels of children with English as an additional language. Pre-tests showed that the CA and control samples were not significantly different in starting levels of cognitive development. Here the testing programme is as shown in Table 2:

Group	9/1999	1 year	6/1987	6/2000
CA	Pre test of levels of cognitive development	CA intervention	Post tests of levels of cognitive development	Delayed:Raven's matrices & KS1 levels*
Control		Normal teaching		
* These are levels obtained on tests which were taken at the end of Year 2.				

Table 2: Experimental design for CA at primary school

As before, we have used residualised gains of individual children to assess any cognitive and academic gains made by the CA children over and above what would be expected on the basis of control children's gains. In the immediate post-test the experimental children showed significant gains in levels of cognitive development compared with controls, in tests on schema which were included in the intervention and, for transfer, of schema that were not included (Adey, Robertson, & Venville, 2002).

We also looked at the mean residualised gain scores of each class individually in the CA and control schools. This is sensitive data as it points directly at individual teachers, and must therefore be treated with considerable caution. In particular, the numbers are often small, allowing for much random variation around any true mean. Even if the impact on a particular class can be attributed immediately to the way that the teacher delivers the intervention, delivery will be the result of a complex of variables including teacher variables (comprehension of the intervention, beliefs about teaching and learning, classroom management competence, etc.) and school variables (resources, senior management support, timetabling issues etc.).

Some questions

Now I must turn to some questions about what valid conclusions can be drawn from results obtained using the methods outlined above. These fall into two categories: technical threats to validity, and more general questions about just what it is that is being evaluated.

Threats to validity

If I had 20 Euros for every time someone said 'Is it a Hawthorne effect?' I would have retired to Barbados long ago. Generally, the questioner has no knowledge of the original Hawthorne paper (Mayo, 1945) which reported short term gains in output from office workers who were told that a particular colour paint on the office walls would make them work more effectively. The point of this effect is that it is *short term*. With CASE we have, not just a long term effect, but perhaps one of the longest follow-up studies that has been conducted within education. (We are however overshadowed in the long-term stakes by Joan Freeman's work on gifted children growing up (Freeman, 1991), and by the Head Start people who tracked rates of adolescent drop-out, pregnancy, and court appearances of children who had experienced the Head start programme when they were four and five years old.)

Another version of the Hawthorne question is "Wouldn't any special attention be paid to pupils over one or two years have the same effect?", to which the answer is "Please describe your special attention". CA has a substantial theory base and a set of procedures and activities based on this theory, trialled, and made explicit for teachers' use. It is open to anyone else to devise alternative intervention strategies perhaps based on different theories and to trial them against CASE or against 'normal' education and they might well prove to be more effective and more efficient. The theoretical possibility of alternative intervention strategies does not invalidate the evidence that CASE is effective.

A related question is "How do you know it is CASE, and not some other thing in the schools which is producing the effect?" This could be a reasonable question if our sample was of just one or two schools. The whole point of looking for the effect in as large a number of schools as possible is to randomise other variables, so we can say that the only systematic difference between CASE and non-CASE schools is that the latter do CASE.

There are also issues around the sampling. For the experimental studies, were classes or departments in the experimental groups ones which were chosen for their effectiveness, and which would have produced such gains anyway, without the intervention? I hope that my description of the sample selection above has answered this. For the value-added studies, our CA sample is of schools which have opted to buy into the CASE PD programme. Maybe these schools have a generally more proactive and forward looking school ethos which might be expected to produce better academic results anyway. The answer to this is that the 'control' schools themselves used for these value-added analyses are actually new CASE schools for whom we have the pre-test data but whose CASE students have not yet come through to the GCSE. The same expectation might be held for these control as for the experimental schools.

Just what does "CASE" consist of?

This is a more interesting question. The simple model looks like this:

CASE: pre-test ....   intervention   .... post-tests
Control: pre-test ....   no intervention   .... post-tests

Given sufficient numbers of classes and schools to randomise other differences between schools, any difference in post-test-pre-test gains are attributable uniquely to the intervention. But what did the intervention consist of? In fact, it is a complex of various inputs, including:

- A theoretical model of what should cause cognitive stimulation based on Piagetian ideas of cognitive conflict and schema theory, Vygotskyan ideas of social construction, and Catholic ideas of metacognition (reflective abstraction from Piaget, language as a mediator from Vygotsky)
- A set of printed materials for teachers and pupils which (a) spell out this theory and relate it to the pedagogic practice which supposedly follows and (b) provide a set of exemplar activities which provide excellent contexts for cognitive conflict, social construction, and metacognition (Adey et al., 2001a; 2001b).

- An extensive professional development programme for teachers, including seven centre based days training and five half day coaching visits over two years.

So what is our experimental test testing? The theory base? The printed materials? Or the professional development? I suggest that this question is not just difficult to answer experimentally, but may be impossible to answer in principle. One needs to go back to Stenhouse's (1975) ideas of what constitutes a curriculum – essentially everything that happens within a school including those actions which are purposeful towards particular learning and development objectives and those which are incidentally provided by the environment. Those of us socialised into CASE methods can distinguish between high and low quality CASE teaching with some reliability, assessed by inter-judge measures. But describing high quality CASE teaching in an unambiguous manner is another matter. This should not be surprising to anyone who has tried to record something as seemingly simple as one science lesson. With, say one teacher and 25 students within 60 minutes there is immediately the potential for thousands of bits of verbal dialogue. And the verbal dialogue is just one aspect of the interactions, which occur: think about the looks, actions, and richness of body language which characterise all human discourse.

Being difficult to describe does not mean that it does not have recognisable characteristics. Good CASE lessons provide students with cognitive challenge, they exhibit a high level of social-cognitive interaction between students and between teacher and students, and they contain significant metacognitive activity by the students. These are the three main 'pillars' we look for and aim to develop during coaching sessions with new CASE teachers. I believe that in principle these characteristics could be exhibited in lessons which make no reference to the particular set of activities we developed as exemplar materials. I also know, because I have often seen it, lessons can be taught from the printed materials without exhibiting the characteristics of Cognitive Acceleration to any serious extent. What we are evaluating could not be the printed materials themselves.

We are evaluating a method of teaching. But is it sufficient to describe this method in terms of the three 'pillars' of cognitive conflict, social construction, and metacognition? In terms of methodology, cognitive psychologists tend to be rather more rigorous and scientific than science educators. When I present our work at psychology conferences, they ask "But which of the three pillars is doing the work? Could it all be metacognition, which would produce effects without any cognitive conflict or social construction?" I can see the rationale for their questions, but in trying to even imagine (let alone get funded) an experiment to tease apart these three pillars, I am confounded by reality. You cannot be usefully metacognitive (reflect on your own thinking) if you have not been engaged in thinking, in some sort of problem solving. This means that you must have encountered some sort of cognitive conflict. And not many people can encounter a problem without wanting to discuss it with someone else – a teacher or more able peer. In other words, cognitive conflict entails social construction, and productive metacognition requires cognitive conflict. So the experiment to separate those pillars cannot be done, and we should look on CASE pedagogy as an integrated, if complex, whole.

Evaluation and Uptake

To what extent is the uptake of a curriculum innovation dependent on high quality evaluation? It would be nice to think that, especially in science education, purchasers of curriculum materials looked for research which showed that the material being purchased did in fact have positive effects on academic achievement or some other desirable outcome. That they seldom seem to do so is no criticism of science teachers, since real evaluation of curriculum effects is a very rare phenomenon, and if heads of science departments waited to see rigorous measures of the effects of a textbook or curriculum scheme before they purchased it they would never be able to buy anything.

Perhaps some of the issues raised in the last section explain why this should be so. It turns out to be extremely difficult to pin down just what counts as a 'curriculum', and so to assess the effects of its various components. With CASE we were in the fortunate position of having a substantial research grant to run a proper evaluation, and we were also unusual in having a well-articulated theoretical model which translated directly into a pedagogic model. Notwithstanding the difficulty of teasing apart the separate effects of its different components, CASE does present as a unified 'package' of materials associated with a strongly characteristic pedagogic style. It is certain that CASE has maintained a high profile within the British science education scene since 1991. At the time of writing (2004), the demand for CASE professional development continues to be very strong. Probably two-thirds of British secondary schools have the CASE materials in their science department, and one-third are making some serious attempt to use them as intended. This is the more surprising when one considers that the first edition of the print materials, *Thinking Science*, was published before we had a National Curriculum in England and Wales, and even subsequent editions make no explicit claim to meet National Curriculum requirements. The positive side of this separation of the materials from a particular curriculum is that they are more internationally acceptable, and *Thinking Science* has been translated into Dutch, German, Danish, Finnish, Welsh, American, Arabic, Korean, and probably unofficially into other languages as well.

Has the rigorous evaluation of CASE contributed to its success? We cannot be certain about this, but anecdotally I can report that while many science teachers look at our evaluation results and say "With those effects, how could one NOT do CASE?", there are plenty of others who take a blanket sceptical view, dismissing the reported effects as "lies, damned lies, and statistics". As with any other human endeavour, embarking on a new and challenging task such as shifting one's teaching method in the way required by CASE, requires more than an intellectual decision to try it. It requires some commitment and a shift in one's beliefs about the nature of teaching and learning. How one brings about such shifts is a question too large to embark on here, but I have essayed a comprehensive answer in Adey, Hewitt, Hewitt, & Landau (2004). The reality is that the success of CASE is unlikely to be explained by its evaluation alone. Although the evaluation does play an important part, other features such as the clear pedagogy and the focus on 'thinking' rather than on scientific content seems to make CASE attractive to many teachers.

References

Adey, P., Hewitt, G., Hewitt, J. and Landau, N. (2004). *The Professional Development of Teachers: Practice and Theory (in press)*. Dordrecht: Kluwer.

Adey, P., Robertson, A. and Venville, G. (2001a). *Let's Think!* Slough, UK: NFER-Nelson.

Adey, P., Robertson, A. and Venville, G. (2002). Effects of a cognitive stimulation programme on Year 1 pupils. *British Journal of Educational Psychology*, 72, 1-25.

Adey, P. and Shayer, M. (1993). An exploration of long-term far-transfer effects following an extended intervention programme in the high school science curriculum. *Cognition and Instruction*, 11(1), 1 - 29.

Adey, P. and Shayer, M. (1994). *Really Raising Standards: cognitive intervention and academic achievement*. London: Routledge.

Adey, P., Shayer, M. and Yates, C. (2001b). *Thinking Science: The curriculum materials of the CASE project* (3rd ed.). London: Nelson Thornes.

Freeman, J. (1991). *Gifted Children Growing Up*. London: Cassell.

Hautamäki, J., Kuusela, J. and Wikström, J. (2002). CASE and CAME in Finland: "The second wave". Harrogate: 10th International Conference on Thinking.

Mayo, E. (1945). *The Social Problems of an Industrial Civilization*. New Hampshire: Ayer.

Shayer, M. (1996). *Long term effects of Cognitive Acceleration through Science Education on achievement*: November 1996: Centre for the Advancement of Thinking.

Shayer, M. (1999a). Cognitive Acceleration through Science Education II: its effect and scope. *International Journal of Science Education*, 21(8), 883-902.

Shayer, M. (1999b). GCSE 1999: *Added-value from schools adopting the CASE Intervention*. London: Centre for the Advancement of Thinking.

Stenhouse, L. (1975). *An introduction to curriculum research and development*. London: Heinemann Educational Books.

Chapter 7

Science education for citizenship: Introducing the discussion of socio-scientific issues into the curriculum

Stein Dankert Kolstø
Department of Physics and Technology, University of Bergen, Allégaten 55, N-50207 Bergen, Norway

Summary

What is the innovation? A small-scale (13 lessons) curriculum project called "Consensus projects" aiming at science for citizenship, implemented in a general science course in the upper secondary school.

What need does it address? The importance of preparing students to deal thoughtfully with socio-scientific controversies encountered in daily life.

What is its scope? Based on a teaching model proposed in the literature, the Consensus project model was implemented in a science class in Norway in their compulsory science course.

What evaluation data have been collected? The discussion in the article is based on the described objectives for the project and on the teacher's evaluation report. The teacher's report focused on students' issue knowledge, participation in discussions and personal decision-making.

What are the key findings? The students increased their issue knowledge and took part actively in discussions related to a controversial issue, including questions of the reliability and validity of knowledge claims. In evaluating the relevance of the project, it was found that prerequisite knowledge needed to examine the controversial issue was under-emphasised. It was also found that evaluation of students' dealing with socio-scientific controversies needs to relate to the value aspects of personal decision-making in a more explicit manner.

Introduction

Many commentators on school science curricula argue that this should nowadays include some opportunities for students to discuss current issues and controversies concerning the application of science and technology, of the kind that appear regularly in the news media.

This chapter focuses on the impact and effects of short teaching interventions ('Consensus projects') designed to improve students' capability to argue and reason, using scientific information. The background and rationale for the intervention is explained, and the implementation described.

The relevance of the project's aims and the foci of the evaluation are discussed. Based on this discussion, general issues concerning the evaluation of curriculum innovations with 'citizenship' aims of this sort are discussed. A primary focus in the discussion is the role of values and personal perspectives in students' responses to socio-scientific controversies and the consequences of this for the evaluation of student learning outcomes.

Society today is faced with a number of controversies with a science dimension. Ability to examine information related to socio-scientific issues have been recognised as an important aim for science education (for example, NRC, 1996; Millar and Osborne, 1998). During the last decade there have been several curriculum initiatives aiming at bringing controversial issues and decision-making into the science classroom (Eijkelhof, 1990; Geddis, 1991; Solomon, 1992; Gayford, 1993; Fullick and Ratcliffe, 1996; Kortland, 1996; Ratcliffe, 1996; Harms et al., 1997; Lewis et al., 1997; Waarlo, 1997; Christensen & Kristensen, 1999; Kolstø, 2000a; Simonneaux, 2001). The evaluation of curriculum projects aiming at science for citizenship is a new area for science education. With an emphasis on students' decision-making skills and relevance for dealing with the science dimension of controversies such projects poses-new challenges to evaluation. The focus of science for citizenship projects might differ according to the developers', and implementers', perspective on controversies, on the nature of science and on science-society interactions. However, if the aim is to support students' analysis and decision-making on socio-scientific issues, not all perspectives will be of equal relevance to this goal. It is therefore important to evaluate *the relevance* of a project's perspective and articulated learning goals in addition to the evaluation of students' *learning outcome.*

This article is concerned with a Norwegian curriculum project aiming to foster students' ability to make knowledge-based decisions on socio-scientific controversies. The project focuses on examination of the science dimension of controversial issues through a teaching model called 'Consensus Projects' (Kolstø, 2000a). An evaluation indicates the existence of several challenges for the evaluation of science for citizenship projects. Aikenhead (1985), in describing the concept of "thoughtful decision making" as the main goal for a science curriculum for citizenship, warns that a potential pitfall when trying to develop students' decision-making skills is not to include necessary prerequisite knowledge about the characteristics and limitations of science and technology. This aspect will be included in the perspective described through an emphasis on characteristics of the science dimension of controversial issues typical given media coverage.

Building on this perspective, a framework is described, which gives the main learning goals on which to build evaluations of science for citizenship curriculum projects. The framework enables an identification of challenges related to evaluation of such projects. In turn, it becomes possible to discuss the strengths and weaknesses of the evaluation made of the Consensus project.

The basic claim in this article will be that the evaluation of science education for citizenship curriculum projects presupposes specification of both perspective and learning goals.

Consensus projects

The 'Consensus project' is a teaching model aiming to provide students with "experiences, knowledge, skills and attitudes that empower them to deal with science, expert statements and knowledge claims with a science dimension emerging in socio-scientific issues" (Kolstø, 2000a). It is a small-scale curriculum project in a lower secondary school situated in a suburban area on the West Coast of Norway. The science teacher implemented the teaching model in the general science course. As part of a university level course in science education the same teacher made a summative evaluation of the project on which this discussion is based.

A main goal in Consensus projects is to train students in information-based argumentation and evaluation of knowledge claims. Through practising this it is hoped that students will be encouraged to study and evaluate information prior to their decision-making, including scientific subject matter. It is also hoped that students will understand why conflicting views exist. A final goal is to make the students understand and appreciate that disagreement and debate are legitimate and important aspects of frontier science.

The teaching strategy used in the consensus project model is a combination of project work in the tradition of Dewey and Kilpatrick and the Danish consensus conference model for democratic technology assessment (Kolstø, 2000a). The consensus project model uses a topical socio-scientific controversy as a focal point. The controversy selected was the debate on whether Norway should allow the building of power plants using natural gas, making it more difficult for Norway to fulfil the Kyoto agreement on release of carbon dioxide. The class was divided into groups, which were to become 'experts' on different aspects of the issue, including scientific, technological and socio-scientific dimensions. All groups were to present their findings at a 'conference' in the science classroom. One group, the 'lay group', had a special task, to scrutinise the other groups' presentations, and make a report presenting a consensual view on the issue, including recommended action. The view had to be consensual in order to avoid simple voting and stimulate argumentation within the group. The 'expert groups' were assigned roles (as subject matter experts, politicians, industry involved, and a well-known local environmental group), allowing them to promote ideas without having to be personally convinced. These 'expert groups' worked for five science lessons, reading information and identifying arguments, and then for one additional hour, preparing a presentation, which aimed to convince the 'lay group' that their views was important. The conference, lasting two school lessons, was supposed to be a kind of 'summit' where all arguments from different perspectives met. Based on the presentations, the 'lay group', which were placed in front, were supposed to reach a well-founded conclusion. The different groups were allowed to comment and discuss the presented information and arguments, and this opportunity was used actively. The teacher chaired the conference, and had an important role in exemplifying how to ask scrutinising questions like: "Is this a knowledge claim or value position?", "Why do you trust these sources?", "Could you explain that concept/mechanism?". After the conference, all groups had to compile a report on the information and arguments they had found and presented.

Learning outcomes

The students filled in a questionnaire prior to, and three weeks after, the project. Beforehand, only one half of the students knew that 'gas-plants' produce electric power and they knew very few arguments. Three weeks afterwards, all the students knew what the issue was about, and knew several of the arguments involved. The most prominent finding, however, was that most students actively participated in debating the arguments put forward at the conference. From the debate and the reports from the different groups it could be seen that the students used arguments, which included scientific concepts. It is not possible to state whether they understood fully the concepts they used, but they were able to use them adequately ways in their arguments. Concerning personal decision-making at the end of the project, fewer students had a clear opinion than beforehand. They stated there were good arguments "on both sides", which indicates that the students learned about more arguments and attained increased respect for a conflict of interests.

The teacher reported that questions related to reliability or validity of knowledge claims was frequently discussed during the project's conference (even though the value aspect of the issue and the desirability of the different alternatives were more prominent). Through these discussions, issues related to competence, expert disagreement, frontier science and possible interests were illuminated.

In this project, there were no obvious signs of increased understanding of the nature of science. This was probably due to the lack of an explicit focus on such knowledge. Issues related to both social processes within science and science's external social relations, nevertheless, seem to have been debated. Also, the students' competence and confidence in their own ability to formulate arguments and to state a view in public probably improved. In fact, several students expressed their pleasure in participating in the conference, both immediately afterwards and unsolicited on later occasions.

The strength of the project was probably its focus on the need for both an information base and evaluation of knowledge claims in relation to both the societal and scientific aspects of a controversy. Findings from the frontiers of science were thus debated inside the classroom. The processes undertaken, therefore, probably exemplified critical examination of knowledge claims involved in a controversy and thus provided the students with the basic idea of what constitutes a critical attitude.

The combination of expert groups and a conference probably also implied practice in the reworking (Layton, 1991) of information from different knowledge domains to articulate with complex real-world issues.

The relevance of the Consensus project

The foci for the evaluation of the project were the students' understanding of what the issue was about, the students participation in discussions related to arguments, the development of personal opinions on the issue and on the reliability of scientific knowledge claims. (The evaluation also considered the students' learning of science concepts and on motivation, but these aspects were not judged to be relevant for this article.) The question then arises as to what extent these four foci represent science for citizenship.

The evaluation of the outcome of the implementation of the Consensus project model was not based on a specified framework describing main learning goals related to science for citizenship. The implication is that even if some relevant learning seems to have taken place, it is difficult to evaluate the relative importance of the outcome in relation to the stated general goal of science for citizenship. The evaluation of the project could probably have benefited from a clarified view on the concept of science for citizenship and the relevance of different learning goals and this will be discussed in terms of identifying the strengths and weaknesses with the Consensus project.

A framework for evaluation of curriculum projects

The concept of science for citizenship might be defined as related to the cultural and the democratic arguments for science education for all (for example, Driver et.al., 1996; Millar, 1996; Sjøberg, 1997). The cultural argument states that science is an important part of our culture and has contributed to our worldview and our way of living. Science is therefore an important frame of reference in our culture, and thus relevant to include in compulsory education. The democratic argument is based on the fact that many issues in public and private life have a science dimension. Knowledge in science might increase the quality of peoples' evaluations and decisions in such socio-scientific issues. This chapter concentrates on consequences of the democratic argument for science education for citizenship.

I will take as a premise that science for citizenship should both be responsive to society's need for knowledge-based decisions and empower the laity to analyse and act in accordance with personally held perspectives. The concept of thoughtful decision-making proposed by Aikenhead (1985) might be seen here as a concept unifying these two different aims. This concept includes aspects of decision-making related to values and ideology, in addition to emphasising the role of knowledge, evaluation and argumentation. This broad definition with inclusion of value-related aspects will, however, result in challenges when it comes to the evaluation of students' learning outcome.

To fulfil their purpose, learning goals for a science curriculum for citizenship have to be relevant in the context of socio-scientific issues. An understanding of these real-world contexts will therefore guide the development of curriculum projects for citizenship.

Socio-scientific issues

A characteristic aspect of socio-scientific issues is the frequent focus on a possible risk to the environment or to human health. Socio-scientific risk issues also often evolve into controversies. The science dimension of socio-scientific issues is typically related to the potential risk. An important aspect of such risk-focused controversies is that they often contain not only one, but two central issues. One issue is the political, ethical, societal or personal question on what action to take, for example, 'Should it be legal to sell food that has been irradiated?'. The second issue relates to the science dimension. In many risk-focused controversies a scientific question related to e.g. the existence or size of the risk is not clarified or may be disputed. In the 'food-irradiation' issue the scientific sub-issue could be: "Does the nutritional value of food become reduced by irradiation?". Controversies where an important scientific sub-issue is unresolved might be termed *double issues* (Kolstø, 2001). In double issues, it will be relevant to look up results from the frontier of science when trying to argue for a specific view. Ongoing research, however, is usually not emphasised in compulsory school science courses.

Several scholars have claimed the existence of two different types of science (Latour, 1987; Ziman, 1991; Cole, 1992; Bauer, 1994). On the one hand, we have ongoing research at the frontier of science. Hypothesis and results from this research will normally be disputed within the scientific community. This science might be denoted as 'frontier science' (Cole, 1992) or 'science-in-the-making' (Latour, 1987). On the other hand, we have the established scientific knowledge typically found in textbooks. This science is consensual and regarded as neutral, objective and reliable within the relevant discipline. Cole denotes this science as 'the core'of science and Latour denotes it as 'ready-made-science'. Subjective and unreliable frontier science is transformed into core science, or out of science, through different social processes which includes publication, criticism and argumentation.

This description implies that claims for the reliability of scientific knowledge vary. Awareness of this variation is important when examining controversies. This variation and the fact that scientific knowledge is based on argumentation, in addition to empirical evidence, also makes it relevant for ordinary citizens to examine the reliability of scientific knowledge claims.

When the scientific dimension of a double issue is disputed, it is relevant to look up results from research when trying to argue for a specific view. The result is that tentative scientific knowledge claims are required, and actively used, by actors in controversies. Claims from the frontier of science are thus applied without waiting for the knowledge claims to be evaluated and judged as either reliable or as dead-ends by a scientific community. Awareness of characteristics of knowledge claims from research thus becomes even more important.

However, it is also important to be aware that scientific knowledge is not produced in a social vacuum. Neither is the old picture true anymore where science was seen as produced at universities by scholars with the development of a discipline as the main objective. Aikenhead (1994) claims that science has been undergoing a process of 'socialisation' whereby "Government, industry, and the military have become the dominant patrons of scientific activity." (p.16). This 'new'science has been denoted by Ravetz (1995) as 'industrialised science'. Typical scientists have lost their independence, and have become employees or contractors. They thus work either in industry or governmental agencies, or have to make dispositions that might give them research contracts.

In industry, the competition in the market might result in less openness towards methods and less emphasis on publication and open debate. Regarding risk issues, industry, governmental agencies and others might have interests connected with certain results. This could, for example, be findings showing that no, or just small, risks are connected to certain technologies and practices. The question then emerges as to whether scientific research, or communication of research results, can be influenced by interests. In scientific research, there is always some room for diverging interpretations, for example due to uncertainties.

If we combine the use of contract-based research to provide arguments, hopefully in line with one's own interests, with the use of results from single studies in the public debate, we get a situation where important social processes in science are overthrown. This leaves more of the evaluation of reliability of results to the lay man and woman, and thus also greater demands on curriculum projects focusing on science for citizenship. This view of modern science is also echoed by studies of lay people's relation to science (Layton, et al., 1993; Irwin, 1995; Irwin and Wynne, 1996). The view of science as "a force to be struggled against" (Irwin, 1995 p.46), sometimes found in these studies, indicates that the neutrality of science and scientists is no longer taken for granted.

Thoughtful decision-making as a learning goal

The inclusion of the concept 'thoughtful' in relation to decision-making indicates that science for citizenship is not only about arriving at a personal decision, but also includes the quality of the decision-making process.

A basic claim in this article is that decision-making on controversial socio-scientific issues is a complex task. As the descriptions in the above paragraph indicates, such issues typically involve several open questions, different kinds of scientific knowledge claims, several different actors with different interests. Thus knowledge from several social domains and disciplines might be relevant. In such a complex landscape it is highly desirable that students in a decision-making situation examine the issue in order to acquire a firm knowledge base for their evaluations.

Decision-making involves the comparison and weighting of arguments and values involved. However, the presence of disputed questions and different actors with different interests implies that decision-making also includes decisions on what information to trust. Ability to evaluate the relevance and trustworthiness of claims with a science dimension therefore becomes necessary.

When participating in a discussion it is necessary not only to present and explain arguments, explain and often but also to adjust these in the light of comments and counter arguments. It is also important to be able to examine the relevance and validity of antagonists' claims, for example through asking scrutinising questions.

In addition, one might want to communicate ones' viewpoints to decision-makers or a wider public. Skills in argumentation therefore need to be included in the concept of thoughtful decision-making.

The concept of thoughtful decision-making thus needs to involve the following three main aspects:

- Knowledge-based *examination* of a controversy, to gain understanding of the issue and alternatives, arguments and values involved.
- Personal *evaluations* based on the outcome of the examination, and focusing on the relevance and trustworthiness of arguments (Kolstø, 2000b), evaluation of alternatives (Janis and Mann, 1977) and personally held values (Ratcliffe, 1994), and hopefully also including a personal decision.
- *Ability to participate in argumentation* in relation to viewpoints involved in the controversy.

Although these three aspects are process-related, they necessarily involve both

1. prerequisite *general knowledge*,
2. *issue related knowledge* based on a personal examination of the controversy,
3. *skills* related to the performance of the examination, evaluation and argumentation, and finally
4. *attitudes* which underpin these processes.

Each of these four dimensions of knowledge involves a challenge to the evaluation of science for citizenship projects that need to be discussed.

Challenges related to evaluation of prerequisite knowledge

Prerequisite knowledge relates to knowledge needed to perform an informed examination of the science dimension of a controversy. As Aikenhead (1985) has warned us, if this examination is to be meaningful, it has to be based on some understanding of the nature of science and science-society interactions.

These learning goals are fact-oriented as long as we do not include the ability to apply this knowledge when examining controversies or in other contexts. Thus they will not represent any challenge to external evaluators of curriculum projects. They might, however, represent a challenge to teachers as they imply evaluation of partly new subject areas.

In the evaluation of the Consensus project, this dimension was missing. With no knowledge of students' ideas about science and science-society interactions, it is difficult to evaluate students competency in applying this knowledge in the context of the controversy. Data could, of course, have been gathered both on aspects of students' knowledge in, and about, science, and of the science dimension of what we might term their 'issue knowledge'. By comparing two such sets of data it may be possible to gain insights into the students' ability to apply prerequisite knowledge to a complex real-world controversy.

Challenges related to identification of issue knowledge

Thoughtful decision-making obviously presupposes issue knowledge: knowledge related to the controversy to be dealt with. To gain issue knowledge, the decision-maker has to examine the controversy using his or her general knowledge (for instance 'prerequisite knowledge'). This examination involves a process, the examination itself, and a product, issue knowledge. This product might include knowledge of alternatives involved, main arguments, main actors and their views, interests and values, possible risks involved, and the disputed and undisputed scientific knowledge claims involved. The outcome of the evaluation, issue knowledge, will to some extent be a consequence of the personal perspective used by the student. Thus this issue knowledge will not be a collection of 'facts' agreed upon by all involved actors, by the student's teacher or by an external evaluator. The evaluation of this examination therefore involves a challenge due to the subjective dimension of the students' issue knowledge.

One choice when performing an evaluation of the students' examination skills could be to focus on the outcome of the examination process, neglect the subjective dimension, and compare the outcome with a standard established by the evaluators. The evaluators might, for example, state that four different actions are involved in the controversy, and use a list of seven main arguments involved. Another choice could be to focus on the process itself, and evaluate the presence of examination activities and results of the examination.

In the evaluation of the Consensus project, the first strategy used was a pre- and post-questionnaire focusing on issue knowledge. However, the questionnaire and the analysis of students' answers did not allow for variations in the knowledge gathered due to differences in students' values and perspectives. The second strategy used the teacher's observation of the whole-class debate. The content, the issues knowledge gained through the examination, was not given attention here.

Challenges related to evaluation of process skills

An important aspect with decision-making is the personal *evaluation* of arguments and alternatives. These evaluations might relate both to relevance and trustworthiness of arguments and knowledge claims, and to the comparison and weighting of arguments, values and alternatives. Learning goals related to such evaluations focus on the development of skills. The evaluation of students' skills in this regard involves a challenge, as some of the students' evaluations will be based on values not agreed upon. There exists no neutral judgement regarding the trustworthiness of a knowledge claim or the desirability of different alternatives. People put different trust in different sources of information for instance. One option could be to focus on the *presence* of evaluation processes and the outcome of this, and neglect the *content* of the evaluations.

The ability to present a*rguments* in debates also involves skills. Examples here could be the ability to identify and articulate one's own views, or to use evidence to underpin a claim. A question here arises as to whether one should evaluate the *quality* of the arguments and the evidence put forward, or whether to focus on the *presence* of articulated arguments and evidence.

The neglect of content implies saying that no quality differences exist between different evaluations and arguments. This is not a comfortable position. The dilemma between content and process might be "solved" through focusing on process in formal evaluations, and on content during the teaching process, leaving room for the teacher to challenge students using quality oriented feedback.

In the Consensus project the students had to write reports presenting the controversy, give an overview of arguments involved, and explain a conclusion to be drawn. This report represented an opportunity to study the quality of the students' evaluations. The study of quality of evaluations would have presupposed the development of a framework for the analysis which defines high and low quality evaluations. The challenge remains, however, of finding quality indicators that do not favour certain perspectives and values.

As regards students' argumentation skills, the evaluation of the Consensus project focused on the presence of argumentative activities rather than on their quality. By looking at the students' reports, or by taping the discussion, it would have been possible to analyse the quality of the arguments put forward. To avoid an analysis biased by the evaluators' perspective on the issue, this analysis probably has to focus on the presence of certain quality indicators like use of evidence or warrants. The work of Driver et al. (2000), based on Toulmin's argumentation structure, represents an interesting opportunity for this.

Challenges related to evaluation of underpinning attitudes

If students are to perform knowledge-based *examination* also outside school, the activity has to be embedded in attitudes which lead to underpins or stimulate this. Examples of such attitudes might be open-mindedness combined with scepticism, and curiosity and interest to understand.

Evaluation of knowledge claims has to be underpinned by an attitude towards knowledge claims, or epistemology, where claims are not seen as true or false, but as supported by arguments. Other attitudes underpinning thoughtful evaluation might be the willingness to consider both pros and cons. Further, the evaluation dimension therefore needs to involve goals related to attitudes.

Concerning the goal to increase students' ability to participate in debates and *argumentation* we might want to develop the students' attitudes to include a commitment to evidence and to values.

Ramsden (1998) states that attitudes "cannot be measured directly, but only inferred from words and action". However, in relation to thoughtful decision-making it is not the attitudes per se we are interested in, but the consequences for processes of examination, evaluation and argumentation involved. It might therefore be wise to base the evaluation related to attitudes on data from the decision-making process, and focus on the consequences for the students' evaluations and decisions more than on the attitudes themselves.

Open-mindedness and willingness to consider both pros and cons might thus become studied by focusing on the presence of and the time spent on views and arguments not in line with the student's own sympathies. This strategy will also make it possible, through the use of such quality indicators, to make an analysis that is responsive to the students' own positions.

In the evaluation of the Consensus project the issue of attitudes was only briefly touched upon. It was found that fewer students held a clear opinion on the controversy towards the end of the project, and that several students explained that they now saw good arguments on both sides. Together these findings were taken as an indicator for students' attitudes regarding willingness to consider both pros and cons, and thus represent an example of the use of perspective independent quality indicators.

Biggs and Collis (1982) proposed a taxonomy for assessment purposes called Structure of Observed Learning Outcome (SOLO), based on Piagetian stage theory. The SOLO taxonomy was devised as a subject-independent tool for the evaluation of learners' responses to open-ended questions. As quality indicators, the SOLO taxonomy uses the student's ways of using information. Thus it provides an interesting opportunity for assessing the quality of students' examination, evaluation and argumentation in relation to socio-scientific controversies. However, more work is needed on whether students' different values and perspectives affect evaluation using this taxonomy.

Conclusions

Evaluation of curriculum initiatives aiming at science education for citizenship have been identified through a discussion based on Aikenhead's concept of thoughtful decision-making. There are two main challenges. The first relates to the relevance of the perspective from which the project evaluation is performed. It is suggested that the evaluators' perspective regarding the concept of science for citizenship needs to be made explicit, and should be included in the foci of the evaluation. In evaluating this perspective its relevance for the context in focus, socio-scientific issues, needs to be emphasised.

The second challenge relates to the role of personally-held values in the decision-making process. Values influence both the student's examination of a controversy, evaluation of knowledge claims, arguments and alternatives, and argumentation in relation to a controversy. The challenge then becomes to find ways of evaluating the quality of the students' decision-making without the perspectives of the evaluators biasing the evaluation.

One way to tackle this is to focus on the presence of certain activities, for example, the presence of debate and argumentation. However, it seems superficial to state that a decision is thoughtful only because there was an examination of the controversy, an evaluation of information involved and a debate over viewpoints. Content sensitive quality indicators therefore need to be developed. Such quality indicators need to focus in more specific ways on the content or the quality of the processes. This strategy will not make evaluation a value-free activity. The quality indicators will represent a value-based perspective. But quality indicators have to be sought whose sensitivity to the values that influence students' decision-making about socio-scientific controversies is as low as possible.

References

Aikenhead, G. S. (1985). Collective decision-making in the social context of science. *Science Education*, 69(4), 453-475.

Aikenhead, G. S. (1994). The Social Contract of Science. In J.Solomon and G. Aikenhead, (eds.), *STS Education. International Perspectives on Reform* (pp. 11-20). New York: Teachers College Press.

Bauer, H. H. (1994). *Scientific Literacy and the Myth of the Scientific Method*. Urbana, Illinois: University of Illinois Press.

Biggs, J. B. and Collis, K. F. (1982). *Evaluating the Quality of Learning*. London: Academic Press.

Christensen, K. G. and Kristensen, T. (1999). *Fra naturfag til politikk. Mot et paradigmeskifte i miljøundervisningen? (From Science to Politics)* (Forskningsrapport fra MUVIN 2 i Norge). Tønsberg: Statens Utdanningskontor i Vestfold.

Cole, S. (1992). *Making Science. Between Nature and Society*. Cambridge, Massachusetts: Harvard University Press.

Driver, R., Leach, J., Millar, R. and Scott, P. (1996). *Young Peoples' Images of Science*. Buckingham: Open University Press.

Driver, R., Newton, P. and Osborne, J. (2000). Establishing the norms of scientific argumentation in classrooms. *Science Education*, 84(3), 287-312.

Eijkelhof, H. M. C. (1990). *Radiation and Risk in Physics Education*. Utrecht: Centre for Science and Mathematics Education.

Fullick, P. and Ratcliffe, M. (eds.) (1996). *Teaching Ethical Aspects of Science*. Southampton: The Bassett Press.

Gayford, C. (1993). Discussion-based group work related to environmental issues in science classes with 15-year-old pupils in England. *International Journal of Science Education*, 15(5), 521-529.

Geddis, A. N. (1991). Improving the quality of science classroom discourse on controversial issues. *Science Education*, 75(2), 169-183.

Harms, U., Kross, A. and Bayrhuber, H. (1997, 2. - 6. September). *Teaching gene technology to secondary school students*. Paper presented at the First International Conference of the European Science Education Research Association (ESERA), Rome, Italy.

Irwin, A. (1995). *Citizen Science – A Study of People, Expertise and Sustainable Development*. London: Routledge.

Irwin, A. and Wynne, B. (eds.). (1996). *Misunderstanding Science? The Public Reconstruction of Science and Technology*. Cambridge: Cambridge University Press.

Janis, I. L. and Mann, L. (1977). *Decision Making*. New York: Free Press.

Kolstø, S. D. (2000a). Consensus projects: teaching science for citizenship. *International Journal of Science Education*, 22, 645-664.

Kolstø, S. D. (2000b). "To trust or not to trust, ..." Students' ways of dealing with a socio-scientific issue. *International Journal of Science Education*, 23, 877-901.

Kolstø, S. D. (2001). *Science Edication for Citizenship – Thoughtful Decision-Making About Science-Related Social Issues* (Vol. 1). Oslo: Unipub forlag.

Kortland, K. (1996). Decision-making on science-related social issues: the case of garbage in physical science - a problem-posing approach. In G. Welford, J. Osborne and P. Scott (eds.) *Research in Science Education in Europe. Current Issues and Themes*. London: Falmer Press.

Latour, B. (1987). *Science in Action: How to Follow Scientists and Engineers through Society*. Milton Keynes: Open University Press.

Layton, D. (1991). Science education and praxis: the relationship of school science to practical action. *Studies in Science Education*, 19, 43-79.

Layton, D., Jenkins, E., Macgill, S. and Davey, A. (1993). *Inarticulate science? Perspectives on the Public Understanding of Science and Some Implications for Science Education*. Nafferton: Studies in Education Ltd.

Lewis, J., Driver, R., Leach, J., and Wood-Robinson, C. (1997). *Opinion on and attitudes towards genetic engineering: acceptable limits* (Working paper 7). Leeds: Centre for Studies in Science and Mathematics Education.

Millar, R. (1996). Towards a science curriculum for public understanding. *School Science Review*, 77, 7-18.

Millar, R. and Osborne, J. (1998). Beyond 2000: *Science Education for the Future*. London: Nuffield Seminar Series: Interim Report V3.

NRC [National Research Council]. (1996). *National Science Education Standards*. Washington, DC: National Academy Press.

Ramsden, J. M. (1998). Mission impossible?: Can anything be done about attitudes to science? *International Journal of Science Education*, 20(2), 125-137.

Ratcliffe, M. (1994). *Decision-making about science-related social issues*. Paper presented at the 7th IOSTE Symposium, Enschede, The Netherlands.

Ratcliffe, M. (1996). Adolescent decision-making, by individuals and groups, about science-related social issues. In G.Welford, Osborne, J. and Scott, P. (eds.). *Research in Science Education in Europe*, pp. 126-140. London: Falmer Press.

Ravetz, J. R. (1995). *Scientific Knowledge and its Social Problems* (2nd ed.). New Brunswick, NJ: Transaction Publishers.

Simonneaux, L. (2001). Role-play or debate to promote students' argumentation and justification on an issue in animal transgenesis. *International Journal of Science Education*, 23(9), 903-928.

Sjøberg, S. (1997). Scientific literacy and school science. Arguments and second thoughts. In E. Kallerud and S. Sjøberg (eds.). *Science, Technology and Citizenship.*

The Public Understanding of Science and Technology in Science Education and Research Policy (pp. 9-28). Oslo: Norwegian Institute for Studies in Research and Higher Education.

Solomon, J. (1992). The classroom discussion of science-based social issues presented on television: knowledge, attitudes and values. *International Journal of Science Education*, 14(4), 431-444.

Waarlo, A. J. (1997). *Biology students' forming and justifying of opinions on predictive genetic testing. Towards a practicable and effective teaching strategy.* Paper presented at the First International Conference of the European Science Education Research Association, Rome, Italy.

Ziman, J. M. (1991). *Reliable Knowledge: An Exploration of the Grounds for Belief in Science.* Cambridge: Cambridge University Press.

Chapter 8

Evaluation of 'Children Challenging Industry': A primary school science-industry links project

Joy Parvin
Chemical Industry Education Centre, University of York, York, YO10 5DD, UK

Summary

What is the innovation? A four-week programme of primary school science lessons set within an industrial context with a linked visit to a chemical company.

What need does it address? (i) To support primary teachers in teaching nationally prescribed science curriculum, and (ii) to create a public that is more informed about the scope of activities within the chemical and allied industry.

What is its scope? The project has been running since 1996 and now operates in four northern regions of the UK. Each year, an advisory teacher in each region carries out the programme with approximately 1000 children and 300 teachers.

What evaluation data have been collected? Extensive data have been collected, using pre- and post-project interviews with 44 teachers and 100 children, and pre- and post project questionnaires with a further 120 children. Teachers were also interviewed one year after the intervention. Data were collected on views of science, the chemical industry, and the links between the two.

What are the key findings? Children Challenging Industry has been received enthusiastically. Children have been motivated by the style of activities used (small group, practical investigations) and by the industrial context; there has been a 'purpose' for doing science. The vast majority of children have gained a more informed attitude to industry, and have appreciated the important place of science. Teachers have been enthused by the industry-context and its effects on the children's motivation. Most teachers felt they gained confidence and/or knowledge to improve their science teaching, and either carried out the same activities with their next class or planned to do so in the second year of their curriculum cycle.

Introduction

The Children Challenging Industry (CCI) project arose out of the previous experience of the Chemical Industry Education Centre (a constituent of the University of York Science Education Group), and the desires of the Centre and a chemical company in the north of England to effect change in the way in which (i) science is taught in primary classrooms and (ii) the chemical industry is perceived by the public.

In order to explain fully the evaluation of this project, I will start this chapter by describing a little more of the background to this project, its aims, and the model that was developed.

I will then discuss the project evaluation in more detail. The evaluation techniques will first be described, which included audio-taped and transcribed interviews with children in half of the schools and with all of the teachers before and immediately after the intervention, questionnaires with children in half of the schools, and telephone interviews with half of the teachers one year after the intervention. The discussion will go on to whether, with the use of these evaluation techniques, the impact on the children and teachers can be ascribed to the relatively short intervention rather than other experiences that young people and their teachers have.

The evidence of change during this focused intervention will be discussed in the light of the notable characteristics of the intervention, including the industrial context used for the sessions, the delivery of the activities by a visitor to the school, the use of practical equipment in each session, and the visit to industry.

The chapter will conclude with a discussion of the effectiveness of the intervention and of the evaluation itself.

Project background and aims

The project design incorporated characteristics to meet the needs of both the sponsor and the Chemical Industry Education Centre (CIEC), carrying out the programme. The Chemical Industry Education Centre was established in 1988, to support the mutual understanding of the chemical industry and schools, whilst maintaining independence from each sector. The CIEC achieves this increased level of understanding via the creation and use of a wide range of written and website-based science materials aimed at teaching science to 5-19 year olds using a context-led approach and via a variety of training methods and courses for teachers and industrialists.

The development and evaluation of the project was sponsored almost wholly by a privately-owned chemical company, the owner of which was keen to change the low public perception of the chemical industry (MORI, 1994). There was also a desire, on the part of the Centre, which was carrying out the project, to develop a cost-effective model of staff development. Both parties hoped to develop a model that would be successful enough to offer to schools and companies nationwide. It was therefore important to evaluate the effectiveness of the model and to discover what national implementation might be possible.

The **aims of the project** were to:
- improve the perception of primary school teachers and children of the chemical industry and its relationship with science
- increase enjoyment of science for children
- provide classroom-based training for teachers in the teaching of the UK National Curriculum for science, using industrial contexts.

Offering children exciting and stimulating experiences of science is a key aim of the CIEC, which aims to promote science to all young people, whether or not they wish to take up science-based careers. Science offers them an opportunity to investigate the physical world in which they live and to take part in debate involving scientific issues in an increasingly mature way as they move through the education system.

From industry's viewpoint, enthusing children about science also improves the chances of them choosing to study science, as they get older, and a science-based career when leaving school or university and, as important, to help them appreciate the role of the chemical industry in a modern society.

Offering training for teachers is another key aim of the CIEC, and this was felt to offer an important dimension for schools at a time when the work carried out in the classroom must fulfil National Curriculum requirements. Teachers would only choose to participate if they felt that the activities helped to cover science concepts they were required to teach.

Although science has been a legal requirement in UK primary schools since 1989, there are still many teachers who wish to benefit from training of this nature, and who may not have participated in some of the 20-day type courses offered by the government in the early 1990s. Only a third of the teachers in this study had received training of this nature.

Project Model

The project model was designed in such a way as to build upon the experience of the Centre, and therefore made use of CIEC 'science units'. A typical CIEC science unit provides detailed written information on how to carry out a short series of practical investigations, including teachers' notes, photocopiable activity sheets, and links to the science curricula of the UK. Three were selected for their strongest industrial links, appeal to the age group, coverage of relevant concepts specified in the National Curriculum, and high level of practical and investigative activity.

The topics covered by these units, and from which each teacher could select, were:

Water – how industry transports and uses water on site
Plastics – properties and the manufacture of common plastics
Salt – how salt is obtained and used as a de-icer.

An example of a practical activity is the investigation in the plastics unit on the shock-absorbing properties of a wide range of commonly available packing materials such as bubble-wrap, expanded polystyrene pellets, newspaper and straw. The children devised, conducted, recorded and drew conclusions from these tests.

My role within the project was multi-faceted. I worked along side the Centre manager to develop the project model. This project model included the use of science units which I had written and which had been tried and tested in schools and had been published. I then put the project into action (as the 'advisory teacher') by delivering the project in the schools involved. As the advisory teacher, I carried out classroom activities with 9–11 year olds. During these sessions, the classroom teachers could either observe or teach collaboratively. I would provide most of the resources, manage these and the lessons, lead classroom discussions at various points during the lessons, and ensured differentiated approaches and resources were used.

In discussion with a wider advisory team, I devised the research methodology, and conducted the research.

The duration of the intervention that this project model offered was:

- 7–8 hours of classroom activities in three weekly sessions, plus 3–6 hours of optional activities for the teacher to carry out (training for the teacher, and science for the children)
- 1–2 hours for the class teacher (and sometimes other members of staff, such as newly-qualified teachers and science coordinators)
- 2 hour visit to industry, where possible.

This may seem a short intervention, but it offered an intense period of science activity within a primary classroom. After discussion and planning with me, and the loan of project equipment, the classroom teachers were offered, and frequently carried out, additional follow-up and extension activities each week.

As already mentioned, the intense period of activity was characterised by hands-on practical activities, often of an investigative nature. From data collected, many of the children participating in the project felt that this was unusual in their science lessons. Teachers stated that the lack of science equipment in the school reduced the chances of children having hands-on experience.

The intervention was also characterised by a visitor, with knowledge of both primary teaching and industry, carrying out the activities each week. The novelty of a visiting 'teacher/scientist' excited many of the children who looked forward to the return of the project officer each week.

To enhance the industrial storyline rolling through the practical activities, I used large photographs, videos, pieces of industrial 'kit' and demonstration experiments to depict and exemplify chemical sites and their processes.

Finally, the site visit was a totally new concept for the schools taking part. 57% of children involved visited a relevant industrial site. None of the teachers had taken classes to visit the chemical industry before. Indeed few had taken their classes to industry of any kind! Therefore, the visit, carefully planned to follow on from the classroom activities, offered a totally new experience for the youngsters. All companies involved received detailed project information, and, in most cases, also received training for site personnel on effective site visits for the age range that were relevant to the classroom topics covered.

I carried out the site visit training. I toured the site first, to enable me to tailor the training, The training session was typically two hours in duration, and included a brief overview of the National Curriculum, carrying out a primary science investigation, learning interactive discussion techniques/questioning with this age group, use of artefacts, culminating in the design of a suitable tour.

Evaluation methods

The evaluation of the project was large in scale, involving over 1300 children (9–11 year olds) and 44 teachers from 38 schools over a three-year period (1996–98). The intervention to be evaluated was short, consisting mainly of three half-day sessions of science activities, over three weeks in each school. In over half of the cases, children visited an industrial site after the final classroom session.

As one of the aims of the project was to develop a model suitable to extend to other areas of the country, the study was intended to be a formative evaluation for similar future projects. It was also intended to be illuminative, as a large quantity of data were collected representing teachers' and children's views of industry and how science relates to the world of work (see Chapter 1 for discussion of these dimensions of evaluation). As very little work has been done in this field, the specific learning outcomes were not determined in advance (see the discussion of Stenhouse's work in Chapter 1) but it was hoped that a range of responses could be studied as a result of the intervention. In addition, it was felt that the resulting bank of data would provide new and detailed information on these views.

The research questions, and therefore chosen evaluation methods, link most closely with one aim of the project; namely to implement a project model that would result in change to people's perceptions of the chemical industry and its relationship with science.

The research questions were:

- *What are children's views of science and of industry?*
  – this area incorporated questions on children's enjoyment of science
- *What are primary teachers' views of science and of industry?*
  Does the use of industry-focused science lessons alter these teachers' or children's views?
  – including teachers' views of the training components of the CCI project
- *Do site visits alter the children's and teachers' views in any way that differs from changes noted after the classroom sessions?*

The evaluation methods are outlined in Table 1.

In choosing these evaluation methods, consideration was given to:

- *The age of the children concerned*

It was decided to use initially semi-structured interviews with small groups of children. This format was chosen in order to provide a focus, the opportunity to probe some responses, and for children to talk freely. At this age, more detailed responses to questions are obtained though small group discussions than with individuals, as children gain confidence to speak from each other (Hopkins, 1993; Heath, 1999). It was hoped that these audio-taped and transcribed discussions would provide a rich source of data that would inform the questionnaire design used with the second half of children involved in the project. As some 9–11 year olds still struggle with reading and writing, it was felt to be important to use the two methods in this way, in order to offer an effective and focused questionnaire that would also minimise the necessary reading and writing (predominantly closed questions).

Both the interview and questionnaire questions asked of the children were structured so as to develop gradually their picture of industry. The progression of questions allowed children to relax into the discussion, look at the 'props' used during the

with whom	method of data collection	purpose of data collection	when collected (pre- or post-intervention)	number collected
teacher	questionnaire	to obtain information about the school and the teachers' background	pre/background	43
			pre	41
			post	40
teacher	interview	to ascertain views of industry and of science	post - one year later	23
teacher	interview			
Teacher[1]	interview	to determine any long-lasting impact	pre	21
			post	21
children	interview	to ascertain views of industry and of science	pre	120
children	interview		post	78[2]
children	questionnaire		pre	3
children	questionnaire			
industrialist	interview			

[1] Telephone interviews were conducted with teachers one year after participation, as I had built up a rapport with each teacher during the previous year.

[2] Children's post-intervention questionnaires were often posted back to the CIEC, hence the lower response rate. The number that could be used for analysis was reduced further to 55% for various reasons.

Table 1: Data collected by different methods

interview, and share their thoughts within the group. Children were asked questions about how and where 2–3 products, which provided the props, were made. The selection of products used during the interviews depended upon which series of activities the class were about to do and which site they were hoping to visit. For example, a school visiting Hydro Polymers would be asked about a plastic product such as a yoghurt pot, whilst a school visiting Thomas Swan might be asked about a Mars bar wrapper, as Swan contribute to the adhesive used to seal the chocolate bar. Other products were selected to gather data on a wide range of products related to the chemical industry, such as headache tablets, washing-up liquid and bleach.

Note: Individual children were not identified during the interviews, so it is onl possible to compare group data before and after intervention. Questionnaire data offered the opportunity to compare pre/post data for individuals.

• The multi-faceted role of the researcher

As I was the researcher and also the advisory teacher implementing the project model with the teachers and children, systematic analysis techniques had to be employed which would maximise the validity of the data, thus ensuring the highest level of objectivity possible. Otherwise, as Harlen (1975) points out:

> "When the evaluator puts himself so much inside the materials or method being tried, there must be empathy between him and those taking part in the experiment, and his attitude must be positive or he would be in danger of undermining the confidence of the participants. Then judgement may become less objective than is desirable." (p.48)

Therefore, triangulation techniques (Hopkins, 1993) were used to ensure the range of data collected determined each category's justification (categories arising from grouping comments from the interviews and open-ended aspects of the questionnaires). Contradictory evidence was also looked for, which might negate categories. Other researchers were asked to apply the categories to the data, and any discrepancies discussed and dealt with.

Systematic analysis was also carried out on children's drawings, by identifying and categorising common features, as with 'draw-a-scientist' research carried out by Newton and Newton (1992, 1997). For example, the drawings of the place of manufacture contained people, chimneys, furnaces, and conveyor belts. The people who worked there were drawn wearing hats, glasses, overalls, boots, suits or laboratory coats. Each of these items was assigned a category in a database, and data from each transcript were duly categorised. Features in drawings that were not clear were discussed with colleagues. Either a consensus was reached on the feature or it was assigned to the 'unidentified' category.

In order to avoid the possibility of children communicating stereotypical images of scientists, even when they may hold others (a criticism of this analytical method spearheaded by Symington and Spurling (1990)), the questionnaire was designed to develop the context of an industrial workplace, and thus set the scene for the children's drawings.

The same process was conducted for post-intervention drawings. As a precedent could not be found in other studies for comparing these drawings Newton and Newton (1992) used a different cohort of children in their comparative study), points were awarded for drawings that showed a more accurate representation of industry than those done pre-intervention. In a similar way, points were deducted for opposite occurrences. Therefore, a high positive score indicates better knowledge of the place of manufacture, and a high negative score indicates poorer knowledge.

A colleague, engaged in science education research, validated the categories, by allocating points in the same way. Agreement between the two was high (84–95%), with the definition of one category being tightened and a few modifications made. These modifications related to whether one or two isolated features indicated a more accurate representation of industry. For example, it was agreed that the change in words one child used to label a chimney indicated greater accuracy. The first chimney was said to 'burn pollution fire' and the second chimney burned 'fumes and gases'.

· *The range of data desired*

The combination of methods was chosen to enable a comparison to be made between the views of all the parties involved in the industry-focused science lessons. Using questionnaires with half of the children also gave me the opportunity to collect children's drawings, to add to the oral descriptions of industry collected during interviews.

· *The numbers of children and teachers involved.*

As four children from each school were involved in the evaluation, interviews were often of 30-60 minutes length. As a result, a great deal of time was required to both conduct and analyse the interviews. Therefore, the more focused questionnaires offered a more efficient data-collection process. It was not felt necessary to do the same with the shorter teachers' interviews. Thus the class teacher from each school was interviewed.

Limitations of the research

It should be acknowledged that the sample size for one area of the research was low. Only 17 teachers were interviewed one year after the intervention. Also, data were collected from children immediately after the intervention, thus ascertaining the short-term effects. The longitudinal study, described towards the end of this chapter, will overcome these limitations, by collecting further data from these teachers and children.

As has already been stated, the researcher also had several other roles within the project development and implementation. Therefore, maximum objectivity was a continuous aim. However, the effects of this position could not be fully negated. I always asked teachers to be completely frank with me during interviews, but the fact that they were being interviewed by the person who worked in their classrooms is likely to have affected some of their responses.

Results

Prior to the project intervention, views of teachers and children of industry appeared to be based predominantly on media images. This is in keeping with the results from studies on teachers' views of industry (Ball et al., 1995) and from studies on children's views of occupations generally (Hutchings, 1996) are in keeping with MORI polls (Lewis and Broadbent,1992; MORI, 1994), which looked at the wider public perception of the industry.

(a) Changes in children's views

At the start of the project, children held a 19th century view of industry, with their images coming from a range of both fictional and non-fictional sources. School or teachers were rarely mentioned as a source of information on industry. This is not surprising, as the topic was only covered in relation to issues such as pollution, land use or the 19th century, and rarely what happens in industry today. Therefore, the children's everyday experiences, especially in school, offered them little information on industry.

A common image was of a large mill-style 'factory' or warehouses that housed large numbers of noisy machines and people working on production lines in inhospitable and dangerous environments. They described a factory taking the 'ingredients' and mixing, heating and cooling them until they had the finished product, which was boxed up and transported to shops and supermarkets in lorries. Science had very little to do with the whole process, and the vast majority of jobs did not require scientific knowledge. Here are two examples of children's written descriptions:

> *"I would say its a very big building with lots of pipes and smoke, and there'll be double glazed windows. Inside there's lots of machines and there's one that goes straight in the air and it looks like a drill and its working. There's another one that looks like a tractor and its pumping up and down and there's lots of smoke coming out of it. And if you go down a pathway there's a table with lots of people there and they're boxing the plastic bottles and things like that." (S3/C1/222)*

> *"[There would be] churning, like when it was churning around to mix it [bleach] all in. The machines might make noises, like the conveyor belt sometimes makes a buzzing noise when it goes across. And there'd probably be quite a lot of talking and shouting to other people." (S9/C1/348)*

Changes to these views varied considerably from child to child. Some children expressed global changes to their thinking, describing an industry that was completely different to their original perception, whilst others described specific new ideas – such as knowledge of a new job, or a different piece of safety wear.

After the project intervention, all children described changes to the way in which they perceived industry. Where changes to the views of individual children could be measured, 90% expressed a change of view in some way. Increased awareness of industry was measured predominantly in the following areas:

- raw materials used
- processes involved and the number of processes per site
- equipment/machines used to carry out the processes
- general physical appearance of a chemical site
- working environment
- jobs that existed and were desirable – especially those requiring scientific or technical knowledge
- sources of scientific and related information.

The drawings in Figure 1 provide an example of one child's drawings, and his changed perception of a 'factory' that makes plastics. This child had a high positive score for the variety of more informed features in his second drawing.

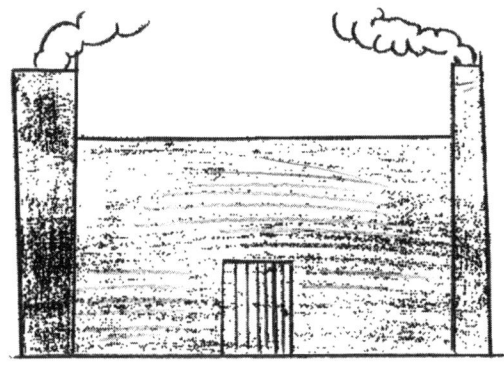

Figure 1:   An example of a child's pre- and post-intervention drawings

These changes were further enhanced by well-planned industrial site visits that met the needs of primary school children. Teachers were enthusiastic to incorporate a site visit into the project. They felt it was an important element in completing the industrial input during the project; the visit rounded off the classroom activities by seeing a real situation with people carrying out real science-linked work.

In all areas where the influence of a site visit was measured, it was found that a greater appreciation had resulted. The comparison of individual children's data revealed that 90% had altered their views to encompass more accurate information about the chemical industry, though some in a very limited way. Those who experienced the greatest change were as a result of visiting a site that had been adapted to suit the needs of the class and their science curriculum. Where children visited a site that had not carried out site visit training, it resulted

in a change of view similar to that achieved through the use of video and photographic images used during the classroom sessions. This suggests, therefore, that if a site is going to invest time and money in conducting site tours for primary children, it does so with the knowledge of the needs of schools and children. If this is not possible, it would appear to be more productive to use a video with appropriate images of the industry, rather than to offer a site visit which leaves the children with an unchanged, or more negative, perception than that with which they started.
There is broad overlap between the areas of learning in which the teachers felt the children had made gains and those measured by the research. Teachers' descriptions of the children's learning of industry fell into four main categories:

- a broad awareness of the existence of such industrial workplaces
- industrial processes
- the links between science and industry
- jobs/people in industry.

Children's awareness of the 'existence' of industry was demonstrated via the many ways in which children described and drew new images of the workplace and the processes involved. Children expressed their new knowledge of the link between science and industry in three ways:

- they realised, after the intervention, that scientists worked in industry, and children frequently wanted to be scientists or 'testers'
- they realised that they could ask people from industry or visit industry to find out scientific information relating to the products a company manufactured
- they appreciated the importance of scientific tests in industry to determine the most appropriate processes, ascertain the quality of the product, and discover new products and processes.

The nature of the intervention was new to the teachers and children alike. The industrial context and the presence of an 'expert' were cited by teachers as the two greatest strengths of the classroom sessions, as they provided children with greater motivation and a purpose for carrying out the tests and investigations.

Therefore, it is highly unlikely that, during this three-week period of intense classroom input, the children would have gained the 'specialised' knowledge that the intervention offered, outside the scope of the project. In some cases, the project encouraged discussion between children and their families about the nature of their relatives' work. This discussion could also be attributed to the project, as it provided the stimulus for the dialogue to take place.

Children were motivated by the nature of the sessions, stating that they enjoyed the vast majority of the activities, and particularly those that had a combination of the following characteristics:

- provide opportunities for learning something new
- are challenging, but not too difficult
- have achievable outcomes
- offer active participation
- provide opportunities to use simple scientific equipment (such as thermometers, funnels, stopclocks and pipettes).

These last two characteristics reflect the areas of science teaching in which teachers had implemented new ideas in the year following the intervention. The use of science activities in which children plan and carry out science experiments independently, was seen by the teachers to be possible, even with classes of thirty or more children.

(b) Changes in teachers' views

Teachers' views of industry come predominantly from news programmes. They held a view of a mysterious, hazardous and polluting industry about which they were unlikely to teach.

50% of teachers were not initially confident enough to describe the chemical industry but the majority made some attempt to do so. Although 50% teachers said that were not confident enough to describe what the chemical industry does, many still made an attempt to do so). These descriptions were predominantly in terms of the site locations, major or local company names, pollution, accidents, and risks. Only 7% of teachers referred to the research and development work of the chemical industry. When asked about the effect of the chemical industry on their daily lives, teachers appreciated that this input was high, and that their limited knowledge came predominantly from media images. One third of these teachers hoped that this project might redress this balance.

Prior to the intervention, most of the teachers who taught about industry, did so in relation to the geography curriculum and concerned themselves particularly with pollution. Half of the teachers made no links with industry at all. Science was linked to industry by only 11% of teachers who covered aspects of pollution, nuclear power and the building industry.

Therefore, during the classroom sessions, teachers hoped that knowledge would be gained (by themselves and by their classes) of industry and of science and the links between the two. Prior to the intervention, equal numbers of teachers had hoped to gain knowledge of science and industry (30% in each case), whereas far more teachers felt they had achieved this afterwards, with 66% citing learning about industry and 41% learning about science. Prior to the intervention, teachers were not specific about the nature of the knowledge they hoped to gain, but after the intervention, teachers felt their learning concerned teaching about science and industry.

The question of attributing changes in adults' views to the project is clearly an easier one to answer than the question of children's changing views. One assumes that the teachers have the maturity to distinguish for themselves where their new knowledge or opinions have originated. That said, the same argument can be applied to the teachers, as well as the children, as in most cases, the teachers' knowledge of the chemical industry came from similar sources. Unlike the children, they had the awareness that their information came from limited sources, which portrayed industry as polluting and dangerous and were willing to find out about industry via its links with the science curriculum and by visiting industry to gain firsthand experience.

(c) Longtitudinal studies

The aims of these longitudinal studies are to find out whether the project has had any long-lasting impact on the teachers and children involved. The main findings are described in the following two sections.

(i) After one year

The next stage of the work, following the classroom interventions and site visit was to contact the teachers a year later. Telephone interviews were conducted with teachers. A designated time to speak to them was agreed, an interview schedule was sent to them at least a week before the telephone interview took place.

The industrial context for the science activities, and the presence of an experienced person to deliver them, were felt by the teachers to be the main strengths of the classroom sessions. The context provided motivation and a purpose for children to do science. This, combined with the opportunity to see the project officer deliver the sessions, motivated teachers to repeat the same activities. 78% of the teachers interviewed one year after intervention either had repeated or planned to repeat the activities in the second year of their curriculum cycle. This repetition of activities was by far the most common way in which industry-links had been maintained by the teachers.

Teachers felt more confident and able to teach practical and investigative aspects of science, and 53% of the same teachers interviewed a year later, had made use of classroom strategies and ideas to teach practical science more effectively. 48% of the children's learning outcomes in science cited by the teachers related to investigative learning. They described this practical and investigative work as particularly important areas of the primary science curriculum, and the work proved to be an important area in which to provide support and learning opportunities for the children and the teachers.

In the year following the intervention, it is possible that teachers received additional training in teaching the science curriculum, as this avenue was not explored during the 'year-on' interviews. Therefore, it may be possible that some teachers had been inspired to carry out more investigative work as a result of such training. However, as many of the changes they described referred to specific techniques or activities carried out by the project officer, it seems logical to assume that the intervention itself inspired the changes to the teachers' practice.

(ii) After five years

In 2002, five years after the original study, questionnaires were used to gather views of the project from 89 children, aged 12–16. Sixteen of these children were later interviewed for more in-depth information. The views of eight teachers were gathered, also using interviews.

Recall of the Children Challenging Industry project

A third of the children remembered the CCI lessons. The element of the lessons that more children remembered than anything else was the carrying out of practical experiments. Only two children said that they did not find the lessons interesting. In addition, 76% of the children who remembered the lessons, thought that the CCI lessons were different from their normal primary science lessons. The main reason was because they contained more practical work, but also because they were new and different. They felt the lessons were real science that was relevant to everyday life.

58% of the children who had a CCI visit could recall it. This is much higher than the number of children who remembered the lessons. Significantly more children remembered visits to the companies that had undertaken training (delivered by the project officer) and had implemented the recommendations. Most of these pupils remembered the size of the site and the product manufactured. Very few children reported negative aspects about the industrial site. Unlike pupil responses 5 years previously, only 8% of the children included scientists in their list of jobs carried out at an industrial site. The gain achieved in this area after involvement in CCI appears to have been lost after five years, with these older children reverting to the perception that work in industry is repetitive.

Secondary school experience of science and industry

Nearly a third of the children remembered an industrial visit during secondary school. Further, those that said that they enjoyed science appeared to have remembered their secondary school visit. Two thirds of the children remembered learning about industry in their secondary school classroom. A significant majority of those who had remembered learning something about industry in their lessons had more positive views about industry. This is similar to the finding by Key for Advanced Level Chemistry students (Key, 1998).

40% of the children felt that the CCI lessons had helped with subsequent science classes. The areas where they had helped included the planning and carrying out investigations, using science equipment and writing science reports. Half of the children also felt that the CCI lessons had helped them in other subjects, in particular in technology and geography.

Views on science and industry

The overwhelming majority, 86% of the children who remembered the CCI lessons, stated that the lessons were enjoyable. Nearly two thirds of the children enjoyed their current science in school, often due to the practical nature of the lessons. On the other hand, the reasons for saying that they did not like the subject was generally that it was 'boring'. The favourite choice of science subject was biology (47%), the most popular reason being that it was 'easy'. Those children who preferred chemistry or physics often said that it was because of the practical work.

When asked whether they would like a career in science, 35% of the children said that they would, with the significant result that more of those who remembered the CCI industrial visit reported that they were more likely to want science careers than the others. Two thirds of these children thought that there were connections between science and industry, frequently stating that industry needs and is based on scientific knowledge.

All the teachers remembered the CCI lessons and found them interesting, useful and relevant to the science curriculum. Half of the teachers were still using the materials after five years. The teachers were also overwhelmingly positive about the CCI site visit.

Teachers reported that there was a positive effect on their teaching methods and three quarters of the teachers had passed on the materials or information to other teachers in the school. Half of the teachers thought that the National Curriculum should contain more information on industry or practical work. Half of the teachers also had links with industry and most of the teachers were positive about industry-sponsored materials. All the teachers were positive about industry five years after the project and three quarters of the teachers felt comfortable describing industry.

All the teachers felt that the project had increased the children's enthusiasm for science and improved their investigative skills. In addition, two teachers were confident that the children's SAT scores (national tests for 11-year olds) had improved as a result of the project.

Implementing the model on a national scale

The CCI project now runs in four northern regions of the UK (the North-West, Tees Valley, Humber Bank and West Yorkshire), and further expansion is planned. Data continue to be collected (questionnaires to children and teachers) to evaluate its effectiveness in these regions. Evaluations will appear on the CIEC website.

A training methodology, based on CCI, developed in 2002–3, has been offered on a national scale since September 2003. As one of the key aspects is that the project officer is removed from the model, the methodology has been planned carefully to incorporate effective quality assurance systems. The evaluation of the methodology and the linked quality assurance, took place in 2003–4. As the project officer is removed, this evaluation encompasses the idea that what teachers and children actually do in the classroom may differ from our (the developers) intentions, an aspect that did not need to be considered in the original evaluation and which is the subject of several chapters in this book, for example in Chapters 9 and 10).

References

Ball, I., Jones, R., Pomeranz, K. and Symington, D. (1995). Collaboration between industry, higher education and school systems in teacher professional development. *International Journal of Science Education*, 17 (1), 17-25.

Bell, J. (1993). *Doing your own research project*. Buckingham: Open University Press.

Harlen, W. (1975). Science 5-13: *a formative evaluation*. London: MacMillan Education.

Heath, L. (1999). Do we always know what is best for learners? *Primary Science Review*, Mar-Apr, 30-32.

Hopkins, D. (1993). *A teacher's guide to classroom research*. Buckingham: Open University Press.

Hutchings, M. (1996). What will you do when you grow up? : The social construction of children's occupational preferences. *Children's Social and Economics Education*, 1 (1), 15-29.

Key, M.B. (1998). *Student perceptions of chemical industry: influences of course syllabi, teachers, firsthand experience*. University of York:, unpublished DPhil thesis

Lewis, S. and Broadbent, M (1992). *The corporate image of the chemical industry: Research study for the Chemical Industries Association*. London: MORI.

MORI (1994). *The corporate image of the chemical industry*: Research study conducted for the Chemical Industries Association. London: MORI.

Newton, L.D. and Newton, D.P. (1992). Young children's perceptions of science and the scientist. *International Journal of Science Education*, 7 (2), 331-348.

Newton, L.D. and Newton, D.P. (1997). Has the national curriculum changed children's minds about scientists? *British Journal of Curriculum and Assessment*, 14 (3), 24-26.

Parlett, M. and Hamilton, D. (1976), *Evaluation as illumination: a new approach to the study of innovative programmes*. Occasional paper no. 9. Centre for Research in the Educational Sciences: University of Edinburgh.

Symington, D and Spurling, H (1990). The 'Draw a scientist test': interpreting the data. *Research in Science and Technical Education*,.8 (1), 75-77.

For more in-depth information on these studies, please visit www.ciec.org.uk and select 'research'.

Acknowledgements

I thank Thomas Swan & Co. Ltd for their most generous funding of the project and Hydro Polymers, Bonar Polymers Ltd, GlaxoSmithKline PLC, Imperial Chemical Industries PLC , Mono Containers Ltd and Thomas Swan & Co. Ltd for the part they all played in arranging site visits. I also thank the Durham Business Education Executive for their support and help.

I have had great encouragement from Tom Swan and Dai Hayward of Thomas Swan & Co. Ltd and much advice on the research design from Dr Judith Bennett and John Lazonby (University of York) and from Rosemary Feasey.

Chapter 9

What can we learn from different forms of evaluation? Experiences from a quality development program in science and mathematics instruction

Christian Ostermeier and Manfred Prenzel*

Leibniz Institute for Science Education at the University of Kiel, D-24098, Kiel, Germany

Summary

What is the innovation? A problem-oriented quality development approach to improve mathematics and science instruction in lower and upper secondary education.

What need does it address? To promote cooperative quality development at the individual school level, foster the professional development of teachers and in a long term approach to improve student outcomes (competencies, interest, motivation) in science and mathematics with an emphasis on deeper understanding.

What is its scope? The pilot program was conducted from 1998 to 2003. The participating 180 schools came from 15 German federal states and were organized into small school networks each comprising 6 schools.

What evaluation data have been collected? The evaluation approaches within the program comprise (a) formative evaluation by the teachers themselves, (b) studies on the acceptance of the program, (c) studies on implementation and (d) summative evaluation. An overview of these four approaches will be given, followed by a more detailed description of the second approach, the studies on implementation.

What are the key findings? The findings indicate that there are relevant differences among the teachers participating in the program. These differences might have a substantial impact on their engagement in cooperative quality development activities to be incited by the program. Regarding the program's implementation strategy the teachers seem to be on different levels of understanding learning and teaching as well as their role in the process of quality development. A crucial facilitative role is taken up by coordinating teachers that serve the local school networks.

Introduction

Whoever acts intentionally, checks again and again whether or not the measures are effective and that aims are achieved. Consequently, evaluation is a natural part of educational actions. It is especially important when new approaches are being developed and tested. Innovations can be evaluated in various ways and according to many different aspects. Using a quality development program in science and mathematics instruction as an example, four approaches of an accompanying evaluation research are reported in this chapter. One approach dealing with the evaluation of the implementation strategy is described in more detail. However, the features of this quality program will be presented first.

'Improving science and mathematics instruction' – a pilot program
Background

In 1997, the German 'Federal and State Commission for Educational Planning and Research' (BLK) decided to start a pilot program to improve the quality of science and mathematics instruction in schools. The initial cause for this decision was the TIMSS finding that the performance of German students in science and mathematics was only mediocre (Beaton et al. 1996a; 1996b; Mullis et al., 1998). Detailed analyses of the German results revealed particular deficiencies which turned out to be even more troublesome than the mere low ranking (Baumert et al., 2000). It appears that German students in science and mathematics do reasonably well when solving tasks that require routine procedures. They fail, however, to solve the more demanding and complex tasks requiring conceptual understanding or flexible application of knowledge. Considerable weaknesses also become apparent when scientific and mathematical thinking and argumentation are needed.

Framework

Against this background, the German 'Federal and State Commission for Educational Planning and Research' asked a group of experts to design a framework for a quality development program. This framework is based on a review of research findings from various sources (BLK, 1997; Prenzel, 2000).

This review identified that the key problems of German curricula concern the limited vertical linking and coherence of science instruction as well as insufficient alignment between the science and mathematics subjects. Additionally, the TIMSS video study (Stigler et al., 1996; Baumert et al., 1997; Stigler & Hiebert, 1997) revealed teaching patterns of mathematics instruction in three different states, Germany, Japan, and the US. The predominant teaching pattern in German classrooms, the 'questioning-developing-approach' (Baumert et al., 1997) which focused on verbal interplay, mainly directed by the teacher. This script of instruction mixes up learning and assessment situations and favours simple routines. The additive (non-cumulative) sequencing of teaching and learning processes hinders students in experiencing growth in competency and disturbs the development of subject-oriented learning motivation and interest (Prenzel, 1997).

These key problems necessitate action on different levels as described in more detail by Prenzel and Duit (2000). Measures directly dealing with science and mathematics instruction in schools are likely to promote improvement faster than measures targeting structures (curricula, teacher training) of the educational system. Accordingly, the program's aim is to improve science and mathematics teaching in the classroom directly.

The framework mentioned above includes the proposal of an intervention program to improve science and mathematics teaching and learning. The program aims to encourage and implement collaboration and processes of quality assurance and quality development at the participating schools. It addresses the key problem areas of science and mathematics instruction in Germany outlined previously. The general aim is to foster science and mathematics literacy in a broad sense. As a first step the program is implemented as a pilot program in a sufficient number of schools. The effects of the program are being evaluated using different approaches.

'Modules' as a frame for quality development

At the core of the program, there are eleven modules, which address the major deficiencies of science and mathematics education in Germany. In a programmatic manner, they indicate which direction the quality development could take. The central ideas of the modules are based on research on learning and teaching in mathematics and science. They concern certain conditions and methods of teaching and learning which can be successfully changed. Thus the modules describe possible starting points and ways for a collaborative effort, which improves mathematics and science instruction. They can be combined or restricted to certain aspects, in any case they have to be adapted to the particular subject matters and problems at hand. At the beginning of the program, the schools and networks had the opportunity to select the subjects and the modules, which addressed the particular needs identified by the groups of teachers.

The participating schools could choose one or more of the following 11 modules to start quality development:

1. Further development of the task culture
2. Toward more adequate views of scientific work and experiments
3. Learning from mistakes – dealing with students' conceptions
4. Securing basic knowledge – Meaningful learning at different levels
5. Cumulative learning – making students aware of their increase in competence
6. Making students aware of the limited view of a particular subject – Towards integrated features of instruction
7. Promoting girls and boys
8. Development of tasks for co-operative learning
9. Strengthening students' responsibility for their learning
10. Assessment: Measuring and feedback concerning the development of competencies
11. Quality development within and across schools

In the following section we describe one module in more detail. Having a central role for science instruction, *Module 2* 'Toward more adequate views of scientific work and experiments' was chosen to explain how this module was identified using TIMSS results and other empirical findings as a starting point.

TIMSS showed that German students show particular weaknesses in scientific reasoning and argumentation in an international comparison (Baumert et al., 1997; 2000). The students often fail when they have to analyse research designs, plan experiments, interpret evidence or when they are required to argue and discuss scientific data. These findings correspond with results from educational research concerning the use of experiments and scientific work in classroom instruction (Harlen, 1999). The results of TIMSS/III further showed that German students experience highly teacher-centered physics instruction (Baumert and Köller, 2000). Even if experiments are being used, they are mainly teacher demonstrations (Seidel et al., 2002). It seems almost impossible for teachers to allow students to plan, carry out and evaluate their own experiments. Indeed, even when students do the experiments, the experiments are often used ineffectively with teachers frequently integrating experiments in lessons without preparing the students sufficiently for the central ideas before starting to work. Frequently, experiments are insufficiently related to students' competencies and interests, and, indeed, are often trivial. Students work through a manual without thinking for themselves.

Accordingly *Module 2* suggests, for example, the following principles to integrate experiments and scientific inquiry in science instruction in a way that positively affects students' cognitive processes and motivation (Harlen, 1999; Hofstein and Lunetta, 1982; Lunetta, 1998):

• Experiments should be challenging. The purposes and goals of the experiments have to be clear to the students.

- Experiments primarily aim at understanding. This implies that students have to work with an idea. It is not the objective to have students merely manipulate equipment.
- Students need the option to plan and interpret their own experiments. Students should not just follow cookbook-like recipes.
- An adequate control over the plan of the work has to be ensured.
- Experiments should encourage self-directed work.
- Planning, execution, analysis as well as the products of laboratory work should elicit experiences of competency for students.

Schools which decided to improve the understanding of scientific processes find a framework for the next steps within the description of Module 2 as well as in additional material. This frame also provides the teachers with a language to communicate about specific aspects of scientific work applied in classroom instruction.

Typically, the groups of colleagues begin their work by setting priorities and deciding which aspects should be dealt with. They identify specific problems, they encountered with practical work and reflect on the use of experiments by using didactical criteria as presented e.g. in the description of *Module 2*. The colleagues identify experiments considered central to their course. Together, they clarify which experiments are better suited for teacher demonstrations and which experiments should be carried out by the students themselves. Teachers report their experiences after testing these new approaches. They reflect on effective ways to integrate experiments, and discuss, for example, under what conditions the experiments are suited best.

In a similar way, other methods of scientific work (e. g. the comparative method as a mode of scientific inquiry in biology instruction) are also encouraged by *Module 2*.

Collaboration and quality development

The program is school- and teacher-based. At school level, processes of quality control and quality development are introduced and supported. Research findings on school innovation show that changes of professional actions occur primarily if they are accepted by the teachers (Brown, 1997; Knapp, 1997; Stake et al., 1997; Anderson and Helms, 1999) and that these new approaches will only work successfully when they become part of the teachers' routines. The aim is an evolutionary development of teachers' views and routines, but also of the lesson scripts shared by teachers and students.

Generally, co-operation among teachers is not very common at German schools (Terhart, 1987) and so an important feature of the program is to encourage co-operation among them, especially those teaching mathematics and science. Examples of occasions, structures and support for collaboration have to be offered. Co-operation includes collaboration within schools and within a network of schools in which every school is embedded. It concerns the joint development of new ideas and materials as well as the collaborative evaluation and documentation of results.

Significantly, the program relies on the constructive, inventive and active participation of the teachers. First of all they need an understanding of the problems they are confronted with in their classroom or school. They also have to develop ideas for possible solutions, helpful materials or instruments. As experiences from teacher training or school innovation approaches show, teachers without such a comprehension will fail when they try to apply available tools, tasks, instructional techniques, or materials.

Organisation

The program began in 1998, with 180 schools from different federal states participating. The schools are organised in 30 so-called 'school sets', i.e. networks of six schools which co-operate closely. Every school set is supported and organised by a co-ordinator. The co-ordinators are released from half of their normal teaching duties, and stay in contact with the whole network. The participating teachers are given a small amount of reduction in their normal teaching duties.

Different approaches to evaluation in the program

Evaluation plays a key role in the pilot program. The different evaluation approaches each serve different functions and can be used at different levels. These approaches comprise (a) formative evaluation by the teachers themselves, (b) studies on the acceptance of the program, (c) studies on implementation and (d) summative evaluation. An overview of these four approaches will be given, followed by a more detailed description of the second approach, the studies on implementation.

(a) Formative evaluation by the teachers

One of the goals of the program is directed at familiarising teachers with simple yet useful evaluation procedures. These can be used to test whether or not the newly developed tasks or teaching approaches are suitable and useful. The teachers, however, should not examine their lessons like empirical researchers with sophisticated designs and instruments. The emphasis should be placed on easily applied investigation techniques and on procedures of peer evaluation. In order to profit (to be able to learn) from formative evaluation it is necessary to document procedures and results in a systematic way. Short summaries of the results and possible recommendations or consequences for further work or use in class are sufficient. Naturally, the possibilities of collaborating at school and through the school networks are excellent for exchanging new developments and for mutual evaluation. Formative evaluation thus is a crucial part of the teachers' professional development that the program intends to instigate.

(b) Evaluation studies on the acceptance of the program

A second level of evaluation refers to the co-ordination of the pilot program and the provision of support. Studies are undertaken to find out to what extent the teachers identify themselves with the program and its aims, accept the provided support and express criticism and special needs concerning future assistance. In order to answer these questions we conducted a survey at the 180 participating schools in 2000. The information obtained from this study led to a better understanding of which value different resources had for the teachers. The program coordinators received important advice on possibilities to provide materials, which seem to be most helpful for the teachers' work. The data also indicated that local and central coordinators play different roles concerning the consultation. It seemed to be helpful to discern the different functions, and to foster the cooperation between the local (set and school level) and the central (program level) coordinators.

(c) Research on implementation

A third level concerns the implementation. It is of great interest to find which school characteristics and which kind of activities and support by the regional and central coordinators are essential or critical for successful implementation (Fullan, 2001). It is also an aim of such analyses to identify crucial conditions for the realisation of quality development, and for the possible dissemination of the program conception beyond the schools involved in the pilot phase. Research on implementation is not only a crucial tool for the program coordinators to learn but is supposed to result in important scientific insights concerning program implementation. We will look at this area of research and describe it in more detail in a seperate section.

(d) Summative evaluation

Finally, the success and the effectiveness of the program has to be studied critically. The summative evaluation has to study the impact of the program on the expertise of the teachers, measuring the collaborative quality control and development in the schools, and the development of students' competence and interest in science and mathematics. In spring 2000, a baseline data collection was carried out drawing on questionnaires from PISA and additional national test intruments which had been developed by experts from the German PISA-Consortium (Klieme et al., 2001; Prenzel et al., 2001). The data collection in 2000 investigated the schools "starting conditions" in comparison to a representative reference group of German PISA-Schools. In 2003 a second data collection took place in which the program schools were included in the second assessment cycle of PISA to enable program coordinators to estimate developments of student performance, interest, teacher professionalism and processes of quality development twice (with a span of three years).

How research on implementation can be realised: An example

Investigations of the implementation of the program in the schools, for example, on conditions that support or hamper the process of putting the aims of the program into practice are an essential part of the evaluation. From a theoretical perspective it is of interest which characteristics of the participating schools and teachers and which kinds of activities and support by the regional (set of schools) and central coordinators are essential for the program to be successful (Fullan, 2001). It is the aim of the implementation studies to gain information on the conditions needed to implement the concept of quality development beyond the schools involved in the project.

Questions concerning conditions and processes of implementation were part of the survey in 2000. Besides the question concerning the acceptance (use and evaluation of support), teachers were asked to describe or rate how content they were with their engagement, in which way they were cooperating on different levels and to what extent they could perceive a development of competence or interest amongst both students and teachers. Also included in the survey were scales which referred to the professional experience relating to the standards of teaching (Oser, 1997). Finally, teachers were asked which needs they had concerning future support and assistance by the program coordinators. In the following section, data from this part of the questionnaire will be briefly reported and discussed to give an example of the kind of implementation research in the program (Ostermeier and Prenzel, 2002).

The investigation of the use of resources and the needs for further support was interesting for two reasons. First, we wanted to have feedback from teachers to optimise the resources of support and for the further steering of the program. Second, we wanted to obtain indicators for how teachers accept a program relying heavily on self-directed planning, problem-solving and individual as well as collective use of learning opportunities. In the questionnaire, teachers were, therefore, asked to rate to what degree they would need more of the following aspects: autonomy for program work, supply of written materials, more training meetings, more possibilities of mutual exchange, precise instructions and an exact determination of the goals for the program-work at one's school.

The data showed an ambiguous picture of needs (Table 1). Nearly half of the teachers expressed needs for more degrees of freedom, more resources, more conferences, chances for exchange or more prescription of goals and ways, whereas the other half seemed to have opposite ideas or wishes.

need for ...	I strongly disagree	I disagree	I agree	I strongly agree
... more autonomy for program work	136	199	94	64
... more written materials	67	118	161	161
... more in-service meetings	76	193	131	97
... more possibilities for mutual exchange	76	161	167	105
... more precise prescription to program work	85	172	152	97
... more precise prescription of goals	91	160	145	110

Table 1: Needs of teachers concerning future support and assistance from central program coordinators (answered by participating teachers, N = 557, frequencies)

From a coordinator's point of view these data are puzzling. There is no clear message of how to proceed. However, such a data set are well suited for data analysis which could help identify different sub-groups or types regarding patterns of needs.

A latent class analysis (Lazarsfeld and Henry, 1968) resulted in three groups of teachers who differ significantly in the amount of assistance required (Figure 1). Differences concern, for example, the extent of further materials needed, the need for precise instructions and a detailed setting of goals for the work within the program. We interpreted the classes in the light of the implementation strategy. In this respect, the first group of teachers (Group A 'explorative'; size: 48.4 %) seems to get along rather well with a conception that relies heavily on the self-directed work of the participating teachers. This group seems to be widely content with the support measures provided. The profiles of the remaining two groups (Groups B 'guidance-oriented' and C 'input-oriented'; sizes: 29.9 %, 21.7 %) seem to indicate more problems with this conception. Characteristics of both of these groups are that needs for precise instruction and for a detailed setting of goals as well as needs for further supply of materials are much more pronounced than within the first group mentioned.

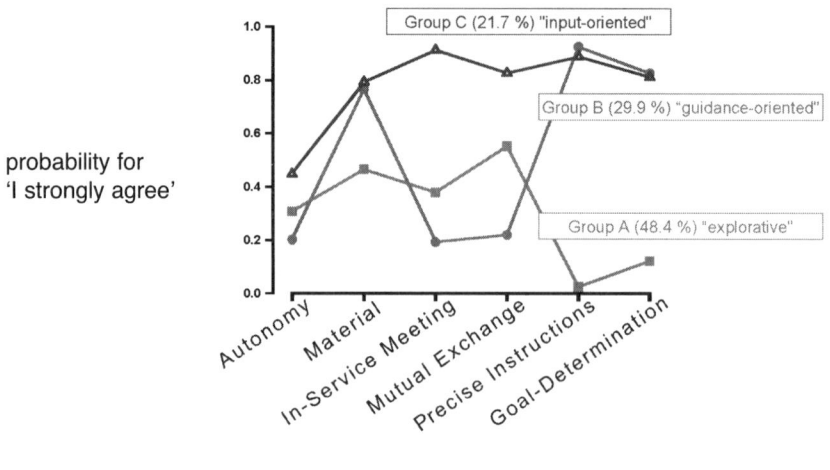

Figure 1: Teachers' needs for additional support (groups identified by LCA; Group sizes indicated in percent)

Further data analysis connected the teachers' actual use of support measures with these three patterns of needs. Our interpretation of the latent classes was validated in that the group most content with the current support is actually using the support measures to a higher degree than either of the other groups (differences for use of written outlines, $F(2,446) = 4.077$, $p < .05$). This group of teachers invests a greater amount of time in program activities as well, $F(2,433) = 8.166$, $p < .01$. In order to identify crucial conditions that might have an influence on the different patterns of needs, we found a significant relationship between the different groups and the perception of local coordination acitivities. The groups differed, for instance, in perceived support of autonomy, $F(2,427) = 5.289$, $p < .01$, and the perceived support of social relatedness through the coordinator, $F(2,422) = 8.054$, $p < .01$ (Ryan and Deci, 2000). In every case, the first group of teachers (48.4 %) seems to perceive the local coordination more positively than either of the other two groups.

What can we learn from these findings? The data show that there are relevant differences among the teachers working in the program that may have a strong impact on their engagement. With respect to the program's implementation strategy, the teachers are at different levels of understanding learning and teaching as well as their own role in the process of quality development.

The program coordinators have to consider such differences and they have to reflect on differential support for the different groups (types) of teachers. The findings indicate that coordinators at the local level serving the small school networks play a crucial role in supporting the work at the schools. At local level, they are able to determine the different needs of teachers. Differential treatments concern areas such as personal consultation, the design of in-service training meetings and the delivery of material. If the coordinator recognises teachers are having difficulties with an aspect of the program, a more intensive form of consultation may be necessary. Among others, the coordinator could encourage teachers to try out new methods that are more easily applied. Starting with easier approaches makes success more likely and raises the possibility that the teachers begin to feel more secure and competent with the innovation. It is important that the local coordinators convey the support that teachers need and communicate that information to the central program coordinators.

Conclusion

The quality development program aims to improve mathematics and science instruction systematically. It focuses on typical groups of problems that are treated using the eleven modules. One important characteristic of the program is the close cooperation at different levels – from teachers in individual schools to the groups (sets) of schools and beyond that to nationwide (including virtual) networks. The various forms of evaluation provide feedback for participants at the different levels and indicate where something needs to be done. The participating teachers and schools, the coordinators, the researchers and the decision-makers profit from the evaluation, each in his or her own way. Of course, how the evaluation is carried out influences what can be learned from it. In principle the evaluation tied with the feedback is not only a procedure to assure quality, it is also an important factor in school efficiency (Scheerens, 2000).

From the program coordinator's perspective, evaluation naturally has other additional functions. It also serves to legitimate the program and/or the (politically made) investments in the program. A pilot program must, of course, be critically and methodologically tested for its effect. It is a question of testing a package of measures that could possibly be carried out on a wide scale with a lot of effort and expense. Dissemination only makes sense when the program is successful under normal school conditions or when important pre-conditions for its implementation are known. Knowledge about such prerequisites and conditions can, on the other hand, be obtained within the framework of accompanying studies. We, therefore, hope to obtain scientifically important results from the evaluation research in this program that will enable further development of the quality of instruction and learning in mathematics and science education.

References

Anderson, R. D. and Helms, J. V. (1999). The ideal of standards and the reality of schools: Needed reaearch. *Journal of Research in Science Teaching*, 38, 3-16.

Baumert, J., Bos, W. and Lehmann, R. (Eds.). (2000). *TIMSS/III. Dritte Internationale Mathematik- und Naturwissenschaftsstudie. Mathematisch und naturwissenschaftliche Bildung am Ende der Schullaufbahn. Band 1 [TIMSS/III. Mathematics and science literacy at the end of school education. Volume 1]*. Opladen: Leske + Budrich.

Baumert, J. and Köller, O. (2000). Unterrichtsgestaltung, verständnisvolles Lernen und multiple Zielerreichung im Mathematik- und Physikunterricht der gymnasialen Oberstufe. In J. Baumert, et al., (Ed.), *TIMSS/III*. Band 2 (pp. 271-315). Opladen: Leske + Budrich.

Baumert, J., Lehmann, R., Lehrke, M., Schmitz, B., Clausen, M., Hosenfeld, I., Köller, O. and Neubrand, J. (1997). *TIMSS – Mathematisch-naturwissenschaftlicher Unterricht im internationalen Vergleich. Deskriptive Befunde [TIMSS – Mathematics and science instruction in international comparison. Descriptive findings]*. Opladen: Leske + Budrich.

Beaton, A. E., Martin, M. O., Mullis, I. V. S., Gonzales, E. J., Smith, T. A. and Kelly, D. L. (1996a). *Science achievement in the middle school years: IEA's Third International Mathematics and Science Study (TIMSS)*. Chestnut Hill: Boston College.

Beaton, A. E., Mullis, I. V. S., Martin, M. O., Gonzales, E. J., Kelly, D. L. and Smith, T. A. (1996b). *Mathematics achievement in the middle school years: IEA's Third International Mathematics and Science Study (TIMSS)*. Chestnut Hill: Boston College.

BLK (Ed.). (1997). *Gutachten zur Vorbereitung des Programms „Steigerung der Effizienz des mathematisch-naturwissenschaftlichen Unterrichts" [Expertise "Increasing the efficiency of mathematics and science instruction"]*. Bonn: BLK [Federal and State Commission for Educational Planning and Research].

Brown, A. L. (1997). Transforming schools into communities of thinking and learning about serious matters. *American Psychologist*, 52, 399-413.

Fullan, M. (2001). *The new meaning of educational change*. New York: Teachers College Press.

Harlen, W. (1999). *Effective teaching of science – A research review*. Edinburgh: SCRE.

Hofstein, A. and Lunetta, V. N. (1982). The role of laboratory in science teaching: Neglected aspects of research. *Review of Educational Research,* 52, 201-217.

Klieme, E., Neubrand, M. and Lüdtke, O. (2001). Mathematische Grundbildung: Testkonzeption und Ergebnisse [Mathematical literacy: Test-conception and results]. In J. Baumert, et al. (Ed.), *PISA 2000: Basiskompetenzen von Schülerinnen und Schülern im internationalen Vergleich* (pp. 139-190). Opladen: Leske + Budrich.

Knapp, M. S. (1997). Between systemic reforms and the mathematics and science classroom: The dynamics of innovation, implementation, and professional learning. *Review of Educational Research* 67, 227-266.

Lazarsfeld, P. F. and Henry, N. W. (1968). *Latent Structure Analysis.* Boston: Houghton Mifflin.

Lunetta, V. (1998). The school science laboratory: historical perspectives and contexts for contemporary teaching. In B. Fraser and K. Tobin (Eds.), *International handbook of science education* (pp. 249-262). Dordrecht: Kluwer.

Mullis, I. V. S., Martin, M. O., Beaton, A. E., Gonzales, E. J., Kelly, D. L. and Smith, T. A. (1998). *Mathematics and science achievement in the final year of secondary school: IEA's Third International Mathematics and Sciency Study (TIMSS).* Chestnut Hill: Boston College.

Oser, F. (1997). Standards in der Lehrerbildung. Teil 1: Berufliche Kompetenzen, die hohen Qualitätsmerkmalen entsprechen [Standards in teacher education. Part 1: Professional competencies that meet high quality characteristics]. *Beiträge zur Lehrerbildung,* 15 26 - 37.

Ostermeier, C. and Prenzel, M. (2002, April). Opportunities for teachers to learn: A study investigating teachers' acceptance of support measures within a national quality development program. Paper presented at the Annual Meeting of the AERA, New Orleans.

Prenzel, M. (1997). Sechs Möglichkeiten, Lernende zu demotivieren [Six possibilities to demotivate learners]. In H. Gruber and A. Renkl (Eds.), *Wege zum Können. Determinanten des Kompetenzerwerbs* (pp. 32-44). Bern: Huber.

Prenzel, M. (2000). Steigerung der Effizienz des mathematisch-naturwissenschaftlichen Unterrichts: Ein Modellversuchsprogramm von Bund und Ländern [Increasing the efficiency of mathematics and science education: A nationwide quality development program]. *Unterrichtswissenschaft,* 28, 103-126.

Prenzel, M. and Duit, R. (2000, April). Increasing the efficiency of science and mathematics instruction: Report of a national quality development program. Paper presented at the Annual Meeting of the NARST, New Orleans.

Prenzel, M., Rost, J., Senkbeil, M., Häußler, P. and Klopp, A. (2001). Naturwissenschaftliche Grundbildung: Testkonzeption und Ergebnisse [Scientific literacy: Test-conception and results]. In J. Baumert, et al., (Ed.), *PISA 2000: Basiskompetenzen von Schülerinnen und Schülern im internationalen Vergleich* (pp. 191-248). Opladen: Leske + Budrich.

Ryan, R. M. and Deci, E. L. (2000). Intrinsic and extrinsic motivations: Classic definitions and new directions. *Contemporary Educational Psychology*, 25, 54-67.

Scheerens, J. (2000). Improving school effectiveness. Paris: UNESCO: IIEP.

Seidel, T., Prenzel, M., Duit, R., Euler, M., Geiser, H., Hoffmann, l., Lehrke, M., Müller, C. T. and Rimmele, R. (2002). „Jetzt bitte alle nach vorne schauen!" – Lehr-Lernskripts im Physikunterricht und damit verbundene Bedingungen für individuelle Lernprozesse ["Can everybody look to the front please?" – Patterns of instruction in elementary physics classrooms and its implications for students' learning]. *Unterrichtswissenschaft*, 30, 52-77.

Stake, R., Burke, M., Flôres, C., Whiteaker, M. and Irizarry, K. (1997). *Renewal and transformation*. Chicago: Teachers Academy for Mathematics and Science.

Stigler, J. W., Gonzales, P., Kawanaka, T., Knoll, S. and Serrano, A. (1999). *The TIMSS videotape classroom study. Methods and findings from an exploratory research project on eighth-grade mathematics instruction in Germany, Japan, and the United States*. Washington, D.C.: U.S. Department of Education.

Terhart, E. (1987). Kommunikation im Kollegium [Communication among teachers]. *Die deutsche Schule*, 79, 440-450.

Chapter 10

Teachers' transformations of innovations: The case of visual language

Jaume Ametller[*a] *and Roser Pintó*

CRECIM, Universitat Autònoma de Barcelona, Campus de Bellaterra, Edifici G5, 08193 Bellaterra, Barcelona, Spain

Summary

What is the innovation? Inclusion of a set of images representing energy-related concepts in an innovative teaching sequence for secondary school students.

What need does it address? The idea that the teachers' use of images included in instructional material will affect the effectiveness of any innovation.

What is its scope? The images were included in materials designed for research purposes within the framework of an European Research Project. The resorces were used by seven teachers in their secondary school science courses.

What evaluation data have been collected? The data included three different sources: namely, video recordings of 49 classes, notes collected by researchers during the observation of 22 classes and interviews with the teachers conducted after implementation of the material.

What are the key findings? The analysis of the teachers' transformations of the proposed innovative images revealed that they appear to have had both problems of comprehension of some scientific concepts and problems using visual language. This provides important information to curriculum designers and teacher trainers about both concerns. The results were used in an analysis across three kinds of innovations and five countries within the framework of the Project to obtain generalisable results concerning transformations.

[a] At present at CSSME, School of Education, University of Leeds, Leeds LS2 9JT, UK

Introducing curriculum innovations as a transformative communication process

Putting a curriculum innovation into practice involves a process of communication between designers and teachers. Whether or not teachers are closely involved in the design of the innovation, once designed, the innovation has to be "communicated" to the teachers who will implement it. This can be done by different means ranging from handing them written material to organising training courses. In any case, the communication process does not end here. The teachers have to interpret the material and the instructions given by the designers to adapt them to their own teaching style before implementing the innovation in the classroom. This process of adaptation often has two distinct phases. In the first phase, teachers act as receivers of innovations. This is not a mere transmission of information; it involves understanding the content of the innovation according to the teachers' ideas on the different aspects of the information contained in the innovation. It entails a first kind of transformation that has to do with aspects such as the teachers' knowledge of the subject and their particular interests. Once the teachers have decoded the information contained in the innovation and thereby created their own version of it, they have to adapt and recode it for transmission to students. Teachers do this on the basis of their beliefs on how to teach science and on the needs of the specific group of students with whom they have to implement the innovation. This second phase of transformation is related to the issues usually addressed in teacher-training courses while the first one is often neglected.

The teachers' transformations do not have to be considered as being something to be avoided or eliminated. On the contrary, these transformations are embedded in the process of communication and should be considered essential because teachers have to be involved in the implementation of the innovation. However, some of the transformations can be incompatible with the intentions of the material to the point of "ruining" the innovation. A better understanding of how and what teachers transform when faced with an innovation might be useful to minimise the risk of this happening.

The use of (multimodal) language: a general underlying element of any science curriculum innovation.

It is widely accepted that the use of language is an important aspect of teaching and learning science. Curriculum innovations might not be focused on this aspect but, in any case, cannot avoid it. When designing materials or activities, choices in relation to the use of language have to be made. In many cases, introducing a new conceptual treatment cannot be dissociated from a new treatment of the language used to teach. In the case of science education, this involves taking into account different modes of communication, verbal, mathematical and visual language, since science can be considered a multimodal activity.

In the context of the Information Society, visual representation has become an important channel for transmitting information. This way of encoding information is coming into the classroom through new materials and IT tools, and science instructional material is making increasing use of images in communicating ideas rather than just illustrating the written text.

The framework of the research: the STTIS project

The STTIS (Science Teachers Training in an Information Society) was a European-founded research project involving five research teams. The research spanned over three years and was motivated by the hypothesis that teachers are nowadays undergoing a process of changes that places new demands on them (Pintó et al., 2001a, 2001b).

The general aim of the STTIS project was to study how secondary school physics teachers adapt certain innovations proposed to them. The STTIS project focused on three kinds of innovations, namely those related to:

1. the use of IT tools
2. the use of visual representations
3. the introduction, treatment, sequencing and selection of scientific concepts.

In the following sections, we will focus on some of the results on the teachers' use of some innovative visual representations analysed by the team of the Universitat Autònoma de Barcelona.

The curricular innovation: visual representations of energy concepts

The images used in our research were designed to be an integral part of an innovative teaching sequence on energy. Energy-related concepts are seldom visually represented in traditional instructional material. Therefore, the teachers that implemented the sequence were presented with images that were innovative as regards their specific design, the conceptual approach they represent, and the fact that they were used to teach a concept for which images are seldom used.

The instructional material included several visual representations. For the sake of brevity, we will only describe the case of the proposed visual representations of the concepts of system and surroundings.

The proposed images: visual representations of the systems and surroundings

The designers wanted to provide visual representations that could be used as meaningful tools to enhance the teaching/learning process of scientific contents. This means that the message transmitted by the images had to represent faithfully the scientific ideas as they were approached in the sequence, avoiding reinforcing the alternative conceptions described earlier (Duit, 1985; Pintó, 1991). Once the exact message that was to be transmitted (semantics of the message) had been defined, the designers encoded it into a specific image (the grammar of the message) following the rules of visual semiotics. This process took into account other aspects such as the scientific and mathematical background of the students to whom the images were addressed. In this sense, the designers had the hypothesis that in the context of a comprehensive educational system, where science courses are offered to a wide range of students, some of them with little proficiency in mathematics and more used to receiving information through images, a set of well-designed visual representations could be a good means to introduce and structure concepts, when aiming for a less mechanical and more conceptual approach.

The conceptual difficulties addressed by the images.

It is only possible to say that energy is conserved in closed systems or when considering the open system and its environment together. Understanding and using these concepts properly will help to foster the correct conceptualisation of energy conservation that is one of the most important ideas to acquire not just in secondary school science education but also for the scientific literacy of the population (Solomon, 1983, Duit, 1985, Pintó, 1991).

The choice of graphical symbols to represent the concepts.

In literature, rectangles are often used as the graphical representation of systems. We have chosen rounded rectangles to add the idea of 'natural' systems as opposed to man-made, technological ones (Arnheim, 1984) to represent the concepts of system and environment. Two different representations have been chosen (Figures 1 and 2).

Figure 1 was used to introduce the concepts while Figure 2 was intended to be used when representing energy transfer chains. In the first case, the absence of arrows and the compositional structure of the document establishes a static analytical context reinforcing the idea of a thermodynamic universe composed of a system and its surroundings. In the second representation, the icons representing both concepts are spatially separated and the arrows between them convey the idea of system and surroundings as actors in a process, the energy transfer (Kress and van Leeuwen, 1996). Placing the surroundings below the system instead of encircling it aims at fostering the idea of energy transfers to the surroundings as being the same thing rather than a transfer to "another system" and is thus in contrast to the idea of losing energy, which is often associated with environmental pollution.

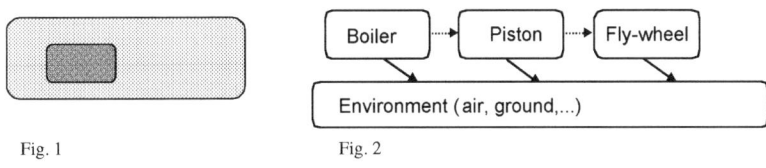

Fig. 1   Fig. 2

Figures 1 and 2:   The two representations of the system and environment concepts proposed to the teachers. The second is used in images representing energy transfer chains

Evaluating the innovation: teachers' transformations

The aim of our research was not to evaluate the teaching/learning outcomes but to analyse the teachers' use of the images. That is, our evaluation was not focused on whether the innovative visual representations work better than others in the process of teaching/learning energy concepts. Rather, we are interested in how teachers use the images, by taking for granted that this use would have a transformative nature. To stress the focus on the transformations, the results do not focus on teachers' case studies but on the way specific images were used by different teachers.

In turn, this facilitates their comparison to results obtained with other images and even with transformations of other kinds of innovations studied within the framework of the STTIS project.

Our analysis is based on the description of the transformed images, comparing the scientific messages which they convey with those intended in the images in the designed instructional material. To what extent these transformations affect the aims intended by the designers will affect the evaluation of the innovative teaching sequence, and thus will help establish the co-ordinates for the evaluation of the whole innovation.

Research questions

We can thus formulate the following research questions:

What transformations do teachers make in the images representing the concepts of system and environment proposed to them?

Why do they transform them as they do and what do these transformations imply?

Theoretical background sustaining the analysis of the teachers' use of the images

Science teaching is a multimodal activity (Jewitt et al., 2001), i.e. the teacher creates the scientific meaning through the integration of different communication modes. Since visual language is one of the communicative modes of the multimodal language of science, the teachers' drawings can be considered quotes of their use of language in a similar way to their verbal language quotes. The joint analysis of both sources of complementary and compatible data can enlighten the understanding of the conceptual implications of the detected transformations in the proposed documents.

The extent to which conclusions are entailed by the collected evidence could become especially controversial in our work, since it involves the analysis of a data source with less tradition than interviews or tests in science education research, namely images. This requires the need to be able to process systematically the visual language (Saussure, 1971; Eco 1985). According to the social semiotic school that informed our research (Halliday, 1978, Kress and van Leeuwen, 1996), we consider a picture the physical representation (grammar), the expression of a specific idea (semantics). The relationship between these two aspects of one and the same message (an image in our case) is such that any change in either of the levels will be accompanied by a change in the other. This implies that any transformation in the proposed images at the grammatical level, that is, when a teacher has changed the appearance of the image, is to be associated with a change on the semantic level, in the *signification* of the message. In this sense, we assume that there are several ways of communicating an abstract physical concept such as system and surroundings. Any of these ways imply a certain choice of a semantic structure founded in aspects such as the abstract scientific concept, the audience to which the message is intended and so on. This choice will determine a specific grammar structure, such as a specific image or verbal explanation. Therefore, the proposed images represent the particular semantic structure reflecting the intentions of the designers. Some of the aspects of this semantic structure constitute the core intentions. The "problematic" transformations are those that do not contain these core intentions in their semantic structure, and therefore make it impossible, for example, to reconstruct the abstract accepted scientific concepts represented by the images.

The teachers' answers to a post-implementation interview provided information on relation to their view on the images and on how they worked as teaching tools. This information may give some insight on the sources of the two kinds of transformations considered: their conceptual understanding and their views on teaching and learning science. Contrasting the information coming from the interviews and the hypothesis drawn from the analysis of the teachers' use in the classroom of the multimodal language may provide a way of validating the conclusions.

Data collection

Seven teachers used the proposed images, included in a didactical sequence on energy, in their secondary school (15–17 years old) science classes. Some written recommendations on the use of images were given to them before the start of the classes.

The data were collected for the analysis through:

1. Observations of the classes. Some classes of the teachers of the sample were observed directly during 22 hours of classes.

2. Video recordings of 49 classes. The classes were video-recorded. An important and extremely delicate sources of data were the videotapes of the images drawn on classroom blackboards.

3. Interviews of the teachers after implementation of the sequence.

Analysis of the transformations

The teachers who implemented the instructional material used the proposed images in different ways. In some cases, they chose not to use them at all and in other cases they used the images as proposed by the designers but we have not studied these situations. However, in many cases teachers made significant transformations as we discuss in the following sections

Omitting the visual representation of the environment

When using the proposed visual representations of an energy transfer chain, teachers often leave out the graphical representation of the surroundings. In this case, the transformed image no longer conveys the information related to this concept (Fig. 3)

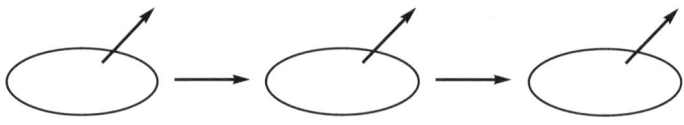

Figur 3: Omission of the surroundings in the visual representation of an energy transfer chain

The choice of the information not present in a message is very important. The omitted information reveals what the transmitter considers unnecessary for the receiver to understand the message (Halliday, 1978), either because the transmitter assumes that it is known by the receiver, or because the transmitter considers this information unnecessary to communicate the message.

The first option would imply that the teacher takes for granted that students will be able to reconstruct the concept of the surroundings when decoding the message. The second option would mean that the disappearance of the surroundings stems from the idea that this concept is unnecessary for the understanding of the message.

Furthermore, the related video-recordings show that teachers who omit the environment usually speak vaguely about the environment as the place where the 'lost' energy goes. Cross-checking the data coming from the visual and the verbal explanations, and considering that the environment is a concept seldom explained to students, it is reasonable to think that the omission of the environment is connected to the second option: Teachers seem to consider the concept of the surroundings unnecessary when explaining the concept of energy transfer chain.

According to Kress and van Leeuwen (1996), arrows are visual elements with a verbal meaning, an action that an actor does on another one. Once the visual representation of the surroundings has been omitted, the arrows originally representing the energy transfer from the system to the surroundings become action without a goal, i.e., an action that the actor-system does on an invisible goal. This transformed image might be read as systems transferring energy to some unknown place and thus energy is being lost. Therefore, this image reinforces the idea that there is a loss of energy associated with energy transfers between systems. This is one of the ideas that the designers wanted to avoid when designing the proposed image. As one teacher said to his students:

> *The important thing is to indicate with an arrow, or by any other means, that some energy is lost*

The teacher clearly states that energy is being lost. Significantly enough, only the energy transferred from the systems to the surroundings is the only energy being lost by the system; therefore they are not treated as open systems. Furthermore, the teacher does not say where the lost energy goes and he does not even name the surroundings. A similar misconception appears in the interview with another teacher, when asked about the energy transfer chains:

The energy chains are OK, but the arrows go out and go nowhere

It has also been observed that, along different class sessions, once teachers have eliminated the graphical representation of the environment, they also leave out the arrows representing the energy transfers from the systems to the environment (Fig. 4)

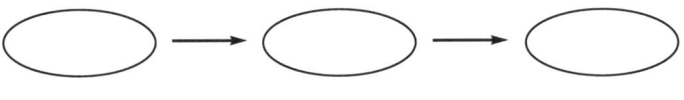

Figure 4:   Omission of the energy transfers to the surroundings

This seems to suggest that the disappearance of the graphical representation of the surroundings might lead to the omission of the arrows representing energy transfers from the system.

The disappearance of these arrows connected to the omission of the surroundings changes completely the scope of the image by making it impossible to introduce the concept of energy conservation, which is stressed in the teaching sequence.

Some teachers do not acknowledge the proposed representation as a good means of talking about energy conservation. When asked if the representation of the energy transfer chains was helpful at introducing/teaching energy conservation, the teachers clearly have this view:

When using the diagrams, the energy conservation concept does not work anymore. (…) That of conservation is never clear to them (…) maybe because it is not bordered, or something like that.

These teachers seem to suggest that energy conservation can only be explained with inclusive surroundings. They had used this type of representation in an earlier lesson to introduce the concept of system-surroundings, but now they seem unable to understand the new representation. This way of reasoning might help to explain the transformation studied in the next section.

In brief, by considering that only the energy transferred to the surroundings is lost by the system, teachers are changing the meaning of the open system. Moreover by not talking about the surroundings, they make it impossible to speak about energy conservation. From this analysis, it can be concluded that the omission of the graphical representation of the environment seriously affects the rationale of the innovative teaching sequence.

Attaching a topographical meaning to the environment

In some classes it has been observed that a topographical character is assigned to the environment, that is to say, information concerning a real physical space is improperly attributed to the environment. In these cases, it is possible to speak properly of a significant transformation from the semantic standpoint.

In the energy transfer chain representation, this transformation consisted of using the visual representation of the surroundings proposed in Figure1. In this visual representation, systems are drawn 'inside' the environment, instead of separated as it was proposed in Figure 2.

Though in such cases the image has clearly been changed, its analysis is not conclusive concerning the relation of the effect of the transformation and the concept of surroundings. This effect becomes clearer when the teacher using such representation of the surroundings include arrows representing energy transfers outside the surroundings Figure 5).

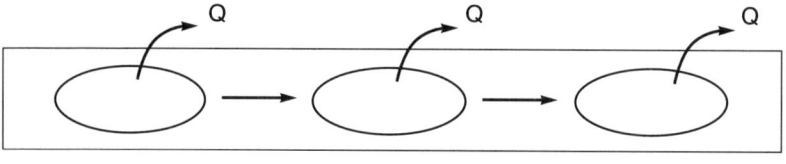

Figure 5: Transferring energy outside of the inclusive surroundings

Some explanations accompanying the blackboard image provide evidence for the following view. When explaining the energy transfers in an industrial process, a teacher considered that energy becomes dispersed in the air inside the factory, the air being its surroundings. But to continue this explanation, the teacher told the students that this energy would finally heat up the air outside the factory. Instead of redefining the surroundings, the teacher indicated this new energy transfer as taking place outside the surroundings.

The existence of energy transfers outside the rectangle representing the surroundings clearly indicates that the large box is not considered the representation of the thermodynamic limits of the universe, that are unsurpassable by definition, but a topographical concept of the physical space around the systems (as was already suggested in a previous quote).

In some cases, the transformed image reinforced the idea of energy losses. That was especially stressed by placing the symbol of heat (Q) at the end of the arrows, wrongly but commonly considered an 'energy form'.

> *This wasted energy is what you (the students) say is going to the surroundings or heating up the apparatus*

These transformations of the graphical representations appear to confirm the relation between the teachers' use of scientific concepts and their graphical representation of these concepts.

Discussion

The analysis supports the idea that changes have occurred to the aims intended by the designers for the images as well as for the teaching sequence in which they were integrated. The designed images aim to provide visual representations to foster the establishment of connections among several related concepts, those that come into play when trying to make sense of energy transfers between systems. By omitting the surroundings, or the arrows representing energy transfers from the systems to the surroundings, or using topographical representations of the environment, multimodal explanations by the teachers focus on just some of the represented ideas. Subsequently, with such transformations, the explanatory capabilities of the visual representations become reduced to explain a few concepts separately. Thus, there is an important gap between the proposed and the implemented curriculum that jeopardises the effectiveness of the innovation.

When looking at the teacher transformations described above, it is unclear to what extent these transformations should be attributed to the teachers' lack of knowledge of the visual language. There is no doubt about the fact that teachers do not necessarily master the grammar of the visual language, but it seems to be equally clear that, just as it happens with the verbal language, a lack of theoretical knowledge does not imply not being able to use it. In any case, whatever the cause of the transformation, the effects on the message conveyed by the images are the same.

The results also suggest that the methodology followed and the theoretical framework chosen has been useful. We have found a good degree of agreement on the analysis drawn from the different sources of data that have been obtained in this study. The analysis has enabled us to study the teachers' use of the visual language and evaluating its consequences on the effectiveness of the innovation. It has been particularly helpful at eliciting some of the teachers' conceptual problems underlying their performance and it may also provide insight on the sources of transformations relative to teachers' views on the process of teaching and learning.

Generality of the results: General trends arising from the transformations

So far, the analysis of the teachers transformations exposed in this study has been restricted to two specific images used in the STTIS project, which is a small part of the research on images conducted by the Barcelona research team. A broader picture of how teachers adapt innovations is obtained when taking into account the transformations observed in five countries when implementing three types of innovations.

Obviously, these transformations have a lot to do with personal characteristics of each teacher. It seems reasonable to think that there might be some commonalities among different teachers in their way of adapting information. In the STTIS project, a cross analysis of the outcomes of the different pieces of research was conducted allowed the detection of common features of the transformations and, in turn, to find general trends of transformation and innovations (Pintó et al., 2001). The results of the STTIS project clarify why these commonalities exist but they show reasonable evidence of plausible mechanisms of transformation.

Implications for the design and evaluation of curriculum innovations

The results reinforce the assumption that the implemented innovation will be different from the designed one. These transformations are an essential part of the communication process and further, they are a fundamental part of teaching because they underlie the capacity to adapt the teaching process to changing situations. It is neither feasible nor desirable that science teachers act as mere driving belts of the proposed innovations. In the light of such considerations, effectiveness, meaning a high level of consistency between the intended curriculum and the implemented curriculum (Goodlad et al.,1979), becomes more complicated.

Understanding how and why teachers adapt the innovations in the way they do might be useful when establishing to what extent it can be said that the designed innovation is fruitful or not. We think that a better understanding of how teachers transform the language used in the instructional material gives valuable information on how this affects the effectiveness of the innovation itself, thus providing a valuable element for any evaluation, which is concerned about why do innovations work as they do.

The research results could help designers when making a specific choice on the use of language in the instructional material and on more general aspects of the design of instructional material. Curriculum developers have to play an active role in proposing images that can be used as effective teaching/learning tools in the classroom and avoiding the design of visual representations that are guided mainly by aesthetic criteria, which undermines the conceptual message that they should convey.

Furthermore, the results suggest that the relevance of these features and their (foreseen) implications in the teaching/learning process should be made very clear to teachers through training sessions, prior to the implementation of any curricular innovation. The transformations are not to be avoided but their effects could be modulated through a conscious transmission of their aims to the teachers. Taking into consideration aspects referring to the use of the language about curricular innovations in teacher training programs, it may improve the communication between the designers and the teachers and reduce the gap between the designers' intentions and actual classroom activities, if aspects are considered in teacher training programs, which refer to the use of the language about curricular innovations.

Further development of the evaluation

The aim of any curriculum innovation is to improve students' learning and, therefore, evaluating the success of a curriculum innovation means studying whether or not the proposed innovation succeeds in this aim. In this sense, the study of teachers transformations conducted by the STTIS project does not help us to decide if an innovation is effective. Effectiveness (2) as described by Millar in Chapter 1, is understood as a match between the intended and the attained goals. However, analysis of transformations gives much information about the gap between the intended and the implemented curriculum, i.e. about effectiveness (1).

We consider that the results of STTIS project suggest that the changes undergone by the images are related to the conceptual aspects represented by them. But how does it really affect the performance of the students? How do they deal with these transformations? To what extent do these effects at a conceptual level affect the students' understanding of the topic? To answer these questions, the evaluation should collect data on the students' learning outcomes. Paying close attention to the students' interaction with the teacher and among themselves during the class sessions could inform us to what extent their construction of the meaning is in agreement with the approach of the concept transmitted by the transformed images. This evaluation should provide information on the effectiveness of the innovation, understood as a good correlation between the designers' intentions and the students' performance. Future research on these issues will be welcome.

References

Arnheim, R. (1984). *El poder del centro*. Madrid: Alianza Editorial, S.A.

Duit, R. (1985). In search of an Energy Concept. Conference on Teaching about Energy within the Secondary School Science Curriculum. Leeds.

Eco, U. (1985). *Tratado de semiótica general*. Barcelona: Editorial Lumen, S.A.

Goodlad, J. I., Klein, M. F. and Tye, K. A. (1979). The domains of curriculum and their study. In J. I. Goodlad and associates (eds.), *Curriculum Inquiry. The Study of Curriculum Practice* (pp. 43-76). New York: McGraw-Hill.

Halliday, M. A. K. (1978). *Language as social semiotic. The social interpretation of language and meaning*. London: Edward Arnold (Publishers) Ltd.

Jewitt, C., Kress, G., Ogborn, J., and Tsatsarelis, C. A. (2001). Exploring Learning Through Visual, Actional and Linguistic Communication: the multimodal environment of a science classroom. *Educational Review*, 53(1), 5-18.

Kress, G. and van Leeuwen, T. (1996). *Reading Images: the Grammar of Visual design*. London: Routledge and Kegan Paul.

Pintó, R. (1991). *Algunos conceptos implícitos en la 1^a y la 2ª Leyes de la Termodinámica: una aportación al estudio de las dificultades de su aprendizaje*. Universitat Autònoma de Barcelona, Bellaterra.

Pintó, R., Gutierrez, R., Ametller, J., & al, e. (2001a). *Teachers' Transformations Trends when implementing innovations. STTIS Transversal Report WP4.*: Directorate Generale Researche. European Commission . TSER Projects.

Pintó, R., Viennot, L., Ogborn, J., Sassi, E. and Quale, A. (2001b). *STTIS (Science Teacher Training in an Information Society) Final Report* (Restricted). Brussels: European Union.

Saussure, F. (1971). *Curso de lingüística general* (9 ed.). Buenos Aires: Losada.

Solomon, J. (1983). *Learning about energy. A study of fourth year pupils in a school Physics course*. London: Chelsea College, University of London.

The STTIS research teams and its leaders were at the Université Dénis Didérot - Paris VII (Laurance Viennot), Universitá Federico II da Napoli (Elena Sassi), University of Oslo (Andreas Quale), University of Sussex (Jon Ogborn) and the Universitat Autònoma de Barcelona (Roser Pintó), who was the coordinator of the project.

Chapter 11

Critical reflections on the evaluation of small-scale innovations

*Bob Campbell and Fred Lubben**

University of York Science Education Group, University of York, York, YO10 5DD, UK

Summary

What is the innovation? Three aspects of the Matsapha Materials: a curriculum intervention for lower secondary school integrated science education in Swaziland.

What need does it address? The perception that the established integrated science curriculum lacks local relevance and is inappropriate to the needs of the learners.

What is its scope? The curriculum has been trialled with some 300 students in 8 classes in 4 schools.

What evaluation data has been collected? Data have been collected on the professional development of teachers developing and implementing the curriculum materials and on the reactions and attainment of pupils.

What are the key findings? The Matsapha Materials have been well received by pupils who appreciate that they are learning about useful things, that they gain ownership of the curriculum by contributing their own knowledge and experience and that they are discussing relevant issues. There is strong evidence that pupils are engaged by the Matsapha Materials and are active participants in class. This greater degree of class participation has helped to expose misconceptions and misunderstandings. Pupils also appreciate the range of learning activities and have indicated some strong likes (e.g doing a play) and dislikes (e.g writing). In terms of attainment, no significant overall differences have been detected between experimental and comparator groups but the attainment of the highest achieving pupils in the application of their knowledge and in designing experimental investigations was higher in the experimental than the comparator group. Teachers involved in the innovation have improved their knowledge of science and developed professional self-confidence so that they now see themselves as curriculum developers as well as teachers and feel able to adapt lesson materials to meets the needs of their pupils.

Introduction

This chapter presents and discusses approaches to the evaluation of three, small-scale, curriculum interventions with which we have been engaged. We use the three examples to discuss aspects of our approaches to evaluation. In terms of the aspects of evaluation discussed in Chapter 1, it will become clear that we have had a variety of focus points for our evaluations and used a range of data collection methods. What is common to the three examples is that while we have sought to determine if we have *made things better* in ways intended by the innovations, we have also been alert to unanticipated outcomes of the implemented curricula.

The three examples are from our work in Swaziland. It is important to make explicit that some fundamental constructs underpin our work in Swaziland (and elsewhere). We are committed to seeking to achieve relevance in the school curriculum and improvement in the quality of teaching. We embrace the ideal of achieving these goals through partnerships with fellow professionals and recognise and welcome that such partnerships contribute to the professional development of all of us. We listen to the voices of learners. They are the ones that experience innovatory practice and have much of value to contribute to evaluation.

We take a broad view of what is *'making things better'* and recognise many ways of demonstrating progress in this direction. While enhanced achievement must be an important measure of success, we maintain that it should not be the only gauge. Indeed, only one of the examples we describe here features tests of attainment. We see positive changes in such affective attributes as participation, enjoyment and long-term interest as significant indicators that an innovation in science education *has made things better*.

Example 1: Evaluating a Learning Programme

The Swaziland Integrated Science programme (SWISP) has been the junior secondary school science curriculum in the country for some time. In an attempt to move towards a more relevant curriculum we worked with colleagues in Swaziland to develop new materials that, while addressing the same science concepts as SWISP, also built in local relevance. The lesson materials (called the Matsapha Materials) incorporated the following three features:

1. Contextualisation: linking science to everyday life and the experiences that pupils may have or are likely to have;

2. Application: helping pupils to select and apply their science knowledge to solve problems;

3. Investigation: including science investigative skills to help pupils use their knowledge to design valid tests.

The lesson materials were introduced to teachers and evaluation data were collected through observations in the classrooms of teachers using the resources. Observation data were supplemented by semi-structured interviews with groups of pupils. Pupils were also asked to reflect on the materials by writing about their reactions to the new teaching approach. The data from the observations, interviews and writings were collated. All these primary data were analysed for common patterns of pupil response. In addition, the qualitative data were triangulated with teachers' reports of pupils' reactions in further lessons collected through semi-structured individual interviews with teachers and in two reflective group discussions. These secondary data were used to attempt to refute claims based on the pupil data set (Lubben et al., 1996).

In addition, we collected evidence of student achievement in six schools. We administered standard tests to an experimental group of 104 pupils in four classes using the Matsapha Materials and a comparator group of 184 pupils in four classes using SWISP resources to support their learning of the same syllabus topic on Electriciy (EL), and with both groups using SWISP for the topic on Detecting the Environment (DE). The achievement of experimental and comparator groups on both topics was analysed (Lubben et al., 1997).

Did the Matsapha Materials make things better and if so how do we know?

Qualitative evaluation (I)

What emerged from the observation data was increased pupil participation in science lessons. We contend that an increase in pupils' participation **is** *making things better.* Increases in learner ownership are particularly significant in African classrooms where tradition allocates firmly fixed roles to the older authority figure (the teacher) as the oral provider of knowledge and the ignorant youngster (the pupil) as the absorber. With the Matsapha Materials, pupils enthusiastically offered examples and suggestions in response to teachers' questions and were ready contributors to discussion. Further analysis of the classroom observations pointed to the fact that such participation occurred particularly when the materials allowed pupils to:

- learn about immediately useful things;
- gain ownership of lesson activities by contributing their own knowledge and experience;
- discuss issues (particularly contentious issue where science knowledge conflicted with cultural beliefs).

For example, in discussing the study of electricity in the Matsapha Materials one student reported:

> *Some of these things are dangerous but they can be prevented. By reading the stories and doing the experiments, we have learned how to prevent these sorts of things from happening.*

However, on the less positive side, pupils rarely offered scientific explanations for their ideas. Also, their contributions were not always relevant. Furthermore, the teacher was shown to be a major factor in determining the extent of pupil contributions. Negative feedback to a pupil discouraged further offerings not just by that pupil but also by other members of the class.

Classroom observations were carried out over a period of time and so allowed us to document with some considerable detail how the Matsapha Materials were transacted. While subject to the standard criticisms of classroom observation we feel that the data on pupil participation are sound. On the other hand, criticism of our evaluation method may be levelled at the use of teachers' comments as the sole evidence of 'increased classroom participation'.

What may at first seem less than positive outcomes of this evaluation are the observations on the lack of scientific explanations and the discouraging teacher responses to pupils' contributions. These outcomes have been fed into teacher development programmes and we are optimistic on endeavours to change such behaviour. But lesson observations also indicated an unexpected benefit of the Matsapha Materials. The increased level of pupil participation and invitations to speculate on the explanations on locally contextualised situations brought pupil misconceptions to the fore so allowing teachers to recognise and deal with these. Our open approach to evaluation allowed these unanticipated outcomes to be identified and acted upon so adding strength to the study and thus contributing to *making things better.*

Qualitative evaluation (II)

The data from learner group interviews and writings showed that the Matsapha materials increased student interest in science lessons. We contend that an increase in pupils' interest in science lessons **is** *making things better.* It is our view that pupils' should engage with the school curriculum and be active learners. To do so the curriculum needs to capture their interest. Science lesson that are perceived by pupils to be interesting are more likely to be engaging and lead to active learning.

Critics of our evaluation strategy may point to a main source of data being feedback from pupils. In considering what pupils have said we have been conscious of issues such as the power relationships between learners, teachers and researchers, the language and communication problems related to learners using a second or subsequent language and, perhaps above all, the fact that they are being consulted as stakeholders in their learning: a novel experience for most of them.

While these are indeed legitimate points of criticism we believe that the body of evidence is too strong to uphold this criticism. The respondents had been taught in English and had written English throughout their schooling. Triangulation with classroom observational data shows that the areas of interest mentioned coincide with the instances where high participation takes place. Also, some components of the materials were identified as uninteresting, indicating pupils' power of discrimination. Also, rather than being threatened by the prospect of talking about their learning experiences, pupils embraced this opportunity with enthusiasm and conveyed their views not just in what they said but also in the way that they said it. Being asked to provide oral and written feedback on their learning experiences was seen as a responsible task.

Quantitative evaluation

A third outcome of the study relates to pupils' achievement in conceptual understanding, applying science concepts and designing a practical investigation. All of these are intended learning outcomes of the Matsapha Materials. The data from the experimental group were compared (using t-tests) with the data from the pupils in the comparator group.

Whereas the experimental group performed significantly better on the DE topic (both groups taught using SWISP), there was no significant difference between experimental and comparator group performance for the EL topic (using the Matsapha Materials and SWISP respectively). This seems to indicate that, in terms of knowledge and understanding of subject matter, the experimental group underperformed on the EL topic. This was particularly so for pupils taught by teachers who only partly adopted the approach of the Matsapha Materials. This finding points towards a possible weakness in the evaluation procedure, i.e. the judgement of a new teaching approach without allowing teachers time for 're-skilling' from the old approach and 're-skilling' for the new approach. The 'dip effect' leading from this has been noted in other innovations (Fullan, 2001).

The test responses showed no significant overall differences in the ability of learners in the experimental and comparator groups to apply science concepts and design investigations. Since the Matsapha Materials include activities that aim to develop both of these abilities this outcome was disappointing. However, further analysis of achievement for concept application for different levels of conceptual achievement shows that concept application was higher within the Matsapha Materials group than the comparator group, but for high conceptual achievers only. So, for such pupils the Matsapha Materials have *made things better* in the sense that they have an improved achievement in a scientific ability. While this is encouraging in terms of the intended outcomes of the Matsapha Materials, it also indicates that the test items on application were too dependent on pupils' conceptual achievement to provide a comprehensive picture of pupils' ability to apply their knowledge.

Our data on investigations indicate that about half the pupils in the comparator group could produce adequate designs for investigations without any explicit teaching. Many of those that could not do so focused on expected outcomes rather than procedures. About one in four in the experimental group mirrored this. As for application of knowledge there was a link between the ability to plan and design investigations and conceptual achievement. It is thus possible that while the Matsapha Materials have helped the high achievers to describe valid methods of investigation, and so *made things better* for them, they may have confused the low achievers.

In our evaluation we put great store on what was said and written by pupils and what was observed in class as well as what test results indicated. Our data point to improvements in participation and interest in learning science. In terms of achievement we recognise that while the initial implementation of the Matsapha Materials did not produce an overall gain in conceptual achievement, the higher achieving pupils developed improved abilities in applying their knowledge and understanding and in designing investigations. The evaluation also demonstrated aspects of classroom practice that were recognised as important to *making things better.*

Example 2: Evaluating Teachers' Professional Development

The purpose of curriculum innovation is to create improvement. This is most effective where the innovation has value congruence with the teachers who implement it, when they can identify with the process and also claim ownership of the new curriculum. Thus one way of *making things better* is to prepare teachers to work effectively with a new curriculum and to help them towards value congruence.

While recognising the importance of the traditional forms of professional development, in the creation of the Matsapha Materials described above we involved teachers in all stages of the curriculum development process and studied their professional growth. Field notes were kept during development workshops. Each participant was interviewed and also completed feedback questionnaires. Each was also visited in school. On each visit, there was classroom observation and discussion of the new curriculum. At the end of the implementation period an evaluation workshop discussed and recorded teachers' experiences and perceptions of the activities Lubben et al., 1995).

We report here on three aspects of teacher growth as an outcome of involvement with curriculum development and intervention:

- self-perception as curriculum developers;
- professional self-confidence, and
- understanding of science.

Self-perception as curriculum developers

At the initial curriculum development workshop, teachers were generally hesitant contributors to brainstorming sessions. This was not because of a general reluctance to contribute *per se,* as they generated many suggestions for teaching strategies but because they felt uneasy with the imaginative nature of the process. During materials development sessions, even the more confident brainstormers opted to develop areas requiring little imagination and some showed a low level of engagement with their tasks. However, three quarters of the teachers expressed positive opinions about writing materials. By the end of the induction workshop in which developed lessons were presented and discussed, the teachers displayed considerable ownership of their materials with several claiming increased confidence in teaching lessons that they had been involved in developing. Following teaching trials of the lessons teachers readily contributed suggestions for improvement, including ways to link the science concepts and contexts – the aspect to which they were initially most reluctant to contribute. The teachers thus seemed to be better prepared to *make things better* in their classrooms as they progressed to teach with the new curriculum. Comments by teachers such as the following support this view:

> *Now, I am able to even change the structure of a lesson. Now I know how to do it, to use applications from daily life to start a lesson off.*

Professional self-confidence

Few Swazi teachers have the self-confidence to participate in open critical debate. This may in part be a reflection of the cultural norm of respect for the views of others. Despite our efforts at building good interpersonal relationships, the quality of professional debate remained modest during the curriculum development phase of the project. It was thus to our surprise that during the induction workshop the teachers readily embraced peer teaching and offered supportive and critical remarks to their colleagues.

In terms of confidence in the three aspects of the innovation we noted that initial visits to schools to observe the teaching of the new materials were welcomed as an aid to resolving concerns over appropriate teaching but later visits were seen as opportunities to report on student reactions and on plans for extensions of the approach to other topics. The teachers had grown in professional self-confidence and were perceived to be well placed to *make things better* in their classrooms.

Understanding of science

Discussion of the lessons being developed gave the teachers opportunities to share their experience of student misconceptions and learning difficulties and, through this, their own science ideas. The task of designing lessons that explored the science of everyday activities rather than presenting textbook examples required teachers to reflect on their science understandings, challenged them to use their science knowledge in new ways and forced them to consider new approaches to providing pupil explanations. The teachers soon realised that by contextualising lessons they had to fully understand the science of the situations before they could consider how best to explain the science to their pupils. During the lesson writing workshops and peer teaching sessions, teachers were frequently observed explaining the science of a situation to a less knowledgeable colleague, some occasionally correcting points of detail. In addition, points of scientific understanding were discussed among the group as a whole. Further evidence of growth in science understanding was obtained during the trials of the lessons. Here teachers remarked that their involvement in the project had placed them in a stronger position to teach the topics and that they were more confident to answer pupils' question. Again, strong evidence that they could *make things better.*

Looking critically at the approach taken to evaluate teacher professional development, it is clear that it is much dependent on the records of the Matsapha Materials development process, the induction workshops and the school visits undertaken to monitor and support the infusion of the innovative materials. These records were made by the same team that supported the development of the materials and introduced the innovation. It could be argued that it was difficult for these evaluators to maintain sufficient critical distance from the development that they were encouraging. This criticism can be countered in part by the fact that except for schools visits (made by an evaluator alone) notes were kept by team members independently and the collated records used to provide the documentary basis for conclusions. Conclusions required the support of more than one record. In this way, the outcomes were not related to a single set of field notes and thus subject to any possible bias of an individual recorder. Also, the team did not set out with a preconceived set of behaviours that they wished to document but took an open-ended approach to the evaluation. The evaluators were participant observers rather than external viewers. Furthermore, an important constituent of the database for the evaluation was contributed directly by teachers through written feedback and open-structured discussion towards the end of the project. These data are considered to be strong and supportive of those gained from the other sources.

In this example, we are claiming to witness teacher professional growth with evidence of participation in workshop and teaching in school. We support our claim with the written evidence of the teachers. Our approach to evaluation was an open one: a co-ordinated team effort employed a multi-method strategy and engaged with the curriculum innovation over time. In terms of making a difference to the quality of teaching and learning in school, it is our view that more knowledgeable, self-confident teachers who consider themselves able to modify curriculum activities to suit their school circumstances and their pupils can *make things better* for their pupils.

Example 3: Evaluating Learning Activities

In Swaziland and in other developing countries, there is a concern that an insufficient number of learners progress with their studies of science and so not only restrict their own education but also limit the development of science-based industry and the localisation of its staffing. One of the factors contributing to low interest in the sciences is pupils' negative perception of these school subjects. Pupils claim not to like what happens in science lessons. Thus one way of *making things better* is to introduce learning activities that pupils' claim to like.

One of the reasons given for the negative perception of school science is the mismatch between the curriculum content and the everyday experience of learners. A second suggested reason for negative attitudes towards science education is the conflict between the pedagogy of enquiry characteristic of science education and the social and cultural values of African society (Ogunniyi, 1995). Thus, in evaluating the Matsapha Materials we also attempted to provide a systematic survey of pupils' preferences for various types of learning activities (Dlamini et al., 1996).

Almost 300 pupils from various schools were taught in trials of the new curriculum materials and returned a questionnaire after completing each of two units. The first part of the questionnaire listed 13 types of learning activities included in the curriculum materials and asked pupils to identify the three types of activity that they liked most and least with an explanation of their choices. Some of these activities were specific to the materials but others were common to the Matsapha Materials and their normal SWISP science lessons. The frequencies with which various activities were ranked amongst the three most and least liked learning activities were determined. The reasons provided by pupils were analysed and clustered into a number of categories of explanation.

By looking at the rankings of popularity and unpopularity of the various learning activities (see table below) each could be categorised in terms of pupil perception as one of contentiousness, mainly liked, slightly liked, mixed, indifferent or mainly disliked.

Learning Activity	Most Liked Ranking	Least Liked Ranking	Student Perception
group discussion	high	high	contentious
reading stories	high	mid	mainly liked
listening to the teacher explain	high	mid	mainly liked
doing a play	high	mid	mainly liked
recording experimental results	mid	low	slightly liked
solving practical problems	mid	mid	mixed
group practical work with instructions	low	low	indifferent
explaining what happens around us	low	low	indifferent
observing practical demonstration	low	low	indifferent
identifying science in everyday life	low	low	indifferent
planning an experiment	mid	high	mainly disliked
labelling diagrams	mid	high	mainly disliked
writing reports	low	high	mainly disliked

Table 1: Popularity of learning activities

In looking for explanations of likes and dislikes, group discussion emerged as a contentious activity. While the merits of group discussion in exchanging ideas, clarifying understanding and encouraging participation in learning were recognised, it was also seen as an opportunity for some pupils to disengage from learning, for allowing some pupils to rely too much on the knowledge of others and because it left uncertainty as to the correctness of outcomes. On the other hand, listening to teacher explanations was recognised as a reliable way to acquire the correct knowledge but also disliked as it restricted independence of thought. Labelling diagrams was mainly disliked for its finality in that the activity exposed knowledge (or lack of it). In the same way, writing reports was disliked as it allowed the teacher to check correctness. The notion of correctness was also evident in the explanations as to why planning experiments was mainly disliked. Half the pupils who gave reasons for disliking this activity focused on the uncertainty of the correctness of their planning and the other half on the need for demanding thought.

Unlike the previous two examples that we have discussed above, this evaluation of learning activities depended entirely on pupil reading and writing. We recognise that unsupported reading and writing can pose difficulties for many pupils who, although receiving schooling in English, do not see this as their natural language of communication. With this in mind, the evaluation instrument was constructed to be simple in structure and language and was piloted before use. Nevertheless, several pupils did not complete the second section of the feedback document that asked them to select their three least liked learning activities from the list provided. Thus the data for this aspect of the evaluation were less than for that on liked activities. Also, the challenge of writing free prose that explained why they liked or disliked a learning activity was too much for some pupils and there were fewer explanations than choices of activities (or they did not know why they liked or disliked something or if they did, then they could not put it into words). While we consider that this does not undermine our findings, it does flag up the importance of language and the need to be sensitive to the demands that this places on the contributors to evaluation studies. The recognition of experiences (in this case learning activities) and expression of views by respondents (in speech as well as writing) are restricted by their command of language. This takes on greater significance with respondents who are working in other than their first language and is probably more significant for writing than speech. In this evaluation, it is of note that the least liked classroom activity is writing yet we asked pupils to provide written feedback! Pupils may see stating a view in writing as making a more significant statement than giving a spoken response. While writing provides a permanent record for the evaluator, in a culture with an oral tradition it may be a daunting challenge for pupils.

Unlike the other examples we have presented, this example took a less open approach to the evaluation. This was done as a deliberate strategy to collect data on quite specific aspects of the innovation. It is not seen as a weakness, particularly as our instrument allowed for pupils to add further learning activities and to express opinion on these if they so wished. What may be a more important consideration is the seriousness with which pupils provided feedback. We have no reason to believe that pupils were not diligent respondents but as in all such studies there must be some lingering concern about the extent of thought that went into the completion of the feedback form. What we did, as others have done, is to appeal to the pupils to provide their considered views and to assure them that these will be valued and used to inform the development of the curriculum for the benefit of future generations of pupils.

By way of concluding this example, we wish to return to the starting point of the study and consider if we have *made things better*. The answer here may be a mixture of yes and no. On the no side, we have developed a curriculum that includes activities that are disliked. On the other hand, we have also provided more liked activities than the normal SWISP curriculum. Also on the yes side we have information on learning activities that if incorporated into science lessons can *make things better*. By *make things better*, we mean that it will be liked by pupils. We do not know for sure whether or not liked learning activities make a more positive contribution to learning than less liked activities, but we do know that activities that are liked are motivators to learning.

Concluding Points

In presenting these example evaluations of curriculum innovations in Swaziland, we have attempted to point out what we consider to be the strengths and limitations of our approaches. We have learned the value of a multi-method approach to data collection and that unanticipated outcomes can be of value to improving the curriculum further. However, we also recognise that evaluations are judgements based on evidence and while the evidence may be robust (but of course subject to the data collection decisions of the evaluators), the conclusions are interpretations of the evidence and may be more personal to the evaluators. This is particularly so where the approach is more qualitative than quantitative as is the balance in our work. Here it may be of value to stress the importance of the collaborative nature of our studies. In working together with colleagues in Swaziland, we have an in-built safeguard against individualism of interpretation and also the valued strength of cultural knowledge and insight so adding an important local dimension to our evaluations. We have also drawn attention to the importance we have placed on the views of the pupils who are the recipients of curriculum innovations. This is an aspect that, to the best of our knowledge, is not common in curriculum evaluations in Africa.

In the UK we are hearing more of education serving customers or clients (= pupils and their careers); yet it does not seem odd that we do not routinely seek their views. Duffield *et al.* (2000), writing about curriculum implementation in Scotland, draw attention to the importance of listening to learners' voices if we are to really understand classroom processes. While it is of note that the influential study on the role and value of the science curriculum in England by Osborne and Collins (2001) relied on evidence from focus groups of learners, there is work to be done if we really wish to take note of 'customer opinion'. We feel that within the African context there is even more work to be done to develop further the methodologies to enable learners as well as teachers and other adults to have a stronger voice in the evaluation of the science curriculum. While we may have taken some note of what they have to say, curriculum evaluators need to do more to empower these stakeholders to help to determine if *things have been made better.*

Acknowledgements

The research and development activities on which this contribution is based could not have taken place without the active participation of pupils, teachers and other professionals in Swaziland and, in particular, our colleagues at the University of Swaziland, Betty Dlamini, Tizzie Maphalala and Bongi Putsoa. We also wish to recognise the financial support of The British Overseas Development Administration, The British Council and The Swaziland Educational Research Association.

References

Dlamini, B., Lubben, F. and Campbell, B. (1996). Liked and disliked learning activities: responses of Swazi students to science materials with a technological approach. *Research in Science and Technological Education.* 14, 221-235.

Duffield, J., Allan, J., Turner, E. and Morris, B. (2000). Pupils' voices on achievement: an alternative to the standard agenda. *Cambridge Journal of Education,* 30, 263-274.

Fullan, M. (2001). *The new meaning of educational change.* London: Routledge Falmer.

Lubben, F., Campbell, B. and Dlamini, B. (1995). *In-Service Support for a Technological Approach to Science Education.* Serial No 16 in Education Research Papers. London: Department of International Development.

Lubben, F., Campbell, B. and Dlamini, B. (1996). Contextualising science teaching in Swaziland: some student reactions. *International Journal of Science Education,* 18, 331-320.

Lubben, F., Campbell, B. and Dlamini, B. (1997). Achievement of Swazi students learning science through everyday technology. *Journal of the Southern African Association for Research in Mathematics and Science Education*, 1, 26-40.

Ogunniyi, M. (1995). The development of science education in Botswana. *Science Education*, 79, 95-109.

Osborne, J. and Collins, S. (2001). Pupils' views of the role and value of the science curriculum: a focus-group study. *International Journal of Science Education,* 23, 441-467.

Chapter 12

A long-term and systemic approach to science curriculum development, implementation and evaluation

Bat-Sheva Eylon and Avi Hofstein*
Department of Science Teaching, The Weizmann Institute of Science, Rehovat 76100, Israel

Summary

What is the innovation? (1) A sequence of units (e.g. the atomic model) for 7– 10th grade students that promote long-term conceptual understanding. The curriculum is spiral, and employs constructivist and STS elements stressing conceptual progression and knowledge integration. (2) Integrating domains in physics high school education. These initiatives were carried out at the Department of Science Teaching in the Weizmann Institute of Science employing a long-term systemic approach to science curriculum development.

What need does it address? The chapter addresses the following needs: The importance of employing a systemic and long-term approach to the development of learning materials in science to ensure continuity, coherence and effective implementation. This approach is characterized by longitudinal, dynamic, and progressive refinements of program development school and classroom organization, teacher professional development assessment, and cognitive research. All these are conducted together under one integrated institutional roof.

What is the scope? These topics are part of the national curriculum in Israel for junior and senior high school. 10,000-30,000 students are studying the programs about the atomic model each year.

What evaluation data has been collected? A series of diagnostic investigations led to the design of the curricula, and evaluation data of its effectiveness involved: diagnostic questionnaires (verbal and visual), clinical interviews investigating in-depth conceptions and their sources and interviews with teachers. In addition, attitude questionnaires were administered to students and teachers.

What are the key findings? Based on the diagnostic findings, the new curricula in the 10th grade (*Chemistry: A Challenge*) improved students' understanding of different aspects of the atomic model and its applications to chemical reactions significantly.

In addition, the new (*MATMON*) junior high school spiral curriculum on materials led to a significant increase of students' understanding macro-micro relationships in chemistry and their long-term retention, providing a sound foundation for the 10th grade.

Introduction

In this chapter, we take a comprehensive view of "curriculum development" and claim that it is necessary to include under this concept the following components: research, development, implementation, teacher development and evaluation. Moreover, we suggest that it is impossible to separate these components in any meaningful way. Instead, these components and their interrelationships should function as a whole and be part of a systemic approach. This approach should be an academic endeavor conducted as a continuous and renewable project.

It is suggested that in order to be able to inform other curriculum- development groups about different aspects of a given curriculum project and applicable results of its evaluation, the long-term and systemic approach to the science curriculum process is recommended. In particular, curriculum development centers using this approach are able to provide reliable, and adaptable information regarding the implementation of a certain innovation or curriculum in a manner that can be easily applied by other educational systems and other curriculum development groups. Changes and innovations in the educational system especially at the national level are not a trivial exercise. It is, therefore, worthwhile to examine and analyze past experiences worldwide in order to learn about the successes and failures of curricular efforts in the sciences (Walberg and Fraser, 1995, Black and Atkin, 1996, Ganiel, 1997; Van den Akker, 1998).

Science curriculum reform started in the US and in the UK in the late 1950s when science education began to be the subject of serious policy making, and when large-scale curriculum development was initiated (Van den Akker, 1998). The reform in the 60s in the US resulted from dissatisfaction with the poor output of the education system in terms of meeting the increasing demand of scientists and engineers. The science curricula developed were academic in their nature and were intended mainly for those students who planned to embark on scientific careers. These programs were based largely on the idea of the *"structure of the discipline"* and very often neglected psychological, practical, and technological applications. The problem with these projects was that after one or two trial versions, the grant provided to the developers was terminated and the project came to an end. Several comprehensive studies (Helgeson et al., 1977, Weiss, 1978), and also Project Synthesis (Harms and Yager, 1981), aimed at summarizing these studies, were conducted to evaluate the effectiveness of these projects. The results provided a rather gloomy picture, in spite of the fact that high quality subject-matter experts and many enthusiastic teachers were involved. Goodlad (1984) stated that the gap between the expectations and what happened in schools was formidable. In retrospect, it seems that one of the key reasons for this situation is the fact that one of the more important phases of the curricular process, implementation, was almost entirely neglected or omitted. For the purpose of this chapter, we will use Leithwood's definition (1991) that

> *"Implementation is the process of reducing the differences between existing practices and practices suggested by the innovation." (p.445)*

Fullan (1991) suggested that the implementation phase probably has the most significant impact on the outcomes of any efforts to bring about change. Effective implementation of a certain educational innovation often requires a change in the behavior of people. This requires the acquisition of new skills, knowledge, values, attitudes, and interests. It is suggested that the acquisition process, is slow and time-consuming processes, and is developed only gradually over a long period of time. In addition to time constraints, effective implementation requires expertise, resources, and organizations that contribute to the implementation processes. Anderson (1992) suggested that successful implementation of an innovation rests on the cultivation of organizational conditions and on the use of broad-based approaches. In this view, implementing an innovation can be seen as growth on the part of those who wish to use the innovation, from their existing practices through a relatively simple approximation of practices suggested by the innovation to relatively sophisticated use of the innovation (Leithwood, 1991). The case study in the next sections gives a detailed example.

Whether the educational system is centralized or decentralized, it is clear that in order to foster innovation there is a need to provide for a *systemic approach*. This approach is characterized by longitudinal, dynamic, and progressive refinements of program development, school and classroom organization, teacher professional development, assessment, and cognitive research. All these aspects are considered and activated together under one integrated institutional roof (Ganiel, 1997).

Evaluation of implementation

More than 50 years ago, Tyler (1949) suggested that evaluation and curriculum development (curriculum research) must be closely integrated in the continuous cycle of curriculum planning, development, and implementation. According to Leithwood (1991) and Leithwood and Montgomery (1980), implementation evaluation may assist in making accountability and management decisions. Accountability decisions are aided when information is provided about whether, or the extent to which, an innovation has been put into practice according to design; and whether what was delivered or paid for is being undertaken as planned. In addition, implementation evaluation may help specify the practices implied by the innovation; identify those conditions under which implementation is likely to succeed; explicate problems likely to be encountered and strategies available for their resolution; and determine the feasibility of innovation implementation.

Several issues need to be considered in carrying out implementation of evaluation. The first issue is concerned with who should conduct the evaluation. Many of the curricular innovations developed during the 1960s tended to integrate small-scale evaluation (research) activities. These were mainly conducted following standard procedures. In general, the impact of these evaluation studies on further developments, decisions, and the enhancement of implementation initiatives were rather limited. Tamir (1985) suggested that one of the reasons for this was that, in general, the information resulting from assessment and evaluation was obtained *only late* in the curricular process.

A second issue concerns the transfer of knowledge within a given development group and between groups. Implementation contexts are complex and the results of evaluation provide rich data. It is important to identify the most influential variables, with the greatest impact on future curriculum development that can serve other groups who are involved in similar efforts in the area of science curricula development and implementation (Welch, 1985).

A third issue is a dilemma associated with the conception of professionalism. A central goal of teacher professional development is to foster independent learning skills and construction of practice. Thus the success of implementing an innovation is not necessarily measured in reducing the gap between intended and actual practices as advocated above. An innovation may lead to an unexpected change in practice, conceptions and attitudes of teachers that result in improved student learning. This is a more subtle desirable influence of the innovation that may be more difficult to detect.

These issues are easier to resolve in a long-term and systemic approach in which there is continuity and responsibility of a development team for longer periods of time. Such an approach provides the conditions for on-going learning of the team from teachers and responding to the many avenues they choose to take.

Coherence in curriculum research

A conclusion that can be drawn from the previous sections is that lack of coherence between the various components of the curricular cycle may be a central determinant in the lack of impact on decision-making. Van den Akker (1998) suggested that since previous curricular efforts were only partially successful in attaining the goals of reform, there is a vital need to achieve a correspondence between curricular goals and guidelines, learning materials and curricular frameworks, as well as the approaches and emphasis on assessing and evaluating students' learning of science. It is useful to carry out in-depth curriculum research from the first stages of the development, to execute some of this research in the context of implementation and to integrate these activities with teacher development. As a result, it is likely that the gap between theory and practice will be reduced, that the resulting curriculum will be of higher quality, and the scale up efforts will be more feasible. An example for such an approach, advocated especially for the first stages of the curricular process, is that of "design experiments" following the methodology of the design sciences: project teams engineer innovative educational environments and, at the same time, conduct experimental studies of these innovations (Brown and Campione, 1994). This methodology is essential when a prescriptive theory of instruction is not available (Reif, 1995). In designing actual instruction, even the descriptive background provided by research usually is partial and must be studied in the context of the design project. This kind of methodology is also advocated by educational-psychologists with the goal in mind to advance practice and practical knowledge. For example, Greeno et al. (1996) claimed that:

> *In research and development of this kind, questions about a theory are not limited to whether it is coherent and yields accurate predictions; we also ask a central question, whether reforming practices requires transformations of people's understanding of principles that are assumed.... at the same time, we believe that embedding research in the activities of practical reform, the theoretical principles that are developed will have greater scientific validity..... because they will have to address deeper questions of how practices function and develop. (p. 41).*

The long-term and systemic approach increases the coherence between theory and practice, and between the different pieces of the curricular cycle. As a result, there is a greater probability of gaining more robust practical knowledge, stronger impact and more reliable transfer of knowledge.

Examples of the Long-Term and Systemic Approach

In the Department of Science Teaching at the Weizmann Institute of Science, we often start the development process with *a diagnostic phase* that attempts to identify in detail important aspects relevant to the specific innovation such as investigating the learning difficulties in the domain and studying their sources. The results usually help us to define desirable goals for instruction. Ideally, we then devise some *models of instruction* that take into account previous research and development experience and the findings of the diagnostic phase. In particular, the teaching approaches attempt to avoid, by-pass or remediate diagnosed learning difficulties. These instructional models are then tested in *small-scale instructional studies* under relatively controlled conditions that enable us to undertake a detailed investigation of teaching and learning, and to assess educational effectiveness of the teaching approaches. On the basis of such experiments we modify the model of instruction and after repetitive revisions we undertake *large-scale implementation and evaluation efforts*. Many of these activities are accompanied by work with teachers, and relevant *professional development* is an integral part of the process. It should be emphasized that instead of carrying out the initial phases sequentially, we often carry them out in parallel and attempt to devise the teaching methods in the context of limited implementation (Figure 1). This approach enables us to identify what ideas are feasible and to adapt the curriculum design as it is implemented. To accomplish the steps in Figure 1, there is a need to build cooperation between the four dominant groups involved in curriculum development and implementation: researchers, curriculum developers, decision makers (i.e., inspectors from the ministry of education responsible for implementing national syllabi), and science teachers in schools.

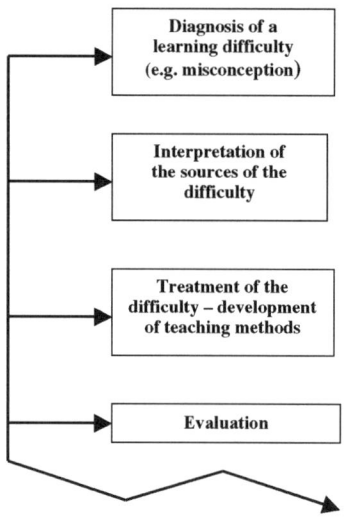

Figure 1:   The cycles of research-based curriculum development

Most of our studies are carried out in actual classrooms aiming at narrowing the gap between research and practice and providing opportunities to investigate basic research questions that cannot be studied in other environments. Hence the research methods that we use to investigate these complex environments consist of both qualitative and quantitative approaches, and we attempt to carry out converging operations to come up with reliable conclusions.

To illustrate some of these ideas, we will describe two case studies from research, development, and implementation projects.

Learning about the atomic model: a case study

As discussed earlier, the identification of students' conceptual frameworks and modes of instruction that bring about a conceptual change is a long-term activity, which involves several cycles. The present case study illustrates the process of research, development, implementation for teaching about the atomic model.

The atomic model is usually taught in Israeli secondary schools several times: the particulate model of matter and some aspects of the atomic/molecular model are taught in junior high school, and the latter is revisited in greater detail in 10th grade chemistry.

In the early eighties, in an effort to reformulate the chemistry curriculum, a series of diagnostic studies were conducted to investigate students' understanding of key concepts of this topic (Ben-Zvi, Eylon and Silberstein, 1988). For example, in one of these studies, a sample of 337 students from 11 tenth-grade classes that studied chemistry for eight months were given a set of formulas (e.g. O_2, $O_{3(g)}$, N_2O_4, NO_2) and were asked to describe them by drawing models and in writing. Most students knew how to represent one molecule of an element. However, many had difficulty representing correctly one molecule of a compound. For example, about a third of the sample drew N_2O_4 as two connected or disconnected fragments - an additive view of structure. Similarly, about a third of the sample represented incorrectly an element in the gaseous state, e.g. they represented the gas $O_{3(g)}$ by one molecule or three disconnected atoms. The performance dropped even more when students were asked to represent a compound in the gaseous state (70% provided incorrect answers).

In another study (Ben-Zvi et al., 1986a) conducted with 288 students at the end of 10th grade, students were given several diagnostic tasks, one of which is described below:

A metallic wire has the following properties:
(a) Conducts electricity (b) has brown color (c) is malleable. The wire is heated in an evacuated vessel until it evaporates. The resulting gas has the following properties: (d) Pungent odor (e) yellow color (f) attacks plastics. (1) Suppose that you could isolate one single atom from the metallic wire, which of the six properties would this atom have?
(2) Suppose that you could isolate one single atom from the gas. Which of the six properties would this atom have?

About 40% of the students claimed that the atom "isolated" from the solid has its properties, and the one "isolated" from the gas has the properties of the gas. Only 15% of the sample understood that an atom could not be regarded as a small piece of material, which carries the properties of the substance.

After analyzing the written questionnaires, we could group students into major classes of conceptions, we then chose randomly representatives from these groups and interviewed them. In these interviews, we re-examined students' conceptions and investigated our hypotheses concerning the sources of students' ideas. For example, some students remarked that:

> *"atoms in molecules of gaseous materials are farther apart than atoms in molecules of the same materials in the liquid state".*

Such ideas could be attributed to deficient prerequisite knowledge acquired in learning about the particulate model in junior high school physical science. Students learned that in the gaseous state the distance between the particles is much larger than in the liquid state, but were not clear how to apply this information correctly to distances between atoms and molecules.

The results of the studies show that even at the end of the 10th grade, many students did not understand clearly the micro-macro relationships regarding the structure and properties of matter. Following these diagnostic studies, the chemistry group in the Science Teaching Department prepared a new curriculum for 10th grade "Chemistry A Challenge" (Silberstein and Ben-Zvi 1986), which attempted to remedy these learning difficulties by using a historical approach and by dealing carefully with the formation of micro-macro relationships. For example, it was found that the emphasis on single molecules in representing materials misleads students and they do not refer to aggregates of particles in trying to explain the properties of materials. Hence appropriate representations involving multitudes of particles with clear relationships between different levels of description were used.

A summative evaluation (Ben-Zvi et al., 1986b) was conducted among 1,078 students from 35 classes to find out about the educational effectiveness of the new teaching materials. Half of the students studied the previously used materials while the other half studied the new curriculum "Chemistry A Challenge". The students were given three sets of questionnaires, consisting of achievement tests and diagnostic questions, similar to the ones described above, to which they had to respond by drawing models. One set was given prior to the beginning of their study, the second in the middle of the year and the third set served as a post-test. The new program had a pronounced effect on the middle and lower achievers while the high achievers were successful irrespective of the instructional program.

Similar studies were conducted on other central topics in the chemistry curriculum. For example, one of the studies investigated students' conceptualization of the structural, interactive and dynamic aspects of chemical reactions. (For more details regarding this study, see Ben-Zvi et al., 1987).

The design of research-based curriculum and teacher workshops had a far-reaching influence on chemistry teaching and learning in Israel. The teachers became more sensitive to students' difficulties in reasoning, to the importance of pre-existing knowledge, and to the fact that students do not always learn what they are taught. Yet some of the students still had conceptual difficulties. For instance, about 30% of the students lacked a satisfactory understanding of structural aspects of matter at the end of 10th grade (Ben-Zvi et al., 1988). Remnants of these difficulties could be found even two years later at the end of the 12th grade in the matriculation examination among students who opted to study chemistry at a higher level (Ben-Zvi and Hofstein, 1996).

One possible reason for the resilience to change could be attributed to the lack of solid foundation acquired in junior high school science. An opportunity to change this situation came in the mid-nineties when, following the *"Tomorrow 98"* (1992) report recommending a reform in Israeli science and mathematics teaching, new science curricula for middle school were developed. Based on the experience that we had accumulated at the highschool level, one major goal of the development team was to establish in the middle school a robust conceptual understanding that would be relevant to later studies of the atomic model. This goal had to be coordinated with other factors posed by the system: a prescribed syllabus with a limited allocation of time devoted to covering many topics, an emphasis on using the STS approach, teachers' previous knowledge and experience in teaching the topic of materials and others.

The resulting MATMON curriculum for middle school consists of several units that develop the atomic model in steps (Margel et al., 2002). The development of these units was based on previous research (e.g. Novick and Nussbaum, 1978). In these units related ideas are revisited several times, thus reinforcing them. The emphasis is on knowledge construction and knowledge integration, which are consolidated by repeating the same ideas in several contexts. The particulate model of matter is studied in the first unit (Nussbaum, 2000) using a constructivist approach involving student's debates about contrasting the continuous and the particulate conceptions of materials' structure. Then follows a unit that develops the basics of the atomic/molecular models, and finally, the concepts are revisited and extended in the context of learning about fibers. Another opportunity for visiting the ideas is provided later in a unit about industry dealing with colors.

A longitudinal study (Margel et al., 2002) investigated the changes in JHS students' conceptions of the structure of matter in studying 'Materials' for three years with these programs. The sample consisted of an experimental group of 1082 JHS students who studied 'Materials' according to a new curriculum, and a comparison group of 218 JHS students who studied this topic according to a traditional curriculum. Questionnaires, in which students were asked to represent the structure of several materials, were administered five times during a three-year period. One of the tasks is shown in Figure 2. Figure 3 shows how the different levels (macroscopic, particulate, and molecular) of representing water, in this task, changed from the 7th to the 9th grade in the experimental and comparison groups. When averaged on all materials, in the 9th grade, about 83% students from the experimental group reached at least a particulate model compared to 28% in the comparison group. In addition, about 23% of the experimental group reached a molecular model compared to 1% of the students in the comparison group. These results suggest that the new curriculum materials led to a lasting progression in students' understanding of material structure. The results also show how the different units contributed to this progression.

> **Consider the following materials:**
> Iron, Water, Air, Nylon, Juice, Wool, Oxygen, and Paper.
> Describe in words and draw the structure of these materials as if you were using a very powerful magnifying instrument.
>   **Explanations**   **Drawings**
> Iron _____
>
> Water _____

Figure 2:   A task investigating students' conceptions of the structure of matter in the JHS study

As was mentioned previously, implementation through long-term development of teachers was an essential step in this endeavor. Teachers who worked with the new series of curricular units in middle school had to undergo extensive training to assimilate the underlying philosophy of constructivist learning and teaching and to appreciate its benefits. They had to acquire skills regarding how to lead students through the new process and had to deal with the natural questions that arose: *Why should we spend all this time on building the particulate model of matter? Why can't we just tell them and convince them by several experiments?* Here we can illustrate Leithwood's (1991) description of 'implementation of innovation' as growth on the part of those who wish to use it. We observed how teachers who initially just 'followed

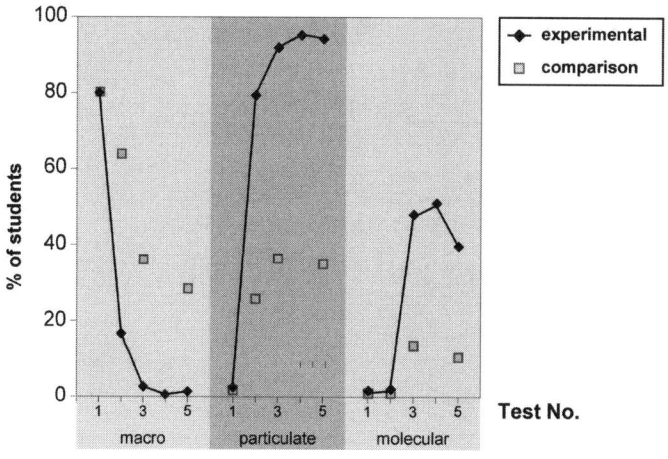

Figure 3: JHS students' representations of the structure of water in five tests administered along grades 7 – 9. N (experimental) = 1082; N (comparison = 218).

the moves' became later more and more keen on allowing students to discuss their ideas and construct their views. However, we still meet many teachers who know that it is the vogue to dwell on students' construction of knowledge. So they adapt pieces of a curriculum such as one of the benchmark experiments, without preparing the necessary background for this activity or carrying out subsequent activities necessary for consolidating the knowledge. It is not surprising that students of these teachers do not gain a solid understanding of the concept.

This case study illustrates the importance of the long-term systemic approach and some of the ideas presented in the previous sections in order to achieve desirable changes in the educational system. The curricular innovation was initiated because of dissatisfaction with student learning about the atomic theory in curricula of the early eighties. A detailed diagnostic study revealed some of the reasons for this, and since the same group that carried out the research was also responsible for the curriculum development, it was possible to build upon the findings in the development process. Several versions were developed, and each was evaluated with the same diagnostic tools, leading to an improved curriculum. The same group was involved in the implementation process and realized the need for genuine changes in teachers' views and their teaching methods. Teacher workshops emphasized the importance of prerequisite knowledge, the development of conceptual understanding in this domain, and the possible remedies to conceptual difficulties that arise in the process of learning. As already mentioned, the impact was considerable but limited until new opportunities were available. The fact that there was a long-term involvement and that the *same* organization was responsible for advancing physical science in secondary school enabled us to influence the syllabus at the national level, and to build on previous experience in the development of the new curriculum for middle school. Taking a long-term view of student learning about the atomic theory in grades 7 – 12 was a central corner stone in the design process.

Knowledge integration in physics: a case study

A similar approach has been used in many other curriculum development projects. The following case study illustrates briefly an example from high school physics focusing on knowledge integration.

An important goal of learning in any area is to be able to go beyond the details and develop a comprehensive understanding of the "big picture" (Eylon and Reif, 1984). Our diagnostic studies (Bagno and Eylon, 1997, Bagno et al., 2000) have shown repeatedly that this goal is usually not attained in high school physics, neither by students nor by teachers. For the last 20 years, we have been engaged in improving this aspect of student learning in different contexts of teaching physics, both at the student and the teacher level. This aspect was treated in relation to all components of the curricular cycle, and different domains of physics: mechanics, optics and electromagnetism.

We discuss here one particular example from this work that focused on forming useful connections between conceptual understanding and problem solving. Following diagnostic studies on this topic, a model of instruction was devised for students to be carried out during, or after studying a certain topic: Students solve simple and familiar problems, they reflect on their solution methods, identify underlying principles and present them in visual form (concept maps). Additional activities deal with conceptual difficulties and application of the information represented in the concept map. The sequence of problems is chosen in a manner that allows gradual construction of the map. This strategy — *SOLVE, REFLECT, CONCEPTUALIZE, APPLY and LINK* — is repeated until all the relevant knowledge is represented in the map. The maps are constructed at different levels of detail, and are applied in further problem solving. The strategy involves active involvement of the students and emphasis on reflection, reformulation of ideas and use of alternative representations.

This instructional model was realized in curricula that were designed in several domains and contexts. For example, it was used as the underlying strategy for helping students to organize their knowledge about Maxwell's equations in electromagnetism (Bagno and Eylon, 1997). It was also used to form a unifying picture of several domains in physics such as mechanics and electricity through the concepts of field and potential (Bagno et al., 2000). In each of the cases, we conducted evaluation studies assessing the contribution of the learning materials. We consistently found, that knowledge integration is not formed spontaneously either by most students or by most of the teachers. The method that we have devised contributed to students' learning as was evident in tasks testing conceptual understanding, problem solving, and organization. Teachers claimed that it improved their understanding of both the details and the overview of the relevant physics topics.

Identifying the lack in teachers' knowledge, we redesigned the modes for using the materials in classrooms before implementing them on a large scale, and also designed different frameworks for related professional development. These frameworks for teacher development are being used repeatedly in different contexts of teacher courses, and the same methods are being used in new areas as they are being developed. For teachers who have been involved in teacher development for longer periods of time, the importance of knowledge integration and the quest for a variety of methods for its promotion has become a routine.

The long-term and systemic approach has enabled us to continually redesign the curricula and support systems to scale up the achievement of this important goal.

Summary

In the past decade we have been witnessing many new reforms in science education all over the world. The scope of these reforms is comparable in magnitude to that of the sixties. Yet there is dissatisfaction with the impact of these reforms on the teaching and learning science.

In this paper, we have described a model of long-term and systemic approach to science curriculum development that includes research, development, implementation, teacher development and evaluation that are conducted under the same roof and often in parallel. We have shown how the features of this model help in overcoming three major elements that provide a barrier for effective implementation of innovations:

- **Lack of continuity.** The fact that the knowledge accumulated within a given project often does not contribute to future-related developments. In particular, assessment results are not integrated into the continuous improvement of the innovation and implementation. Since they become available long after the termination of the developmental stage, they can contribute significantly to our scientific knowledge, but often do not have practical impact.

- **Short-term approach.** Short-term projects do not support the need to improve the curricula on the basis of feedback. It also prevents the need for long-term planning of teacher professional development needed for lasting implementation of innovations. Moreover, attempts for scaling up are inhibited, and the innovations often are limited to experimental and limited trials.

- **Dispersed approach.** The various components of the curricular cycle that have been presented in this paper are often carried out by different educational agents. As a result, the coordination and integration of information and actions are severely impaired.

To sumup, the science curricula developed, using the approach that we have suggested, have a higher likelihood to be ecologically valid and matched to the requirements of the field, and as a result be implemented and sustained over time. The knowledge accumulated from one project is likely to be transferred continuously to new developments and to be communicated more readily to others.

References

Anderson, R. D. (1992). Perspectives on complexity: An essay on curricular reform. *Journal of Research in Science Teaching*, 29, 861-876.

Bagno, E. and Eylon, B. (1997). From problem-solving to a knowledge structure: An example from the domain of electromagnetism. *The American Journal of Physics,* 65, 726-736.

Bagno, E., Eylon, B. and Ganiel, U. (2000). From fragmented knowledge to a knowledge structure: Linking the domains of mechanics and electromagnetism. *The American Journal of Physics*, 68, S16-S26.

Ben-Zvi, R., Eylon, B. and Silberstein, J. (1986a). Is an atom of copper malleable? *Journal of Chemical Education,* 63, 64-66.

Ben-Zvi, R., Eylon, B. and Silberstein, J. (1986b). Revision of course materials on the basis of research on conceptual difficulties. *Studies in Educational Evaluation*, 12, 213-223.

Ben-Zvi, R., Eylon, B. and Silberstein, J. (1987) Students' visualization of a chemical reaction. *Education in Chemistry*, 24, 117-120.

Ben-Zvi, R., Eylon, B. and Silberstein, J. (1988). Theories, principles and laws. *Education in Chemistry*, 25, 89-92.

Ben-Zvi, R. and Hofstein, A. (1996). Strategies for remediating learning difficulties in chemistry. In D.F. Treagust, R. Duit and B.J. Fraser, (eds.), *Improving Teaching and Learning in Science and Mathematics*. New York: Teacher College Press.

Black, P. and Atkin, M. J. (1996). *Changing the Subject*. London: Routledge.

Brown, A.L. and Campione, J.C. (1994). Guided discovery in a community of learners, In K. McGilly (ed.), *Classroom lessons: Integration cognitive theory and classroom practices*. Cambridge, MA: MIT Press (229-290).

Eylon, B. and Reif, F. (1984). Effects of knowledge organization on task performance. *Cognition and Instruction*, 1(1), 5-44.

Fullan, M. (1991). Curriculum implementation. In A. Lewy (ed.), *The International Encyclopedia of Curriculum* (378-84). Oxford: Pergamon Press.

Ganiel, U. (1995). Fostering change in science education: Creation, implementation, evaluation, and research-the Israeli experience.

In A. Hofstein, B. Eylon and G.J. Giddings (eds.), *Science Education: From Theory to Practice*. Rehovot: The Weizmann Institute of Science.

Goodlad, J. (1984). *A Place Called School*. New York: McGraw-Hill.

Greeno, J.C., Collins, A.M. and Resnick, B., (1996) Cognition and Learning. In D.C. Berliner and R.C. Calfee (eds.), *Handbook of Educational Psychology*. Englewood Cliffs, New Jersey: Prentice-Hall, 15-46.

Harms, N. and Yager, R.E. (1981). *What research says to the Science Teacher?* Vol 2. Washington DC: National Science Teachers Association.

Helgeson, S., Blosser, P. and Howe, R. (1977) *The Status of Pre-College Science, Mathematics, and Social Studies Education*. Columbus OH: Center for Science & Mathematics Education, Ohio State University.

Leithwood, K.A. (1991). Implementation evaluation. In A. Lewy (ed.), *The International Encyclopedia of Curriculum*, (444-450). Oxford: Pergamon Press.

Leithwood, K.A., and Montgomery, D.J. (1980). Evaluating program implementation. *Evaluation Reviews*, 4, 193-214.

Margel, H., Eylon, B. and Scherz, Z. (2002). A Longitudinal study of high school students' conceptions of the structure of materials. *Submitted to the International Journal of Science Education*.

Novick, S. and Nussbaum, J. (1978). Junior high school pupils' understanding of the particulate nature of matter: an interview study. *Science Education*, 62(3), 273-281.

Nussbaum J. (2000). *The Structure of Matter: Vacuum and particles*. Rehovot: The Weizmann Institute of Science. (In Hebrew).

Reif, F. (1995). Millikan lecture: Understanding and teaching important scientific thought processes. *American Journal of Physics*, 63(1), 17-32.

Silberstein, J. and Ben-Zvi, R. (1986). "Chemistry A Challenge". Rehovat: The Weizmann Institute of Science. (In Hebrew).

Tamir, P. (1985). The potential and actual roles of evaluators. In P. Tamir. (ed.), *The Role of Evaluators in Curriculum Development*. London: Croom-Helm.

Tamir, P. (1991). Reforms in Science Education, In. A. Lewy, (ed.), *The International Encyclopedia of Education*. Oxford: Pergamon Press.

"Tomorrow 98" (1992). Report of the Superior Committee on Science, Mathematics and Technology Education in Israel. Jerusalem: Ministry of Education, Culture and Sport (in English).

Tyler, R.W. (1949). *Basic Principles of Curriculum and Instruction*. Chicago: University of Chicago Press.

Van den Akker, J. (1998). The science curriculum between ideals and outcomes. In B.J. Fraser and K.G. Tobin (eds.), *International Handbook of Science Education*. Durdrect: Kluwer Academic Publishers.

Walberg, H. J. and Fraser, B. J. (1995). Introduction and overview. In Fraser, B.J. and Walberg, H.J. (eds.), *Improving Science Education*. Chicago: National Society for the Study of Education.

Weiss, I. (1978). National Survey on: Science, Mathematics, and Social Studies Education. Washington, DC: Institute of Education, Educational Resources Information Center.

Welch W.W. (1995). Student assessment and curriculum evaluation. In B.J. Fraser and H.J. Walberg (eds.), *Improving Science Education*. Chicago: National Society for the Study of Education.

Part C:
Conclusions

Chapter 13

Evaluating innovations in science education: Some reflections

Judith Bennett and Robin Millar*
University of York Science Education Group, University of York, York YO10 5DD, UK

The previous twelve chapters of this book are in two distinct groups. Although these are rather unequal in size, both are important to the aim and purpose of the book. Part A consists of two chapters on general issues concerning the evaluation of curriculum packages, programmes and interventions. They are written from what might be termed an 'educational research' perspective, and reflect a concern with some of the issues about the quality and value of educational research that have been prominently and vociferously aired and debated over the past decade (Hargreaves, 1996; Fitz-Gibbon, 2000; Mosteller and Boruch, 2002). Part B, on the other hand, consists of a collection of accounts of specific science curriculum innovations, written from the perspective of the developers.

Within the accounts in Part B, it is possible to identify a number of common features in the approaches adopted to the evaluation of the interventions that were developed. Two are particularly striking. Firstly, the evaluations have all been undertaken by those involved in the design of the intervention. This contrasts with the approach implicit in some of the educational evaluation literature, of an external, 'professional' evaluator, collecting data in order to make judgements about the success or otherwise of aspects of the innovation in question, but with little personal commitment to its success or failure. The absence of an impartial, external evaluator might be seen as weakening claims made for the success of an intervention. For the interventions described in Part B, however, the choice of internal rather than external evaluation may have more to do with practical constraints than with deliberate choices or preferences. Many of the funders of science curriculum innovation place more emphasis on the development of the materials than on external evaluation. Evaluation may be valued for its contribution to 'product development', rather than to exploring more general educational questions and issues. Thus it is not entirely surprising that evaluation data has, by and large, been gathered by those involved in development of the materials, who are eager to gather evidence of their effects.

The second striking feature is that, for those undertaking the evaluation studies, the question 'What works?' has been interpreted largely with reference to meeting the aims of the intervention itself, rather than comparing the effects with those of other approaches. Often the focus is on establishing 'proof of principle' – showing that the ideas the developers had can be translated into activities and supporting materials which 'work' in the classroom. This can be seen in the approaches taken by, for example, Gräsel et al., Boersma et al., Kolstø, Parvin, and Ametller and Pinto. However, all the interventions were made in the belief that they could improve science education practice in some way. So it seems reasonable to ask how we might demonstrate that improvement has (or has not) taken place – and what kinds of data would need to be gathered to do this. The two most obvious possibilities are comparative data from a control group, or from previous cohorts of students before the innovation was introduced.

The studies reported in Part B, which have attempted to gather some comparative data are those which focus on understanding of science ideas, which are arguably easier to specify than affective outcomes, or skills and abilities such as those associated with constructing arguments. Chapters which report studies gathering comparative data on understanding include those by Bennett and Holman, Prenzel and Ostermeier, and Campbell and Lubben; Gräsel and her co-workers also indicate that the gathering of such data is taking place. Hofstein and Eylon compare their data with existing baseline data. In the reporting of some of these studies, however, it would have been useful to know more about how comparator groups were chosen and how well they were matched in terms of factors such as ability and gender.

A significant concern for several of the projects in Part B is the extent to which teachers used the innovation in the ways intended by the developers; this is seen as crucial to the success or otherwise of the intervention. This places the focus on classroom processes rather than (or in addition to) learning outcomes. So, for example, Gräsel et al. have looked in some detail at what is happening in the classroom, as have Boersma et al., Ametller and Pinto, and Campbell and Lubben.

In the context of this book, and the issues it set out to explore, perhaps the most striking feature of Part B, taken as a whole, is the contrast between the approaches to evaluation adopted in these studies and those advocated by some parties in the wider debate about educational research and its quality. In that debate, experimental methods, with randomly selected experimental and control groups, are strongly advocated by some, for all research questions that are really about whether or not something 'works'. Evaluations of innovative curriculum interventions in science most certainly raise the question of whether these 'work' as intended (or hoped), and sometimes of whether they work better than another approach, such as the one currently being used. For those advocating experimental approaches, the randomised controlled trial (RCT) is seen as the 'gold standard' – the research design which can best answer the question, 'what works? The study which comes closest to an RCT is that reported by Adey, who employed an experimental approach, comparing a group taught using the innovation with a matched control group, as a key part of the evaluation strategy. The absence of RCTs is perhaps not surprising, given the logistical difficulty of setting up a trial. Often, however, reports of non-experimental studies could be enhanced by discussing more fully the extent to which the evaluation approach that was used, places limits on the confidence with which conclusions can be drawn.

Another approach to curriculum evaluation that has been much discussed in the recent literature is the 'design experiment' (Brown, 1992; Collins, 1993; Gorard, 2004). This sees curriculum innovation and evaluation as a search for 'designs' that work. The aim is to produce an artefact (a teaching intervention) that 'works', by implementing a prototype and investigating how it works in practice, modifying it as things evolve to try to make it work better. The long-term aim is a design that is robust enough to be seen as successful, perhaps with modifications to fit local circumstances whilst retaining its central characteristics. Out of this may also come an understanding of the contextual factors which appear to be associated with situations in which the intervention works well and those where it works less well. The literature on design experiments is smaller than that on RCTs, and there is much less clarity about exactly what a 'design experiment' involves (how, for example, it differs from teacher action research). Some of the evaluations reported in Part B do exhibit features of design experiments, particularly where they have attempted to gather comparative data, or to modify and improve aspects of the intervention as it proceeded, though they have not characterised themselves as such.

What might be the reasons for this apparent lack of communication between science educators and those involved in more general discussions about educational research and its impact on policy and practice? One is that the debate about the quality of educational research is relatively recent. It is at its sharpest in the United States, where the *No Child Left Behind* Act (US Congress, 2001), which currently dominates educational discussion

> mentions 'scientifically based research' 110 times. It defines 'scientifically based research' as 'rigorous, systematic and objective procedures to obtain valid knowledge,' which includes research that 'is evaluated using experimental or quasi-experimental designs,' preferably with random assignment. (Slavin, 2002: 15)

A target of the US Department of Education (2002) is that 75% of the new research and evaluation projects which they fund should use experimental designs with randomly selected samples. In such a context, it is scarcely surprising that these general issues about research methods exercise and engage science educators. In other countries, whilst questions about the quality of educational research have also been raised, these have not yet led to an imposed orthodoxy. However, the development of many of the contributions predates these specific concerns.

A second reason, however, may lie in the close links that many science educators, and science curriculum developers, have to practice. Many sit in a position between research and practice: they may have previously been teachers and so have a 'feel' for the realities of practice; and many are still involved in teacher education, which involves working in school contexts. Often their involvement in curriculum innovation arises out of their experiences as teachers, and reflects a desire to improve practice, rather than simply to understand aspects of practice better. Having seen what practice is currently like, they believe they can see ways in which it could be better. Curriculum innovation is then a way of trying to achieve these improvements and disseminating 'good practice' more widely. In this sense, their perspective is much more accurately caught by the 'engineering' metaphor that underpins the idea of the design experiment, than by the rigorous testing of causal hypotheses that animates the RCT approach.

There are also sound logical grounds for being wary of experimental approaches to evaluation, and for questioning the strength of evidence that they really can provide on the questions that matter. These become more apparent when we start to look in more detail at where we might use an RCT to evaluate, and how this might be done. Imagine a group of science educators trying to devise an intervention to improve the teaching and learning of a specific topic, or to help teachers use a specific teaching approach (such as small-group discussion, or formative assessment). To design a teaching intervention, the developers must first agree on some general principles, perhaps drawn from research or from professional experience, on which the intervention and materials will be based. These lead to specific design criteria. To apply these general principles and design criteria, the developers must then make many more decisions and choices, about more detailed aspects of the specific subject matter that the lessons will cover. Whilst they might hope (and predict) that the resulting intervention will be better than that currently in use, it is clearly not the only intervention that could possibly be produced using the chosen principles or criteria. There are far too many choices and decisions involved for this to be a plausible claim. The intervention is just one way to 'engineer' the underlying principles into a workable practice. When we evaluate the intervention, it is really the merits (or otherwise) of these underlying principles that we are interested in. If they 'work', we can then hope to apply them to other topics and contexts. An RCT, however, can only provide evidence about *the actual intervention* that is trialled. We cannot, logically, from this infer that the reasons why it worked, or did not work, are due to the design criteria on which it was based.

Another area of difficulty for the experimental approach to educational evaluation concerns the measurement of outcomes. The use of RCTs in education is often advocated by comparing the apparent lack of progress in educational knowledge with the advances in medical and nursing knowledge that have been achieved through the systematic use of experimental studies with randomly selected samples.

In medical and health contexts, however, the outcomes we are seeking, are much clearer and much easier to detect (or measure) than in education. Often they are simply the recovery or survival of the patient. Even where outcomes are not quite so clear-cut, they are invariably much easier to measure than educational outcomes. In educational settings, we are often interested in improving students' 'understanding' of something, or their 'attitudes' towards something. Yet we have no generally accepted measures of these. Measures are therefore developed for each individual study (all of the Part B studies developed their own ways of assessing the outcomes of the innovation; none was able simply to use a pre-existing measure). The lack of sound and generally accepted outcome measures in science education undermines the case for RCTs. It is difficult to justify the effort and cost of these until we have better (and more widely agreed) ways of measuring the outcomes we are interested in.

A related issue is that science curriculum innovations are rarely developed simply to try to teach better the things we currently teach. Much more frequently, an innovation is based on the view that we ought to have new and different emphases in our teaching, for example, more emphasis on understanding rather than recall, or an understanding of some of the ways in which scientists work and the questions that interest them, as well as of the fundamental concepts of the discipline. This then means that the innovative intervention cannot be directly compared with an existing one. They are incommensurable. This does not mean that no comparison is possible. But it does mean that any post-intervention test or measure that is used is likely to favour one or the other – and that this fact may be used to challenge the validity of the conclusions that are drawn.

For all these sorts of reasons, the 'engineering' metaphor and the idea of a 'design experiment' seem rather closer to the reality of curriculum development and innovation. If a design experiment does not involve a control group, however, it is important to be as clear as possible about the criteria that might be used to judge the intervention a success or a failure. It is rather easier to make this kind of judgment about an engineered artefact such as a bridge, than about a teaching intervention. For the latter, it again comes down to having a sound and convincing outcome measure, which provides clear evidence of what students can and cannot do, or about their affective characteristics (attitudes, feelings, etc.) after the intervention. If we are able to say in advance what we would want these outcomes to be, in order to judge the innovation 'a success' (success criteria), and what outcomes we would regard as evidence that the intervention had not worked (failure criteria), then we may be able to draw more compelling and persuasive conclusions, without the need for a comparison or control group. Few of the evaluations of curriculum innovations discussed in Part B, however, attempt to do this in as clear (and daring) a manner. This caution, whilst understandable, limits the impact which the findings might have.

What, then, might be the practical implications that emerge from the overview of evaluation of science curriculum innovation that this book provides? The short answer perhaps is more, and better, dialogue – between developers close to the realities of practice, and those who approach curriculum change from the perspective of educational research and policy. It does not seem to us that either of these groups has all the answers or insights, and that both could benefit from a continuing sharing of views, perspectives and ideas. 'Professional evaluators' need perhaps to develop a fuller and more realistic understanding of the realities of schools and classrooms, and the constraints which these place on the kinds of evaluation designs that are feasible, or which might repay the effort needed to implement them. There also needs to be a fuller recognition of the logical limitations of randomised controlled trials for evaluating complex interventions – those which are multifaceted, difficult to specify exactly or to implement consistently in different settings and, perhaps above all, whose outcomes are difficult to measure in a reliable and valid manner. On the other hand, science educators need perhaps to acknowledge more fully that the impact of their work would often be enhanced by a stronger emphasis on systematic evaluation, including a clearer prior statement of the outcomes that are sought and the ways we might be able to tell if they are realised to the extent that we wish.

This book, and the seminar from which it has arisen, are an attempt to begin to explore these differing perspectives on curriculum evaluation – to use the current debate about educational research quality to hold up a mirror to current practices in science curriculum innovation. The growing perception that improvements in educational practice require research and development (rather than research alone) (Burkhardt and Schoenfelt, 2003) suggests that this exploration is timely. Only by engaging more seriously with the issues and the practical challenges raised by the question 'does it work?' can we begin to understand how best to try to collect the kind of evidence that might justify a claim that any particular science curriculum innovation results not just in change but in improvement.

References

Brown, A. (1992). Design experiments: Theoretical and methodological challenges in creating complex interventions in classroom settings. *Journal of the Learning Sciences*, 2 (2), 141-178.

Burkhardt, H. and Schoenfeld, A. (2003). Improving educational research: Toward a more useful, more influential and better-funded enterprise. *Educational Researcher*, 32(9), 3-14.

Collins, A. (1993). Toward a design science of education. In Scanlon, E. and O'Shea, T. (eds.), *New Directions in Educational Technology* (pp. 15-22). New York: Springer Verlag.

Fitz-Gibbon, C.T. (2000). Education: realising the potential. In Davies, H.T.O., Nutley, S.M. and Smith, P.C. (eds.), *What Works? Evidence-based Policy and Practice in Public Services* (pp. 69-92). Bristol: The Policy Press

Gorard, S. (2004). *Combining Methods in Educational and Social Research*. Maidenhead: Open University Press.

Hargreaves, D.H. (1996). *Teaching as a research-based profession: possibilities and prospects* (Annual Lecture). London: Teacher Training Agency.

Mosteller, F. and Boruch, R. (eds.) (2002). *Evidence Matters: Randomized Trials in Education Research*. Washington, DC: Brookings Institution Press.

Slavin, R.E. (2002). Evidence-based education policies: Transforming educational practice and research. *Educational Researcher* 31 (7), 15-21.

US Congress (2001). *No Child Left Behind Act of 2001*. Washington, DC: US Congress.
(URL: http://www.ed.gov/policy/elsec/leg/esea02/107-110.pdf)
(Visited 02 September 2004).

US Department of Education (2002). *Strategic Plan* 2002-2007. Washington, DC: US Department of Education.
(URL: http://www.ed.gov/about/reports/strat/plan2002-07/plan.pdf)
(Visited 02 September 2004).

Participants at the Conference

Philip Adey	King's College, London
Jaume Ametller	Autonomous University of Barcelona, Spain
Judith Bennett	University of York, UK
Kerst Boersma	University of Utrecht, The Netherlands
Rodger Bybee	BSCS, Colorado Springs, USA
Bob Campbell	University of York, UK
Diana Elbourne	Institute of Education, London, UK
Bat-Sheva Eylon	Weizmann Institute of Science, Israel
David Gough	Institute of Education, London, UK
Cornelia Gräsel	University of the Saarland, Germany [a]
Avi Hofstein	Weizmann Institute of Science, Israel
John Holman	University of York, UK
Stein Dankert Kolstø	University of Bergen, Norway
Bianca Lange	IPN, University of Kiel, Germany
John Lazonby	University of York, UK
Robin Millar	University of York, UK
Peter Nentwig	IPN, University of Kiel, Germany
Ilka Parchmann	IPN, University of Kiel, Germany [b]
Joy Parvin	University of York, UK
Manfred Prenzel	IPN, University of Kiel, Germany
Iris Stracke	IPN, University of Kiel, Germany

[a] Now at the University of Wuppertal, Germany
[b] Now at the University of Oldenburg, Germany

Biographies of authors

Philip Adey
Philip Adey is Professor of Cognition, Science and Education in the Department of Education and Professional Studies at King's College, London and Director of the Centre for the Advancement of Thinking, a research base for work on the development of thinking in children and the associated professional development for teachers. As a secondary science teacher and teacher educator in Barbados, Adey started to question the nature of the difficulty, which his students encountered with science concepts. This led to a London University PhD in 1980, after which he worked for the British Council in London and Indonesia. In 1984, he returned to King's College London for the first of the Cognitive Acceleration projects, working with teachers to maximise the cognitive stimulation, which they provide for their students. While the original work concentrated on Key Stage 3, more recently he has directed projects working with Year 1 and with Year 3 children.

Jaume Ametller
Jaume Ametller graduated in physics at the Universitat Autònoma de Barcelona where he later took a Masters degree in Science Education and is currently finishing his PhD. His thesis deals with the teachers' use of multimodal communication when teaching energy-related concepts at secondary school level. While a graduate student at the Autonomous University of Barcelona, he worked with the European research project STTIS (Science Teacher Training in an Information Society). His work in the STTIS framework included research on the use of visual representations to teach physics, teachers' transformations of curriculum innovations and the design of teacher training materials.
Since 2003 he has been a Research Fellow in CSSME (Centre for the Studies of Science and Mathematics Education) at the University of Leeds. At CSSME, he has worked on the EPSE (Evidence-based Practice in Science Education) project and is working on an evaluation of the 21st Century Science Project. He is a member of TIRE (IT tools and Educational Research Group) and CRECIM (Science and Mathematics Education Research Centre).

Judith Bennett
Judith Bennett is a senior lecturer in science education at the University of York. After obtaining her first degree in Chemistry-with-Education, she trained as a teacher and spent eight years teaching, mainly in London. During this period, she studied part-time for an MA and then a PhD, researching gender issues in science education. In 1988, she moved to York, first as senior editor of the Salters Science project, and then to her current post. She was a member of the writing team of the

Salters Advanced Chemistry project, and the Prime Science project, the US adaptation of Salters Science.

Her research interests lie in the area of attitudes to science and in the evaluation of aspects of curriculum development, particularly context-based approaches to the teaching of science. She has recently completed two books, one on links between research and practice in science education, and the other on educational evaluation. She has just completed her term of office as Chair of the Research Committee of the Association for Science Education (ASE).

Kerst Th. Boersma

Kerst Th. Boersma is Professor of Biological Education at the Centre for Science and Mathematics Education at Utrecht University. He graduated as a geologist and completed his PhD in palaeontology at Leiden University. After working as editor for science education, he trained teachers and lectured on biology teaching methods from 1976-1984 at Utrecht University. In 1984, he moved to the National Institute for Curriculum Development (SLO) in Enschede, where he was engaged in curriculum development for science and environmental education, and in curriculum research. Since 1997 he has held a chair in Biological Education at Utrecht University. His research interests are in learning systems thinking in biology education, and in learning in social practices in biology education. He has published in the fields of curriculum studies, environmental education, science education and biology education. In 2000, he was admitted to the Biological Council of the Royal Netherlands Academy of Arts and Sciences (KNAW).

Bob Campbell

Bob Campbell trained as a secondary school biology teacher and taught in a number of comprehensive schools in Scotland before joining the University of York in 1978. He is one of the founding members of the University of York Science Education Group (UYSEG) and was a member of the management and writing teams for the Salters Science projects. He was also active in the adaptation of the Salters materials into Prime Science for the US and has contributed to several UYSEG projects including school-based research on the implementation of Salters Advanced Physics (SHAP). His work has also focused in Southern Africa where he is active in projects concerned with the professional development of science teachers, the practical skills of university entrants and the development, introduction and evaluation of contextualised curricula for schools. Recent activities have included studies on HIV/AIDS education, the systematic review of research in science education and the development and introduction of science standards for the State of Qatar. From 1995 to 2002, he was Head of the Department of Educational Studies and is currently Acting Director of the University of York Science Curriculum Centre.

Diana Elbourne

Diana Elbourne has a background in social sciences and in statistics. From 1981–96 she worked at the National Perinatal Epidemiology Unit, University of Oxford. She currently juggles two jobs – as Professor of Healthcare Evaluation in the Medical Statistics Unit at the London School of Hygiene and Tropical Medicine, and also as Professor of Evidence Informed Policy and Practice at the Evidence for Policy and Practice Information (EPPI) Centre in the Social Science Research Unit at the Institute of Education.

She was first involved with a single centre trial in healthcare in 1978, and went on to conduct numerous multi-centre trials. She began doing systematic reviews of trials in the mid-1980s, working on both applied and methodological areas. She is an active reviewer for Cochrane Collaboration and member of the statistical methods group, with a particular interest in methods for including trials of alternative designs (such as cluster randomised and cross-overs) in systematic reviews. She is involved in qualitative studies of the views of participants in trials, and is also active in moves to involve consumers in reviews (having long done so in individual trials). A major challenge of her work in the EPPI Centre will be including studies with qualitative and/or non-randomised designs in systematic reviews.

Bat-Sheva Eylon

Bat-Sheva Eylon holds a BSc in physics and mathematics, MSc in physics and a PhD in science education from the University of California, Berkeley. Since 1979, she has been a member of the science teaching department at the Weizmann Institute of Science. Currently, she heads both the junior high school science and technology group and the secondary physics group. She also acts as the academic adviser of the teacher national centers in physics and science and technology for junior high-school. She serves as head of the professional national committee for physics teaching in Israel appointed by the Ministry of Education. For the last few years, she has been directing a national research and development project for learning science and technology in junior high school.

Her research is focused on the relationship between conceptual understanding, problem-solving and knowledge organization in the physical sciences, and she has conducted design studies in this area. Some of these studies have led to innovative programs that are being taught in Israeli high schools, as well as new contexts for learning physics such as 'physics and industry'. Within the context of learning science and technology in junior high school, she has investigated the acquisition of high order learning skills and how to integrate them into the study of content. In recent years she has been active in the area of continuing teacher development and has conducted longitudinal studies of teachers and students.

David Gough
David Gough has a Bachelor degree in psychology, a Masters degree in child development and a PhD in social science. He is a chartered Psychologist, Reader in Social Science and Deputy Director of the Social Science Research Centre and its Evidence for Policy and Practice Information and Coordinating (EPPI) Centre, at the Institute of Education, University of London. Previously, he was Senior Research Fellow at the Public Health Research Unit, University of Glasgow and Professor in the Department of Social Welfare at the Japan Women's University, Tokyo. All of his research has been concerned with the study of professional practice to explicate micro-social policy in action and systematic research synthesis. From 1995-2000, he was Secretary of the International Child Abuse Society (ISPCAN). He is currently Editor of the journal Child Abuse Review, on the editorial board of two other journals and on the advisory boards of the British and Japanese child professional abuse societies (BASPCAN and JaSPCAN).

Cornelia Gräsel
Cornelia Gräsel is Professor of Education at the Department of Research on Education of the University of Wuppertal. After her MA she worked at the University of Munich in the Department of Educational Psychology, where she completed her doctoral thesis on problem-based learning (1996) and her habilitation on environmental education (2001). In addition to these topics she has researched on learning with new media and cooperative learning. In 2001, she went to the IPN in Kiel and worked in the Department of Chemical Education. She joined the research group of 'Chemie im Kontext' and worked on the research projects on implementation and evaluation of this curriculum. At the University of Saarland, she led a teacher education group from 2001 to 2004. Her recent work in Saarland and Wuppertal is concerned with the professional development of teachers.

Avi Hofstein
Avi Hofstein holds a BSc in chemistry, MA in education, and PhD in science education (chemistry) from the Weizmann Institute of Science. For more than 15 years he taught chemistry in two high schools in Israel. For 18 years he was the coordinating inspector of high school chemistry at the Ministry of Education in Jerusalem. He served as the head of the National Center for Chemistry Teachers. Currently, Avi Hofstein is the Head of the Chemistry and the Science and Technology for all groups. For more than 30 years, he was involved in all the aspects of the curricular process in chemistry, namely development, implementation, evaluation, and research. In regard to general science education, he has conducted research in the following areas: the science laboratory, classroom, outdoors, and laboratory learning environments, learning difficulties and students' misconceptions in chemistry, and attitudinal and motivational studies. In recent years, he has been involved in the development of

leadership amongst chemistry teachers to promote reform in teaching chemistry in Israel.

John Holman

John Holman is Director of the National Science Learning Centre, a purpose-built centre for the professional development of science teachers that will open in York in October 2005.

His background is in secondary education: until September 2000 he was Head of Watford Grammar School for Boys, a school for students aged 11 – 18 near London. Before that, he taught science in a variety of secondary schools.

In 2000, he became Salters Professor of Chemical Education at the University of York, teaching chemistry to York undergraduates as well as having a specialist interest in science education, with responsibility for the University of York Science Education Group's major curriculum development projects (21st Century Science, Salters Science, Salters Advanced Chemistry, Salters Horners Advanced Physics and Salters Nuffield Advanced Biology) and the work of the Chemical Industry Education Centre.

His educational interests include scientific literacy, school-industry links, context-led higher education, the interface between science and technology in schools, ICT in support of science education, the implementation of curriculum change and the professional development of science teachers.

Marie-Christine Knippels

Marie-Christine Knippels is a biologist, specializing in health education. From 1998–2002, she was a PhD student at the Centre for Science and Mathematics Education in the University of Utrecht and worked on 'Coping with the abstract and complex nature of genetics in biology education'. After that, she qualified as a biology teacher, participated in a research project on primary science education, and worked in the Utrecht Biology Science Shop. From November 2004, she has been holding a post-doc position at RISBO Contractresearch B.V. Erasmus Universiteit Rotterdam. Her research interest is in informed decision-making in genetics education.

Stein Dankert Kolstø

Stein Dankert Kolstø is Associate Professor in Science Education at the University of Bergen, Norway. He graduated in theoretical physics in 1991. After teaching science, physics and mathematics at upper secondary school for three years, he became a teacher educator. He took his doctoral degree in Science Education in 2000. His main research interest is in scientific literacy and students' examination and decision-making in relation to the science dimension of socio-scientific issues. Currently, he is directing the DIA-project, a small-scale curriculum project within teacher education aiming at increasing students' awareness of social dimensions of science and evaluation of information with a science dimension. He is also involved in the DoCTA-NSS project where computer-supported collaborative learning principles are implemented in a teaching sequence focusing on genetics and ethical aspects of gene technology.

Fred Lubben
Fred Lubben has Masters degrees in Civil Engineering and in Science Education and has taught at secondary schools in Ghana, the Netherlands, the UK and Zambia. Since the early 1990s, he has been a Senior Researcher in the Department of Educational Studies at the University of York. His major research interests and publications centre around the effectiveness of experimental work in science and on the role of everyday contexts in the science curriculum. In addition, he is active in research on the interface between curriculum development and continuous professional development of science teachers. Collaborative research links are maintained with colleagues in universities in the Czech Republic, Mozambique, Namibia, South Africa, Swaziland and the Netherlands.

Robin Millar
Robin Millar is Professor of Science Education at the University of York. He studied theoretical physics at university and then did a PhD in medical physics, before deciding to train as a teacher. After teaching for eight years in secondary schools in Edinburgh, he moved to York in 1982 as a lecturer in education. His research and writing are mainly concerned with the development of students' understanding of science concepts, the role of practical work, the development of scientific reasoning, and the curriculum implications of an emphasis on scientific literacy. He has directed several large research projects, most recently as co-ordinator of the *Evidence-based Practice in Science Education* Research Network funded through the UK Economic and Social Research Council's *Teaching and Learning Research Programme (TLRP)*. He was a member of the management and writing teams for Salters' Science and of the Advisory Committee for Salters Horners Advanced Physics. He played a central role in the development of the innovative AS-level syllabus *Science for Public Understanding*. He currently co-directs the *Twentyfirst Century Science* project, which is producing and evaluating teaching materials to support a new science curriculum model for 15-16 year olds in England, based around a core course for all students with a clear scientific literacy emphasis, augmented by additional optional courses in pure and applied science for those students who wish to study science.

Peter Nentwig

Peter Nentwig has been a researcher at the Leibniz-Institute for Science Education (IPN) at the University of Kiel, Germany, since 1976. He has a diploma in chemistry and has taught for several years in various schools before joining the IPN. He has also been engaged in teacher education at the Educational Faculty of the University in Kiel. For several years he was active in in-service Education for teachers, both giving courses and doing research in that field. Additionally, he was involved in national as well as international associations of teacher educators. More recently his work has been concerned with issues of Scientific Literacy, which has led to several international symposia. He is currently involved in the PISA study and in the development and evaluation of the chemistry curriculum, *Chemie im Kontext*.

Christian Ostermeier

Christian Ostermeier is a research assistant at the Leibniz-Institute for Science Education (IPN) at the University of Kiel. He studied Psychology at the University of Regensburg and Vanderbilt University in Nashville. After his diploma in 1998 from the University of Regensburg, he was engaged in evaluation research at IPN, within the pilot program 'Increasing the efficiency of mathematics and science instruction'. He completed his PhD in 2003, in which he investigated processes of cooperative quality development.
Research interests include the implementation of instructional innovations in schools, cooperative quality development of instruction and standards in teacher education.

Ilka Parchmann

Ilka Parchmann is a professor for education in chemistry at the University of Oldenburg. After finishing her PhD, she spent three months with the University of York Science Education Group, before she started her teacher training for chemistry and biology for secondary schools. From 1999 until 2004, she worked at the Leibniz Institute for Science Education (IPN) in Kiel. Her main research areas are the development and evaluation of context-based teaching and learning and the implementation of new approaches, supported by in-service training courses. She is one of the project leaders of the *Chemie im Kontext* programme.

Joy Parvin

Joy Parvin is the Primary Projects Manager for the Chemical Industry Education Centre (CIEC), based at the University of York. After completing a degree in Chemical Engineering at the University of Nottingham, she trained as a primary school teacher. Her teaching career took her into primary and middle schools in Yorkshire, before beginning work at the CIEC in 1992. Her work at the Centre has progressed from being one of writing science units for primary school teachers and providing short in-service training workshops to managing a team of advisory teachers carrying out the Children *Challenging Industry* (CCI) project, and directing the *Primary Science Enhancement Programme*, a sister programme to CCI. She completed an MA in Science Education in 1996.

Roser Pintó
Roser Pintó, is Professor of Science Education at the Universitat Autònoma de Barcelona. She graduated in Physics, and has a PhD in Physics Education. After teaching in secondary schools in Barcelona for ten years, she returned to the Autonomous University of Barcelona as a Lecturer in Science Education. Her teaching activities include science teacher training for primary and secondary school as well as MA and PhD programmes. Her research and writing are mainly concerned with the development of students' conceptual and procedural understanding in physics, and with issues relating to the introduction of IT tools for science education. She is the leading researcher of the research group TIRE (IT tools and Educational Research) created by the Catalan Government and is the Coordinator of a Science Education Research Centre CRECIM (Centre de Recerca per a l'Educació Científica i Matemàtica) at the Autonomous University of Barcelona.
She has been involved in several European projects. In particular, she has coordinated the research projects, STTIS (Science Teacher Training in an Information Society) and IKUITSE (Integrating Knowledge for the Use of IT tools in Science Education)

Manfred Prenzel
Manfred Prenzel is Managing Director of the Leibniz Institute for Science Education (IPN) and Professor of Education at the University of Kiel (Germany). He graduated in Education and completed a PhD in Education as well as an advanced doctoral degree (Habilitation) in Education and Educational Psychology at the University of Munich. From 1993 he was Professor of Educational Psychology at the University of Regensburg, before going to the IPN in 1997. The main topics of his research relate to issues of learning and teaching in different domains (science, mathematics, medicine, economics), especially on motivation and interest, conceptual change and transfer, patterns of teaching and learning and computer-based learning environments. Currently, he is the coordinator of the Pilot program 'Improving science and mathematics instruction', a major project funded by the Federal and State Commission for Educational Planning and Research (BLK). He is the speaker of the DFG (German Research Council) priority program 'Quality of School', in which he is also participating with the IPN project 'Video analyses of physics instruction'. Additionally, he is a member of the Senate of the DFG and is the National Project Manger for OECD-PISA 2003 and PISA 2006, and a member of the International PISA Science Expert Group.

Arend Jan Waarlo
Arend Jan Waarlo is senior lecturer in biology education and holds a special chair in genetics and health communication at the Centre for Science and Mathematics Education in the University of Utrecht. His PhD thesis was on 'Biology teaching and health education'. In 1999 and 2000, he was seconded, at his own request, to the University for Humanistics in Utrecht.

He has trained biology teachers, life-stance and moral education teachers, professionals in environmental and health education, and is currently engaged in the Utrecht Master's Degree Programme, Science Education and Communication. He has also participated in various curriculum development and research projects.

From 2000 to 2004, he was a member of the Academic Committee of the European Researchers in Didactics of Biology (ERIDOB). His current research interest is in acquiring genomics-related opinion-forming competence.

Waxmann

This volume contains country studies on the school systems in Canada, England, Finland, France, Germany, the Netherlands and Sweden. Important characteristics of the specific social and policy contexts, of the school system and of educational practise are described and analysed by renowned researchers of educational studies, based on a common analytical framework. The reports are original surveys, describing the characteristics of the conditions underlying each country's school systems as viewed by national experts.

Hans Döbert, Eckhard Klieme, Wendelin Sroka (eds.)
Conditions of School Performance in Seven Countries
A Quest for Understanding the International Variation of PISA Results
Studien zur International und Interkulturell Vergleichenden Erziehungswissenschaft, Bd. 3
2004, 484 p., pb., 34,00 €,
ISBN 3-8309-1373-7

The study reported in this volume is focused on a systematic comparison of the school systems in Canada, England, Finland, France, the Netherlands and Sweden. It aims to identify factors of education systems as well as cultural and socio-economic factors that are responsible for the international variation of student performance as demonstrated in PISA 2000. Therefore, in addition to the systematic comparison of the school systems, hypotheses are formulated identifying factors with a major impact on student performance.
This publication addresses specifically the scientific community in the areas of comparative education, school effectiveness research and school system governance.

Hans Döbert, Wendelin Sroka (eds.)
Features of Successful School Systems
A Comparison of Schooling in Six Countries
Studien zur International und Interkulturell Vergleichenden Erziehungswissenschaft, Bd. 4
2004, 168 p., pb., 24,90 €,
ISBN 3-8309-1364-8

MÜNSTER · NEW YORK · MÜNCHEN · BERLIN

Waxmann Verlag GmbH
Postfach 8603 · D–48046 Münster
Fon 0251/26504-0 · Fax 0251/26504-26
E-Mail: info@waxmann.com
www.waxmann.com

Cornelia Kristen
School Choice and Ethnic School Segregation
Primary School Selection in Germany
Internationale Hochschulschriften, Bd. 437
2005, 208 p., pb., 25,50 €,
ISBN 3-8309-1447-4

This publication explores the origins of ethnic school segregation. More specifically, it studies individual school choice processes and how they contribute to segregation. The author develops a general explanatory approach to school choice behavior and applies the theory to the German elementary school system. With the aid of a quantitative survey conducted in the federal state of North-Rhine Westphalia, she shows why families of Turkish origin make different school selection decisions from German families. The book reveals which general mechanisms lead to the emergence and persistence of ethnic and social stratification.

Horst Bayrhuber, Jürgen Mayer (eds.)
Empirical Research on Environmental Education in Europe
2000, 156 p., pb., 25,50 €,
ISBN 3-89325-893-0

The public education system belongs to those social institutions which contribute to fostering competences essential for ensuring Sustainable Development. But which basic competences are required for this purpose and to which extent are the education systems adapted to foster such competences? Aiming at answering these questions, empirical research projects have been carried our in many European countries. The researchers have been concerned with reasoning and acting according to sustainability as well as with the scientific knowledge required for that.

The book presents recent empirical studies in the field of environmental education conducted in various European countries and Israel. The research projects were concerned with the general question of the basic competences required for fostering Sustainable Development.

Die durch TIMSS aufgezeigten und durch PISA bestätigten Probleme deutscher Schülerinnen und Schüler im mathematisch-naturwissenschaftlichen Bereich können auf unterschiedlichen Ebenen bearbeitet werden. Im BLK-Modellversuchsprogramm „Steigerung der Effizienz des mathematisch-naturwissenschaftlichen Unterrichts" (SINUS) begannen Lehrerinnen und Lehrer ihren eigenen Unterricht weiterzuentwickeln und gemeinsam in Prozesse der Qualitätssicherung und Qualitätsentwicklung einzusteigen.

„Kooperative Qualitätsentwicklung in Schulnetzwerken" nimmt die Perspektive der beteiligten Lehrkräfte in den Blick. Es wird untersucht, welche Formen der Kooperation die Lehrerinnen und Lehrer auf der Ebene der Schulnetzwerke etablieren und wie sie die kooperative Qualitätsentwicklung insgesamt akzeptieren und einschätzen.

Christian Ostermeier

Kooperative Qualitätsentwicklung in Schulnetzwerken

Eine empirische Studie am Beispiel des BLK-Programms „Steigerung der Effizienz des mathematisch-naturwissenschaftlichen Unterrichts" (SINUS)

Internationale Hochschulschriften, Bd. 434
2004, 192 S., br., 25,50 €,
ISBN 3-8309-1433-4

Dieser Band berichtet, wie Deutschland in der zweiten Erhebungswelle – PISA 2003 – abgeschnitten hat. Er präsentiert und diskutiert die Befunde über Kompetenzen deutscher Schülerinnen und Schüler im internationalen Vergleich. Es werden familiäre wie schulische Entwicklungsbedingungen beschrieben und die Chancen junger Menschen analysiert, ihre Potentiale auszuschöpfen und ihre Kompetenzen zu entwickeln. Der Bericht stellt dar, wie sich die Situation in Deutschland seit der ersten PISA-Erhebung im Jahr 2000 verändert hat.

PISA-Konsortium Deutschland (Hrsg.)

PISA 2003

Der Bildungsstand der Jugendlichen in Deutschland – Ergebnisse des zweiten internationalen Vergleichs
2004, 416 S., br., 19,90 €,
ISBN 3-8309-1455-5